Additional Praise for *Bin Laden's Legacy*

"At this critical crossroads in U.S. foreign policy marked by the death of bin Laden, the Arab revolutions, and the global debt crisis, Gartenstein-Ross offers a sorely-needed explanation of why spending too much money on counterterrorism plays into our enemies' hands."

—Will McCants, founder and co-editor of *Jihadica*

"With an incisive analysis, balanced argumentation, and sometimes unconventional approaches, Daveed Gartenstein-Ross gives us a refreshing insight into the U.S. strategy against al Qaeda. He raises questions about the U.S. defense posture facing the terrorist threat and on the *feindbild* of Osama bin Laden nourished by the analyst community. He ends this very readable book with useful and sensible proposals to mend the U.S. strategy in the fight against international terrorism."

—Ambassador Thomas Baekelandt, counterterrorism coordinator, Belgium Ministry of Foreign Affairs

"Gartenstein-Ross leaves no stone unturned in this provocative examination of America's decade-long war with al Qaeda. An essential read for any serious observer of America's counterterrorism efforts since 9/11."

—Jarret Brachman, author of *Global Jihadism: Theory and Practice*

"*Bin Laden's Legacy* is important and ultimately a fascinating read. Daveed Gartenstein-Ross tells a story and provides you with an unforgettable detailed insight into the mindset of al Qaeda and how they planned and continue to plan to destroy America financially. It is a must-read for all Americans."

—Barry McManus, former CIA interrogator

"I really wish Daveed Gartenstein-Ross had not made so persuasive a case in this book. Al Qaeda, as Gartenstein-Ross demonstrates, has cleverly convinced the United States to bleed itself dry in response to the threat posed by transitional terror groups. Whether or not the United States can adjust its tactics and priorities remains to be seen, but in the meantime, Americans of all political and ideological stripes should consider the important observations and recommendations to be found in these pages."

—Andrew Exum, Fellow at the Center for a New American Security
and former Army Ranger officer

"There is remarkably little consensus among analysts about the threat now posed by al Qaeda. All agree, however, that the end of bin Laden does not end al Qaeda's campaign of terrorism. We may be chasing al Qaeda for decades and must get a lot smarter about how we do it, which is why this thoughtful book is a must read."

—Brian Michael Jenkins, senior adviser to the president
of the RAND Corporation

1

Bin Laden Is Dead; His Strategy Lives

In the wake of Osama bin Laden's death, a number of people are saying that this does not mean that al Qaeda has been destroyed. Some argue that the organization may, in fact, be thriving. . . . I understand why officials have to say this. They want to be cautious. They don't want to overpromise. But the truth is this is a huge, devastating blow to al Qaeda, which had already been crippled by the Arab Spring. It is not an exaggeration to say that this is the end of al Qaeda in any meaningful sense of the word.

—*Fareed Zakaria, May 2, 2011*

On May 1, 2011, President Barack Obama delivered a rare Sunday night address to the nation. "Good evening," he began. "Tonight, I can report to the American people and to the world that the United States has conducted an operation that killed Osama bin Laden, the leader of al Qaeda and a terrorist who's responsible for the murder of thousands of innocent men, women, and children."[1]

Killing bin Laden was a significant accomplishment. The hunt for the terrorist mastermind, led by Navy SEAL Team Six, will surely become, justifiably, the stuff of American legend. Spontaneous celebration erupted after President Obama's announcement, as citizens flocked to the perimeter of the White House and to ground zero in New York City, where bin Laden had struck U.S. soil almost a decade earlier. One D.C.-based website described the festivities outside the White House as a "massive gathering, drawing hundreds of others in a boisterous, sign-waving, lamppost-climbing, anthem-filled display of happiness."[2] Members of the crowd waved American flags and smoked victory cigars well into the wee hours of the morning.

But what did bin Laden's death actually mean? Did killing one man end the so-called war on terrorism? Was bin Laden actually important to al Qaeda, or had he been relegated to the role of an operationally irrelevant figurehead?

Even if bin Laden had been only a figurehead, he performed that role with deadly competence. Islamist militants who knew bin Laden personally spoke of their love and reverence for him.[3] The fact that he had been able to survive the most expensive manhunt in human history for so long had turned him into a worldwide legend. But the early stream of information that has been released, based on the computer hard drives and other data seized from bin Laden's compound in Abbottabad, Pakistan, suggests that bin Laden was more than a mere figurehead. As an Associated Press report published within a week of his death noted, analysts who examined this information came to believe that bin Laden "was a lot more involved in directing al Qaeda personnel and operations than sometimes thought over the last decade" and that he had been providing strategic guidance to al Qaeda affiliates in Yemen and Somalia.[4] So the view that bin Laden's death had no operational relevance seems overstated.

Yet at the same time, the threat posed by Islamist militancy hasn't passed. The threat posed by al Qaeda hasn't passed. And even though Osama bin Laden is dead, his strategy for combating the United States lives on. This strategy has adapted and evolved over the past decade,

Bin Laden's Legacy

Why We're *Still* Losing the War on Terror

DAVEED GARTENSTEIN-ROSS

WILEY

John Wiley & Sons, Inc.

Published by John Wiley & Sons, Inc., Hoboken, New Jersey
Published simultaneously in Canada

For general information about our other products and services, please contact our Customer Care Department within the United States at (800) 762-2974, outside the United States at (317) 572-3993 or fax (317) 572-4002.

Wiley also publishes its books in a variety of electronic formats and by print-on-demand. Some content that appears in standard print versions of this book may not be available in other formats. For more information about Wiley products, visit us at www.wiley.com.

Library of Congress Cataloging-in-Publication Data:
Gartenstein-Ross, Daveed, date.
  Bin Laden's legacy: why we're still losing the war on terror / Daveed Gartenstein-Ross.
      p. cm.
    Includes index.
  ISBN 978-1-118-09494-5 (cloth); ISBN 978-1-118-15093-1 (ebk);
ISBN 978-1-118-15094-8 (ebk); ISBN 978-1-118-15095-5 (ebk)
    1. War on Terrorism, 2001–2009.   2. Terrorism—United States—Prevention.
3. Qaida (Organization) I. Title.
  HV6432.G375 2011
  363.325—dc23

                                                                    2011021413

10 9 8 7 6 5 4 3 2 1

This book is dedicated to Ross Kennedy Smith, my debate coach at Wake Forest University and a remarkable teacher. R.I.P.

It is also dedicated to Robert Jarrod Atchison, who carries on Ross's legacy as Wake Forest's new director of debate. I wrote the first chapter of this book in Jarrod's office, which had once been Ross's.

This world needs more teachers.

Contents

and—although many observers are loathe to admit it—the strategy has been working. If we mistakenly believe that bin Laden's death signifies the end of the fight against Islamic militancy, or that it vindicates our previous policies and obviates the need to change our approach to counterterrorism, bin Laden may well experience even greater success in death than he ever did while among us.

The "Foiled Plots"

In trying to understand the strategy to which bin Laden helped lead al Qaeda, a good starting point is al Qaeda's own words. For example, the centerpiece article in the November 2010 issue of *Inspire*, the English-language online magazine produced by the militant group al Qaeda in the Arabian Peninsula (AQAP), began as follows:

> Two Nokia phones, $150 each, two HP printers, $300 each, plus shipping, transportation and other miscellaneous expenses add up to a total bill of $4,200. That is all that Operation Hemorrhage cost us. . . . On the other hand this supposedly "foiled plot," as some of our enemies would like to call it, will without a doubt cost America and other Western countries billions of dollars in new security measures.[5]

The publication's cover featured a somewhat blurry photograph of a United Parcel Service plane on a runway, along with the crisp headline "$4,200." This was an unmistakable reference to a terrorist plot that the Yemen-based AQAP had launched the previous month, involving bombs hidden in printer cartridges.

In the plot, AQAP militants shipped these explosive devices via UPS and Federal Express in Yemen. Both packages were addressed to synagogues in Chicago. Investigators seized the explosive device sent via FedEx in Dubai; it contained three hundred grams of the military-grade explosive pentaerythritol tetranitrate (PETN) hidden in a Hewlett-Packard desktop printer cartridge. Although it never left the Middle East, that device had been loaded onto, and subsequently flown on, two different passenger jets—first on a Qatar Airways Airbus A320 to Doha, then on a second flight from Doha to Dubai.[6]

Finding the second bomb, a PETN device sent via UPS, proved disturbingly difficult. As Deputy National Security Adviser John Brennan would later recount, it was truly a "race against the clock."[7] A call from Saudi Arabian intelligence originally alerted U.S. officials to the danger. The Americans then notified the German federal police, because the bomb-carrying plane was to make its first stop at Germany's Cologne-Bonn airport, a UPS hub, before continuing to Britain and ultimately the United States. But by the time the German police learned of the suspicious package, it was already too late. The plane had taken off again.

When it landed at Britain's East Midlands Airport, officials cordoned off the cargo area and emptied the plane. They conducted a thorough search but found nothing out of the ordinary. Even the seemingly innocuous printer cartridge hiding four hundred grams of PETN was cleared by security, and the authorities removed the cordon around 10 a.m. British authorities had inadvertently given a green light to tragedy, for the bomb might have exploded over the U.S. eastern seaboard had the plane taken off.[8]

Then officials called from Dubai. They had just discovered the PETN in the Hewlett-Packard cartridge that had been routed through their country. These officials instructed their British colleagues on how to locate the explosives, which were carefully disguised to avoid detection by an X-ray machine.[9] The British authorities again cordoned off the area, and this time they found the bomb.

After the 9/11 attacks, the United States poured enormous sums of money into bolstering aviation security. Yet time and again, terrorists affiliated with al Qaeda have shown how just a bit of technical ingenuity can thwart these expensive defenses. About three months after 9/11—on December 22, 2001—a British ex-con named Richard Reid boarded the Miami-bound American Airlines flight 63 in Paris with enough explosives hidden in his shoe to blow a hole in the plane's fuselage. His attack was disrupted not by airline security but by flight attendants and passengers who restrained him physically when he tried to light a fuse in his shoe.

Terrorists in Britain attempted to exploit another vulnerability five years later. On August 10, 2006, authorities announced the apprehension of more than twenty suspects who were part of a plot to blow up seven transatlantic flights bound for the United States from Britain. Just as Reid had exploited the inadequate screening of footwear, these plotters realized that they could sneak liquid explosives through security checkpoints by hiding them in drink bottles. The tops of the bottles would be unopened, but the plotters would add false bottoms filled with explosives dyed the same color as the beverage—for example, dyed red if the bottle contained a red sports drink. In this way, the terrorists could pass safely through security even if they were asked to drink from the bottles along the way.[10]

Department of Homeland Security secretary Michael Chertoff commented that if the plot hadn't been broken up, the United States could have experienced devastation akin to 9/11. "If they had succeeded in bringing liquid explosives on seven or eight aircraft," he said, "there could have been thousands of lives lost and an enormous economic impact with devastating consequences for international air travel."[11]

On Christmas Day of 2009, a terrorist again snuck explosives onto a plane. Twenty-three-year-old Nigerian Umar Farouk Abdulmutallab managed to board the Detroit-bound Northwest Airlines flight 253 in Amsterdam with a PETN-based bomb sewn into his underpants. He was able to evade security measures because the explosive material, stored in a plastic container, would not set off metal detectors; because it was hidden in such an intimate place, the crotch of his underwear, he was confident that routine searches wouldn't find the explosive. As the plane prepared to land, Abdulmutallab stuck a syringe into the six-inch-long container in his underwear that held the PETN. Although the substance in the syringe was designed to detonate the bomb, Abdulmutallab succeeded only in starting a small but painful fire rather than triggering an immediate explosion.

Reacting quickly, a Dutch passenger seated next to Abdulmutallab named Jasper Schuringa pulled the syringe out of the terrorist's hands. Other passengers likewise sprang into action, with some pouring water on Abdulmutallab and others using their hands to pat the flames.

Schuringa, afraid that Abdulmutallab might have more explosives, held him in a headlock until a flight attendant arrived with a fire extinguisher. Yet again a plot against aviation was stopped not by security measures but by alert passengers.

Shifting Perceptions

By the time Abdulmutallab succeeded in sneaking a bomb past airport security, more than eight years had passed since the 9/11 attacks, and that traumatic day had receded somewhat from the collective American memory. Islamist militants had succeeded in carrying out other mass casualty attacks in Western countries—a train bombing in Madrid just before Spain's 2004 election killed 191 people and wounded more than 1,800, and a series of July 2005 suicide bombings targeting London's public transportation system killed 52 and injured around 700—but they had not launched another major strike against the United States. Thus, as the story of the would-be Christmas Day bomber dominated the U.S. news cycle for several days, the discussion of the incident was notably different from the punditry that had followed older terrorist attempts.

A conversation that typifies one side of the new discussion after Abdulmutallab's attempt occurred in January 2010 on *Bloggingheads*, a split-screen Internet television show designed to have a diversity of viewpoints and also—in the site's own explanation—to turn "not-very-telegenic people into video pundits."[12] A segment featuring *National Review*'s Jonah Goldberg and *The Daily Beast*'s Peter Beinart began with Goldberg commenting how "it is sort of astounding, the sort of school-boy fixation" that terrorists have with airplanes. Both Goldberg and Beinart agreed that a clear lesson to be drawn from Abdulmutallab's failed attempt was that al Qaeda isn't really the threat that most commentators believe.

Pointing out that Abdulmutallab paid for his ticket in cash and didn't bring luggage with him, Goldberg said, "Surely if al Qaeda's been paying attention, they know that those are red flags. Why this guy couldn't have gone to the Goodwill in Amsterdam or wherever, and filled a ten-dollar bag with some bogus luggage, and if they're all that sophisticated, gotten someone's credit card. . . . There are stories about how he didn't even have a passport. If they're that sophisticated, why didn't they do all of those things?"

To Goldberg, this suggested that al Qaeda is not "as big a threat as we're supposed to believe." He said emphatically that he was surprised that after ten years, this was one of the group's most sophisticated attacks. Beinart agreed, stating that "the lesson of the Christmas Day bombing . . . testifies to the limits of al Qaeda's ability."

The discussion between Goldberg and Beinart was poorly reasoned from start to finish. It began, of course, with the fallacious idea that we can assess al Qaeda's capabilities based on its most recent plot. This assumption was all the more questionable because less than a week after Abdulmutallab's attempted attack, a double agent from al Qaeda named Humam Khalil Mohammed executed a suicide bombing at a Central Intelligence Agency base in Khost, Afghanistan, that killed seven U.S. intelligence officers and a Jordanian. *Washington Post* columnist David Ignatius noted that when measured by loss of life, this event represented perhaps "the most costly mistake in the agency's history."[13] In fact, as former CIA officer Robert Baer wrote, given the size of the CIA, the loss it experienced in Khost "was the equivalent of the Army losing a battalion."[14]

Goldberg's conclusion that Abdulmutallab's paying in cash and not having luggage indicated a lack of sophistication on al Qaeda's part was also rather strange, since the young Nigerian had actually *succeeded* in hiding a bomb from security. Both Goldberg and Beinart assumed, unjustifiably, that this plot represented the apotheosis of al Qaeda's sophistication. Missing from their discussion was any acknowledgment of al Qaeda's actual strategy.

Were America's enemies still trying to execute a catastrophic attack, something that could rival 9/11, or had they instead adopted a model of warfare that emphasized smaller and more frequent attacks? Was Abdulmutallab considered a top operative, highly trained with a relatively large amount of resources devoted to his mission? Or were the terrorists just testing the waters to see whether this particular method—a bomb hidden in an operative's underpants—could thwart

Western security measures? Did they in fact view bringing this particular plane down as *irrelevant* to the success or failure of the mission?

Nor did other commentators do much better than Goldberg and Beinart. Another distinct segment of public commentary came from the triumphalists, those who believed that the plot's failure showed that the pressure the United States had applied to al Qaeda was working and that the group had been significantly degraded.

Then there were those who, reasonably enough, argued that the true significance of Abdulmutallab's attempt was his ability to move a bomb past airport security. This was true: despite billions of dollars spent to protect the aviation sector from terrorists, a twenty-three-year-old had been able to sneak a bomb onto a plane. Yet many of these commentators likewise drew a hasty conclusion. The Abdulmutallab plot, they contended, showed that U.S. security expenditures were not wasteful, that there remained an obvious need to continue to protect the country from the threat of terrorism.

This view left two questions unanswered. First, if terrorist innovations had consistently thwarted our new measures, how could we be sure that further expensive upgrades wouldn't again be overcome by relatively simple adaptations? Second, how did all of these security expenditures fit into the terrorists' strategy? The U.S. economy had dramatically collapsed just a year earlier, in September 2008, and it would be fair to ask if one explicit purpose of terrorist attacks was to drive up America's security costs. To put it differently: Do our security outlays make us *more vulnerable* rather than safer?

After the October 2010 cartridge bomb plot, commentators again launched into the same polarized debates that had followed Abdulmutallab's attempt. These arguments were no more sophisticated than those we had seen the last time around. Some pundits argued that the forces of Islamist militancy were weak because they had failed yet again to destroy their target; others argued that these forces were strong, because they had again managed to get explosives on board airplanes. Missing from these debates once again was what the terrorists themselves thought. Did they see the cartridge bomb plot as a failure or as a success?

Al Qaeda's Game Plan

The terrorists' voices were missing until AQAP released the special issue of its English-language magazine, *Inspire*, commemorating the attacks. That publication outlined the basic disparity between what the ink-cartridge plot cost the terrorists and what it cost their enemies: a $4,200 price tag for AQAP versus, in the magazine's estimation, "billions of dollars in new security measures" for the United States and other Western countries.

In fact, *Inspire* outlined a fundamental shift in strategy that should already have been evident to careful observers. It warned that future terrorist attacks against the West would be "smaller, but more frequent," an approach that "some may refer to as the strategy of a thousand cuts." Under this approach, the fact that the ink-cartridge plot killed nobody did not mean that it had failed. Rather, AQAP's ability to get the disguised explosives aboard planes, and thus drive up the West's security costs, made the plot a success.

Although the magazine's slick packaging was new, al Qaeda's emphasis on bleeding the U.S. economy was not. From the late al Qaeda leader Osama bin Laden's earliest declaration of war on the United States, the group had linked its attacks to the U.S. economy. Key thinkers within al Qaeda had long believed that economic power was the source of U.S. military might, and thus they saw weakening the economy as a critical aspect of victory.

Al Qaeda's economic strategy of jihad would go through several refinements. Before we examine them, it is worth taking a moment to clarify the terminology employed in this book. The Arabic word *jihad*, which literally means "struggle," is an Islamic religious concept with a multiplicity of connotations. For many Muslims, jihad is a peaceful inner struggle to follow the dictates of their faith. Islamist militant organizations, which this book refers to as "jihadi" groups, focus on the physical warfare aspect of jihad and have an interpretation of when such warfare is justified that many Muslims reject and revile.

Although the term *jihadi* is controversial among terrorism researchers—in large part because it is derived from the religious term *jihad*—it has the benefit of being an organic term, the way that those within the movement refer to themselves. Moreover, as the esteemed terrorism researcher Jarret Brachman notes, this label has "been validated as the least worst option across the Arabic-speaking world," including being employed in Arabic-language print and broadcast media.[15]

The refinements to al Qaeda's economic strategy of jihad occurred as the group was forced to respond to external events, as it seized on opportunities provided to it, and as it became savvier. The strategy's initial phase linked terrorist attacks broadly to economic harm. A prime example of this is the 9/11 attacks, which destroyed a major economic target (the World Trade Center).

A second identifiable phase, which al Qaeda pursued even as it continued to attack economic targets, can be called "bleed until bankruptcy." Bin Laden publicly articulated the bleed-until-bankruptcy plan in October 2004, in a video he dramatically released on the eve of the U.S. presidential election—at a time when many Americans believed he was dead.[16] This phase seeks to embroil the United States and its allies in draining wars in the Muslim world. Just as the mujahedin sapped the Russians' economy and will during the bloody Afghan-Soviet war in the 1980s, al Qaeda sees itself now doing the same to the United States.

There would be other phases in al Qaeda's economic warfare strategy. In December 2004, bin Laden began to exhort his followers to carry out attacks targeting one of America's greatest vulnerabilities: its reliance on imported oil. Numerous attacks thereafter were aimed at oil targets, most critically in Saudi Arabia.

In all of these phases of al Qaeda's economic warfare strategy, the group succeeded in cutting the United States and injuring it. The 9/11 attacks were a particularly deep cut: in addition to leaving almost three thousand dead on U.S. soil, the destruction of New York's Twin Towers and a large section of the Pentagon traumatized the nation and forced the mobilization of a great deal of resources for the fight against al Qaeda and other jihadi groups. But after the September 2008 collapse of the U.S. economy, jihadi warfare entered a new period, its "strategy of a thousand cuts." This new phase was brought on in part because America's weakened position made it seem mortal.

"How much more can the U.S. Treasury handle?" the radical Yemeni American cleric Anwar al Awlaki asked in March 2010. Referring to Abdulmutallab's attack on the Detroit-bound plane, he continued, "9/11, the war in Afghanistan and Iraq, and then operations such as that of our brother Umar Farouk, which could not have cost more than a few thousand dollars, end up draining the U.S. treasury billions of dollars. . . . For how long can the U.S. survive this war of attrition?"[17]

In this new phase, even attacks that do not destroy their target, such as Abdulmutallab's underwear bomb and the ink-cartridge plot, can be considered successes by America's jihadi adversaries because of the costs they impose. Al Qaeda leaders, operatives, and sympathizers believe that they are winning their fight against the West, and they have a point. As Abu al Fituh al Maghribi wrote in the online jihadi magazine the *Vanguards of Khurasan*, the U.S. economy "collapsed horrendously for the first time in recent history, and they [the Americans] lost their trust in their system."[18] Jihadi militants have certainly been tenacious and skilled adversaries. But many of the deepest wounds the United States has experienced have been self-inflicted.

America's Errors

It did not have to turn out this way. On September 11, 2001, even after absorbing a dramatic terrorist strike, the United States remained the world's unchallenged military and economic superpower. The 9/11 attacks were a clear moral outrage, and al Qaeda represented a threat to numerous governments. The outpouring of sympathy for the United States was immediate and widespread internationally, with various countries pledging their cooperation in the fight against jihadi militancy. The conventional wisdom among U.S. politicians and commentators was that al Qaeda had underestimated America's resolve: the vigorous response to come would test, and almost certainly overwhelm, the militant group's resiliency.

The past decade of efforts has in fact degraded al Qaeda. Key leaders have been captured or killed, and it is experiencing financial trouble.[19] Yet despite the harm that has been done to al Qaeda, the United States is in a far *weaker* position relative to the jihadi group now than it was ten years ago. There are many reasons this is so, many core errors that the United States has made. The United States has simply never taken the time to fully understand al Qaeda's strategy: its ends, ways, and means.

As a result, U.S. planners failed to comprehend two core goals that al Qaeda possessed: bleeding the U.S. economy and making its conflict with the United States as broad as possible. In part because of this failure to understand al Qaeda's strategy, the United States ended up with a system for fighting the militant group that is almost precisely backward in three important ways.

First, although a great deal of resources was devoted to the fight against jihadi militancy, these resources have been allocated in an incredibly inefficient manner. The most visible example has been airport security. In the immediate wake of 9/11, searches of airline passengers were intensified, but every effort was made to ensure that no group felt unfairly singled out. Rather than having a system that focused its resources on passengers most likely to pose a terrorist threat, we ended up with one where figures like Al Gore received unnecessary scrutiny. Gore was in fact twice singled out for extra screening during a 2002 trip to Wisconsin. A seventy-five-year-old congressman, John Dingell, was forced to strip down to his underwear in Washington, D.C.'s Reagan National Airport in January 2002 to prove that his artificial hip, and not a weapon, had set off a metal detector.[20]

There was, of course, a noble goal underlying the desire to avoid terrorist profiling: policy makers wanted to avoid making people (specifically, those of Arab or South Asian descent) feel unfairly singled out on the basis of their ethnicity. But there are a couple of problems with the way this concern was operationalized. There is no question that singling out someone like Al Gore—a former presidential candidate, vice president, and senator—for extra screening is a plain waste of policing resources. Even though Gore's selection for additional screening represents only a couple of incidents, it is indicative of a broader inefficiency that, aggregated over the entire system, caused airport security to be far more resource-intensive than necessary. The other problem concerns public debates over profiling. When many pundits speak of profiling terrorists, they're talking about racial or ethnic profiling alone. But many other factors can be incorporated into the terrorist profile that will increase the efficacy of the practice while minimizing the risk of unfairly and unnecessarily singling out any one ethnicity. The impoverished public debate on this issue has helped to constrain the range of options available to policy makers.

Compounding the inefficiency of our policing efforts, immediately after 9/11, states, municipalities, and private contractors realized that a vast array of policies could be packaged as "counterterrorism" when they would have a marginal impact at best on the terrorist threat. And politicians thought they could show the public how serious they were about tackling the issue by devoting resources to these various proposals despite their marginal impact.

The second major problem with the way we fight jihadi militancy has been the politicization of the fight against terrorism. Politicians' realization that they could demonstrate their bona fides on terrorism by supporting programs that had little to do with actually addressing the problem was one product of this politicization. The public clearly cared deeply about the issue—but using an issue to win a political campaign is not the same as actually addressing the problem. By making terrorism a hard-fought partisan issue, we have created a climate that produces posturing, bad policy, and squabbling that weakens the country.

A third major error has been an eagerness to broaden, rather than narrow, the war on terrorism. President George W. Bush said in 2002 that "the best way to keep America safe from terrorism is to go after terrorists where they plan and hide."[21] He would later phrase this somewhat differently and more directly: "We're taking the fight to the terrorists abroad so we don't have to face them here at home." Terrorist safe havens in remote parts of the world can indeed directly threaten the United States, and the war in Afghanistan was necessary rather than a war of choice. After all, al Qaeda's safe haven in that country posed a systemic risk of another catastrophic act of terrorism against America.[22] But the United States proved to be too eager to enter wars abroad, in particular the adventure in Iraq that was supposed to advance the war on terrorism but has been so costly in both blood and treasure. The decision to invade Iraq was made with little appreciation of the second-order and third-order consequences that it would produce—and little appreciation of its potential to breathe life into al Qaeda rather than bury it.

Ten years after the 9/11 attacks, our enemies are correct to see the United States as weaker: economically troubled, militarily exhausted, and politically divided. Indeed, although it is difficult to precisely measure al Qaeda's contribution to America's grave economic woes, it is certain that these three core errors—coupled with al Qaeda's own ingenuity and deadly competence—made America's war against the jihadi group incredibly costly.

The 9/11 attacks cost the United States at least $1 trillion through direct property damage and second-order economic consequences, including the impact on the stock market. Thereafter, budgetary outlays for the military operations in Afghanistan and Iraq that were undertaken as a response to al Qaeda's attacks have been about $1.3 trillion. This included the cost of the operations themselves, expenditures to secure military bases, reconstruction costs, and foreign aid.[23] But direct expenditures do not encompass the full cost of these operations. When second-order consequences and opportunity costs are considered, the Iraq War alone may have cost the United States more than $3 trillion.[24] And then there are the costs of escalating homeland security and intelligence measures.

Our response to bin Laden has been incredibly costly, and the present system is likely unsustainable. Bin Laden's strategy for defeating the United States survives his death—and if we don't understand what this strategy is, how it developed, and how America's responses have been so ill-suited to defeating al Qaeda, the United States may find itself locked in combat with bin Laden's legacy for longer than necessary.

If bin Laden's death is to truly represent a turning point in the fight against jihadi militancy, it won't be due just to his importance to al Qaeda. Rather, it will be because his death allowed the United States to reevaluate its paradigms for protecting itself from and defeating this adversary. But to do so, it is first necessary to understand the key errors that the country has made along the way and why these mistakes occurred.

2

How to Beat a Superpower

> If you know others and know yourself, you will not be imperiled in a hundred battles; if you do not know others and do not know yourself, you will be imperiled in every single battle.
>
> —*Sun Tzu,* The Art of War

The United States has suffered for its failure to understand al Qaeda and its late leader Osama bin Laden. Before al Qaeda destroyed the Twin Towers in New York City and a large section of the Pentagon on that fateful Tuesday in September 2001, leaving almost three thousand dead on U.S. soil, few within the government paid any attention to it—this despite the fact that by the end of 2000, al Qaeda had already executed two dramatic terrorist strikes against American targets. The United States was slow to recognize the growing strategic challenge posed by nonstate actors like al Qaeda. Thus, when the U.S. was struck by the deadliest terrorist attack the world has seen, it had no plan at the ready for deposing the Taliban regime in Afghanistan that had been sheltering the jihadi group.

Even after the 9/11 attacks made the threat that al Qaeda posed undeniable, the United States did little to understand the group's strategy for defeating its superpower rival—which in turn retarded American planning. Since then, the United States has often mistaken tactics for strategy. More problematic, the United States has committed to drastic measures—such as the invasion of Iraq, a country that had nothing to do with the 9/11 attacks—without giving sufficient thought to how doing so could strengthen its adversary. Thus, America's failure to understand al Qaeda has made it difficult to avoid self-inflicted wounds. This chapter examines al Qaeda's origins and shows that two major prongs of the jihadi group's strategy—to undermine the economy of its enemy and to make the battlefield on which its war would be fought as broad as possible—were eminently knowable by the time 9/11 occurred.

Bin Laden in the Afghan-Soviet War

Osama bin Laden was born in the late 1950s to Mohammed bin Laden, who from humble beginnings in Yemen rose to become a multibillionaire construction magnate and confidant of Saudi Arabia's royal family. Osama had twenty-four brothers and twenty-nine sisters; his father, who practiced polygamy, had a total of twenty-two wives throughout his life. When Osama was only ten years old, Mohammed bin Laden perished in a plane crash. By all accounts, Osama was pious and religiously conservative when he was growing up in Jeddah, Saudi Arabia. One example of his religiosity in his younger years was his reprimand of a friend for wearing shorts—which bin Laden saw as immodest and religiously proscribed—to play soccer.[1] Those who knew him during this period recall a shy young man, more a follower than a leader.

Bin Laden rose to international prominence after the Soviet Union invaded Afghanistan in December 1979. The Soviet invasion was prompted by multiple factors, including an Islamist insurgency that threatened the country's pro-Soviet regime, concern that the United States might deepen its role in Afghanistan after the

Iranian revolution undermined U.S. regional interests, and infighting among Afghanistan's communists that culminated in bloody inter-necine clashes and the assassination of the Afghan president Nur Mohammed Taraki.[2] Although the Soviet general staff opposed the invasion, Leonid Brezhnev, the general secretary of the Communist Party, insisted that operations in Afghanistan would end successfully in three to four weeks.[3]

The war did not turn out as Brezhnev predicted. The Soviets with-drew only after nine years of costly occupation, during which they experienced stiff resistance from the Afghan mujahedin backed by the United States, Saudi Arabia, and Pakistan. The mujahedin were the beneficiaries of the largest U.S. covert aid program since the Vietnam War, with American support (totaling around $3 billion) matched dollar for dollar by Saudi Arabia. The Americans strengthened the mujahedin by providing supplies and weaponry, including Stinger missiles that helped to negate the Soviet airpower advantage.

Bin Laden traveled to Pakistan in the early 1980s, soon after the Afghan-Soviet war began. Bruce Riedel, a Brookings Institution senior fellow and former CIA officer, notes that once bin Laden arrived, he became "a major financier of the mujahedin, providing cash to the rela-tives of wounded or martyred fighters, building hospitals, and helping the millions of Afghan refugees fleeing to the border region of Pakistan."[4]

Bin Laden and a radical Palestinian cleric named Abdullah Azzam founded an organization known as the Services Bureau (*maktab al khidmat*), which was dedicated to integrating Arabs into the anti-Soviet struggle by placing them with relief organizations or alongside Afghan factions on the battlefield. "Azzam was the critical force both ideologi-cally and organizationally for the recruitment of thousands of Muslims from around the world to engage in some way with the Afghan struggle against the Soviets," writes Peter Bergen, a CNN national security analyst and astute chronicler of al Qaeda's history. "And Azzam would become bin Laden's mentor, the first and most important of a series of father figures that he would find to replace his own father."[5]

Bin Laden's wealth and financial generosity earned him many friends, and many wanted to curry the rich young Saudi's favor. But it was his first trip to the front lines in Afghanistan in 1984 that left a lasting impression on bin Laden and gave him a thirst for more action. In 1986, he established a base for Arab fighters near Khost in eastern Afghanistan, where the Soviets had a garrison. This was a divisive move.

Jamal Khalifa, a university classmate of bin Laden's who also became involved in the anti-Soviet resistance, was concerned about bin Laden's lack of military experience, and he believed that these plans would result in many young Arabs being needlessly killed on the front lines.[6] After a harsh confrontation over bin Laden's plans, the two friends became distant. Azzam also thought that the Arab fighters should be embedded with Afghan units to teach the latter "true Islam," and thus he opposed a separate Arab force.

Bin Laden and his comrades-in-arms, establishing the base near Khost despite the opposition of Azzam, Khalifa, and others, called it al Masada, Arabic for "the lion's den." They were attacked by the Soviets in the spring of 1987—which was rather predictable, given al Masada's proximity to a Soviet garrison. But bin Laden and his comrades unexpectedly held their ground in the face of several attacks by Russian special forces (*spetsnaz*). This intense combat, lasting for about three weeks, launched bin Laden to prominence in the Arab media as a war hero.[7]

In reality, that battle was completely insignificant for the outcome of the Afghan-Soviet war. Although bin Laden subsequently emphasized his role in the conflict, every serious history concludes that the "Afghan Arabs," the fighters from the Arab world who traveled to South Asia to join the war against the Soviets, were not a military factor in Russia's defeat. Nonetheless, bin Laden's time on the Afghan battlefield was a formative experience for him that shaped the approach he would take when running al Qaeda.

Russia didn't just withdraw from Afghanistan in ignominious defeat. The Soviet empire itself collapsed soon thereafter, in late 1991. Thus, bin Laden thought that he had not only bested one of the world's superpowers on the battlefield but had also played an important role in its demise. Regardless of the dubious nature of this belief, it seems to have been bin Laden's perception.

From the view that he had played a critical role in causing the Soviet empire to fall, we can discern a further aspect of bin Laden's thought: the centrality of economics to his fight against a superpower.

It is indisputable, after all, that the Soviet withdrawal from Afghanistan did not directly collapse the Soviet Union. The most persuasive connection that can be drawn between that war and the Soviet empire's dissolution is through the costs imposed by the conflict. Indeed, bin Laden spoke of how he used "guerrilla warfare and the war of attrition to fight tyrannical superpowers, as we, alongside the mujahedin, bled Russia for ten years, until it went bankrupt."[8]

This may seem like an implausible propaganda piece that even bin Laden couldn't have believed. But let's examine one construction of this argument: that the costs imposed by the Afghan-Soviet war prevented the Soviet Union from adapting to other economic challenges. One such challenge was grain shortages. Since 1928–1929, with the expropriation of farmers' property and forced collectivization, bad agricultural policies had left the Soviets with no growth in grain production since the 1960s. Meanwhile, they experienced an urban population increase of eighty million. Once the world's biggest grain exporter, Russia by the 1980s had become its biggest importer instead.[9]

Compounding the problem, Saudi Arabia decided on September 13, 1985, to ramp up its oil production in order to collapse world prices. Oil prices dropped precipitously from around $30 a barrel to just $12 a barrel by March 1986.[10] While being battered by huge expenditures to pay for its grain imports, the Soviet Union's oil export–based economy was also being pressured by a significantly smaller revenue stream. For this reason, Yegor Gaidar—who from 1991 to 1994 served as Russia's acting prime minister, minister of economy, and first deputy prime minister—has written that the combination of grain shortages and falling oil prices ultimately undermined the Soviet Union.[11] Although Gaidar does not blame the Afghan-Soviet war, his arguments are instructive on how someone might see that conflict playing a role in the Soviet Union's collapse by diminishing the resources available to deal with the twin catastrophes of grain shortages and low oil prices.

The Soviet Union ended up with enormous budget deficits, Gaidar writes, and therefore faced difficult choices. To cut costs, it could give up its hold over Eastern Europe, ration food to reduce its grain imports, or massively cut its military-industrial complex. Instead, the government ignored the problem and borrowed money from overseas (a solution that may sound hauntingly familiar to us today). By 1989 the Soviet Union's credit rating had fallen, and its loans dried up.

In need of $100 billion from the West and faced with possible famine in Moscow, Soviet premier Mikhail Gorbachev essentially offered political concessions in exchange for credit, and these concessions precipitated an August 1991 coup by hard-liners. But the economic situation doomed this coup from the outset. Even if the hard-liners crushed the demonstrators who turned out to oppose them, Gaidar asks, "Would the grain appear? Where would they find the food necessary to feed the larger cities? Would the West rapidly give the $100 billion? Their case, like the Soviet state itself, was entirely lost." The Soviet state essentially ended with a November 1991 letter from its Foreign Trade Bank informing the country's leadership that it had no money left.[12]

The point is not that Gaidar's view of how this history unfolded should be accepted over competing accounts. Rather, Gaidar's history is presented to illustrate how economics can be seen as relevant to the Soviet Union's demise—and how one could reasonably believe that the Afghan-Soviet war played a role by imposing costs that, coupled with other problems, overwhelmed the Soviet state's ability to adapt and survive. Indeed, some serious scholars credit the Afghan-Soviet war as being a significant factor, though not the sole one, in the Soviet Union's collapse.[13]

The fact that a major strategic lesson taken by bin Laden from his experiences in the Afghan-Soviet war was the importance of economics to defeating a superpower is underscored by his numerous comparisons of the United States to the Soviet Union. When he did so, the comparison was explicitly economic in nature. For example, in October 2004 bin Laden said that just as the Afghan mujahedin and Arab fighters had destroyed Russia economically, al Qaeda was now doing the same to the United States, "continuing this policy in bleeding America to the point of bankruptcy."[14] Similarly, in a September 2007 video message, bin Laden claimed that "thinkers who study events and happenings" were now predicting the American empire's collapse. Comparing President Bush to Brezhnev, the architect of the Soviet invasion of Afghanistan, bin Laden said, "The mistakes of Brezhnev are being repeated by Bush."[15]

Had American strategists understood from the outset the connection between economics and bin Laden's envisioned path to victory, perhaps the United States could have avoided some of its costly blunders. But it is not clear that U.S. strategists saw this link—even after bin Laden boasted of it on the world stage.

Broadening the Fight

Another aspect of bin Laden's experience in the Afghan-Soviet war that influenced his strategic understanding of his fight against the United States was the breadth of the anti-Russian resistance. The Soviet invasion of Afghanistan outraged the Muslim world, including heads of state, clerics, the Arab media, and the man on the street. In January 1980, Egypt's prime minister declared the Soviet invasion "a flagrant aggression against an Islamic state" and said that it showed the Soviet Union was "but an extension of the colonialist Tsarist regime."[16]

By the end of the month, the foreign ministers of thirty-five Muslim countries, as well as the Palestine Liberation Organization, passed a resolution through the Organization of the Islamic Conference (OIC) declaring the invasion of Afghanistan to be a "flagrant violation of all international covenants and norms, as well as a serious threat to peace and security in the region and throughout the world." The Soviet-installed regime in Afghanistan was expelled from the OIC, the delegates of which urged all Muslim countries "to withhold recognition of the illegal regime in Afghanistan and sever diplomatic relations with that country until the complete withdrawal of Soviet troops." On January 30, 1980, the *Christian Science Monitor* described this condemnation of Soviet actions as "some of the strongest terms ever used by a third-world parley."[17]

The stream of Arabs who flocked to South Asia to help the Afghan cause—about ten thousand—was a testament to the widespread outrage caused by the invasion. Mohammed Hafez, an associate professor in the Naval Postgraduate School's National Security Affairs Department, notes that these Arab volunteers "included humanitarian aid workers, cooks, drivers, accountants, teachers, doctors, engineers and religious preachers. They built camps, dug and treated water wells, and attended to the sick and wounded."[18]

There was, of course, also a contingent of Arab foreign fighters, of which bin Laden became a part. But the volunteers who went to South Asia were not the only Arabs to support the Afghan resistance. The Afghan jihad was also aided by a donor network known as the "golden chain," whose financiers came primarily from Saudi Arabia and other Gulf Arab states.[19]

Essentially, bin Laden sat at the top of a major multinational organization during the Afghan-Soviet war. Its members included fighters, aid workers, and other volunteers. It enjoyed a significant media presence, external donors, and widespread support. Indeed, when al Qaeda was later engaged in a global fight against the United States, bin Laden and his companions understood both the media and the struggle for sympathy and allegiance throughout the Muslim world as crucial battlefields.

In a 2005 letter to al Qaeda in Iraq (AQI) leader Abu Musab al Zarqawi, bin Laden's deputy, Ayman al Zawahiri, noted that "more than half of this battle is taking place in the battlefield of the media." Zawahiri said that when it comes to attaining the caliphate, a goal of al Qaeda's that will be discussed shortly, "the strongest weapon which the mujahedin enjoy, after the help and granting of success by God, is popular support from the Muslim masses in Iraq, and the surrounding Muslim countries."[20] This is a telling statement: it shows how important it is to al Qaeda to win Muslim support and turn the Islamic world against the United States.

Had U.S. strategists understood al Qaeda's goal of broadening its fight against the United States, they might have raised more objections to the invasion of Iraq, which created a far broader battlefield for America.

Al Qaeda's Birth

Al Qaeda was founded in August 1988, in the waning days of the Afghan-Soviet war.[21] At that time, bin Laden and Abdullah Azzam agreed that the organization they had built during the conflict shouldn't

simply dissolve when the war ended.[22] Rather, they wanted the structure they had created to serve as "the base" (*al qaeda*) for future mujahedin efforts. As Azzam and bin Laden repurposed this structure into
an organization that would endure, al Qaeda's founding minutes reveal a
broad mission. They describe the organization as "basically an organized
Islamic faction" with the goal of lifting "the word of God, to make His
religion victorious."[23]

Although Azzam had been the leader in the Services Bureau, by
August 1988 it was clear that bin Laden was the head of al Qaeda.[24]
The group was led by an advisory (*shura*) council in which bin Laden
held the dominant position. Under this council the group had an intri-
cate structure, including military, financial, and political committees,
an intelligence wing, and a media-propaganda wing. In other words,
al Qaeda was a prototypically centralized militant organization up until
the time it executed the 9/11 attacks.

In addition to the group's hierarchical structure, there were specific qualifications for each leadership position as well as for mem-
bership. The commander, for example, was required to have been a
member of al Qaeda for at least seven years, have a sufficient understanding of Islamic law and jihad, and "have operational experience
from jihad." Below the commander were a deputy, who must share the
same qualifications; a secretary, whom the commander appointed; and
a command council.[25]

Early documents also detailed members' duties, salaries, and even
vacation time.[26] Under this system, bachelors qualified for a round-trip
plane ticket home after a year, but they also had the option of using the
ticket for the hajj (the religious pilgrimage to Mecca that is considered
one of the five pillars of Islam) instead. The application to train for
jihad in one of al Qaeda's camps inquired about the applicant's education level, professional experience, medical history, and how much of
the Qur'an he had memorized.[27]

Despite bin Laden's disdain for the United States because of its support for Israel, initially al Qaeda wasn't focused on America; rather, its
mission centered on the threat that communism posed to the *umma* (the
worldwide community of Muslims), especially the communist regime
that then ruled South Yemen.[28] But Iraq's August 2, 1990, invasion of

Kuwait transformed bin Laden's outlook. Saddam Hussein's invasion of the tiny monarchy to his south posed an unmistakable threat to Saudi Arabia. With a hundred thousand Iraqi troops amassed in Kuwait, which shared a border with Saudi Arabia, it seemed that the Saudis could be next. President George H. W. Bush offered to furnish a quarter of a million U.S. soldiers to defend the Saudi monarchy. Bin Laden, however, had a different idea.

Bin Laden approached the Saudi defense minister, Prince Sultan bin Abdul Aziz al Saud, and suggested that an army of mujahedin, veterans of the Afghan-Soviet war, could defend the kingdom. His quixotic proposal was politely declined, and a U.S.-led multinational army succeeded in liberating Kuwait in 1991.[29]

Bin Laden saw the U.S. troop presence in Saudi Arabia as a violation of his faith, a view informed by a famous hadith (part of the collection of the customs and sayings of the Prophet Muhammad) in which the prophet, on his death bed, ordered that "two deens [faiths] shall not co-exist in the land of the Arabs."[30] Rather than seeing the Americans as a friendly force defending Saudi Arabia from Iraqi aggression, bin Laden saw them as invaders.

In the spring of 1991, bin Laden left Saudi Arabia for Sudan, where he resolved to sponsor attacks on the United States. Neither a December 1992 bombing of two hotels in Yemen, which housed U.S. soldiers en route to the Horn of Africa for Operation Restore Hope (a U.N.-sanctioned humanitarian mission to Somalia), nor the indeterminate role that al Qaeda played in the October 1993 downing of a U.S. helicopter in Mogadishu launched bin Laden into the Western public's consciousness.[31] But his involvement in terrorism did come to the attention of the U.S. and Saudi intelligence services, and the resulting pressure on Sudan's government caused it to see bin Laden as a liability.

Sudan seized the construction equipment that formed the backbone of bin Laden's business in that country, giving him only a fraction of its value in return.[32] His business suddenly gone, and clearly on his enemies' radar, bin Laden fled to Afghanistan on May 18, 1996—returning to the country where he had first carved out his reputation. The fundamentalist Taliban regime that controlled about 90 percent of that country agreed to protect him. It said, in one statement,

"If an animal sought refuge with us we would have had no choice but to protect it. How, then, about a man who has given himself and his wealth in the cause of Allah and in the cause of jihad in Afghanistan?"[33]

Al Qaeda's War against America

On August 23, 1996, bin Laden, within a few months of arriving in Afghanistan, issued a manifesto proclaiming himself at war with the world's only remaining superpower. Bin Laden's overarching grievance was the U.S. military presence in Saudi Arabia, which he described as "one of the worst catastrophes to befall the Muslims since the death of the Prophet."[34] Bin Laden also named America's support for Israel and U.S.-led sanctions against Saddam Hussein's Iraq as additional justifications for his fight. (There was no love lost between bin Laden and Iraq's secular dictator, but he blamed U.S. sanctions for a humanitarian catastrophe in that country.) Few in the United States took notice of bin Laden's declaration, either among the public at large or within the government.

As Michael Scheuer, the former head of the CIA's Bin Laden Unit, has written, these political grievances were intended to place al Qaeda's fight within the realm of "a defensive jihad sanctioned by the revealed word of God."[35] That is, in contrast to an "offensive jihad," expansionist warfare designed to enlarge the abode of Islam, this was a case, bin Laden argued, in which the faith itself was under attack by its foes. In such instances, each Muslim has an *individual obligation* to join the battle. It's not enough if some group takes up arms; this must be done by all Muslims. If such a religious duty is an individual obligation (*fard ayn*), young people don't even have to receive permission from their parents to join the fight.

This declaration of war did not represent an aberrant turn within Islamic thought, as some commentators have claimed. Although there are credible, powerful, and widely held interpretations of the faith that find bin Laden's arguments and actions unjustified and immoral, bin Laden does draw on legitimate sources, tap into venerable currents of Islamic thought, and make arguments that resonate with many of the faithful.[36] As previously mentioned, the concept of jihad has variegated meanings, and there are nonmilitary aspects of this struggle. But as Bernard Lewis, professor emeritus of Near Eastern Studies at Princeton University, has written, "The overwhelming majority of early authorities, citing the relevant passages in the Qur'an, the commentaries, and the traditions of the Prophet, discuss jihad in military terms."[37]

As a salafi—an adherent to an austere religious methodology that seeks to re-create Islam as it was supposedly practiced by the Prophet Muhammad and the first generations of Muslims—bin Laden argued that other Muslims should return to the earliest, purest interpretation of the faith. If Muslims do return to the earliest interpretation of Islam, salafi jihadism holds, they will understand the righteousness and the necessity of these calls for violence.

Thus bin Laden tapped into currents of thought that preceded him. These currents of thought have also survived his death. The narrative of al Qaeda and other salafi jihadi groups holds that Islam itself is under attack, both physically and morally, by the United States and other forces of nonbelief (including the corrupt regimes that dominated the Middle East throughout the twentieth century) and that violence is necessary to defend the faith.[38] This is not to say that al Qaeda is correct in its interpretation of the Islamic faith, or otherwise. But it is always a mistake to underestimate the strength of your enemy's arguments, which is precisely what many Western analysts have done in the case of al Qaeda and other salafi jihadi groups.

There has been a division within the jihadi movement concerning whether it should focus on the "near enemy"—the toppling of the corrupt Arab regimes, which jihadis sometimes refer to as apostate governments—or instead target the "far enemy," the United States and other Western powers.[39] Thomas Hegghammer, a senior research fellow at the Norwegian Defense Research Establishment in Oslo, notes that this controversy may be "the most significant political rift in the world of militant Islamism since the mid-1990s."[40]

Although al Qaeda views both the United States and the apostate Arab regimes as its enemies, it has largely focused its warfare against the United States and other Western countries. A study released in the summer of 2009 by a jihadi "think tank" that supports al Qaeda's decision to do so explains that in waging war against the Saudi regime, the group was faced with the decision of fighting Saudi Arabia directly or striking at the American presence in that country. If it fought Saudi Arabia, the attacks would have met with condemnation by the Saudi *ulema* (religious scholars). Al Qaeda's war against the Saudis would have been a losing effort, "given the size and weight of the religious institution, and the legitimacy and prestige it instilled in the people's minds across more than 70 years."[41]

On the other hand, the study viewed striking at the Americans as a wise choice, because the kingdom would be forced to defend their presence, "which will cost them their legitimacy in the eyes of Muslims." Moreover, the *ulema* would be delegitimized if they too defended the U.S. presence. Thus, many of those who favor fighting the United States rather than the "near enemy" think that jihadi groups can weaken both foes simultaneously in that manner.

Although the political grievances that bin Laden and other jihadi thinkers have articulated illuminate their short-term ambitions, the movement also possesses long-term goals. One is to spread sharia, or Islamic law. As bin Laden said in a 1998 letter published in the Rawalpindi-based newspaper *Jang*, he believes that al Qaeda's struggle should continue until "the Islamic sharia is enforced on the land of God."[42] He has repeatedly emphasized the importance of establishing sharia since then, as have other jihadi leaders.[43] Extrapolating from their conception of the religious concept of *tawhid* (the unity of God), these jihadi thinkers argue that if only Allah can be worshiped and obeyed, then only Allah's laws can have legitimacy.[44] The version of sharia that these thinkers embrace is undeniably harsh. Illustrating this, when Peter Bergen asked bin Laden's London media representative Khalid al Fawwaz in the late 1990s what present government most resembled his vision of an ideal Islamic state, Fawwaz replied that Afghanistan's brutal Taliban regime was "getting there."[45]

For perspective, the Taliban's treatment of women was so inhumane that Physicians for Human Rights released a report in 1998 noting that "no other regime in the world has methodically and violently forced half of its population into virtual house arrest, prohibiting them on pain of physical punishment from showing their faces, seeking medical care without a male escort, or attending school."[46] Homosexuals were executed, although there was some disagreement among jurists as to whether they should be pushed to their deaths from a high altitude or crushed beneath a toppling wall. Virtually every imaginable form of light entertainment was banned, including kite flying, movies, television, music, and dancing. Also banned were paintings and the celebration of holidays that were cultural rather than religious, such as the Afghan new year.[47] Afghans were beaten and sometimes killed for flouting this complex and outright absurd set of rules.

Another goal of the jihadi movement is reestablishment of the caliphate, a theocratic government that would rule a united Muslim world. Islam's first caliph (Arabic for "successor," denoting that the caliph follows Muhammad as the faith's political leader) was Abu Bakr, who led the *umma* beginning in 632 A.D., after the Prophet Muhammad's death. One jihadi thinker, in a representative statement, described Mustafa Kemal Atatürk's abolition of the caliphate in 1924 as the "mother of all crimes."[48]

Similarly, bin Laden made explicit reference to the grave injustice of the caliphate's fall in his 1996 declaration of war against the United States and referred to the need to reestablish it multiple times thereafter.[49] Indeed, the introduction to al Qaeda's training manual describes the manual as a "contribution toward paving the road that leads to majestic Allah and establishing a caliphate."[50] And Zawahiri has written that al Qaeda's "intended goal in this age is the establishment of a caliphate in the manner of the Prophet."[51]

Yet the caliphate's establishment wouldn't end the war against the infidels. One work that shows how the jihad would continue is Jordanian journalist Fouad Hussein's influential 2005 book *Al Zarqawi: The Second Generation of al Qaeda*, which Pulitzer Prize–winning author Lawrence Wright has called "perhaps the most definitive outline of al Qaeda's master plan."[52] Hussein shows that in this master plan, al Qaeda's strategists foresee a "stage of all-out confrontation" with the forces of atheism after the caliphate is declared. He writes, "Al Qaeda ideologues believe that the all-out confrontation with the forces of falsehood will take a few years at most. The enormous potential of the Islamic state—particularly because the Muslim population will amount to more than 1.5 billion—will terrify the enemy and prompt them to retreat rapidly."[53]

Some Western analysts fail to appreciate what the caliphate's reestablishment signifies. For example, Michael Scheuer, in his 2004 book *Imperial Hubris*, describes Saudi Arabia as "a regime that, since its founding, has deliberately fostered an Islamic ideology, whose goals—unlike bin Laden's—can be met only by annihilating all non-Muslims."[54] This claim is nonsensical. It is premised on the idea that bin Laden's practice of Islam (and that of al Qaeda) was *more moderate* than Saudi Arabia's. There is not a shred of evidence to suggest that this is the case. Bin Laden turned against the Saudi monarchy not because it was too extreme nor because he had rejected the tenets of its Wahhabi creed, but rather because he believed that the Saudis *were not living up to their strict ideals.*[55] Once Scheuer concedes that Saudi ideology is designed to foster an eternal conflict with non-Muslims—a view supported by a literal reading of Wahhabi scholarship—it makes no sense to say that al Qaeda's conflict with the West is anything but existential.

Scheuer may have been conflating al Qaeda's often invoked political grievances with its overall objectives. Or he may have focused on the fact that bin Laden had declared a defensive jihad rather than an offensive one—and assumed that al Qaeda could not declare an offensive jihad, which in Scheuer's estimation "must be called by a Caliph, the recognized leader of the world Islamic community," a position that has not existed since 1924.[56] If so, Scheuer is overly casual in dismissing the possibility that, like the twentieth-century Pakistani Islamist ideologue Sayyid Abul A'la Maududi, al Qaeda might see the distinction between offensive and defensive jihad as artificial.

Maududi wrote that jihad is "both offensive and defensive at one and the same time": it is offensive because a Muslim undertaking jihad "attacks the rule of an opposing ideology," but is simultaneously defensive because by mounting such an attack, a Muslim can "protect the principles of Islam in space-time forces."[57] Moreover, if al Qaeda were able to create the caliphate that it desires, that superstate would have the necessary authority to declare an offensive jihad. The role of the caliphate in al Qaeda's strategic vision thus cannot be ignored.

America Turns Away

It was not just bin Laden's 1996 declaration of war against the United States that went unnoticed in the West. Even a couple of skilled and deadly terrorist attacks—the August 1998 bombings of two U.S. embassies in Kenya and Tanzania and the October 2000 strike on the USS *Cole* destroyer in Yemen's port of Aden—failed either to make bin Laden a household name for Westerners or to provoke a significant response by the U.S. government. Indeed, while the embassy bombings produced limited cruise missile strikes against al Qaeda camps in Afghanistan, the *Cole* attack engendered no U.S. retaliation at all.

In June 2001, a propaganda video released by al Qaeda claimed credit for the *Cole* bombing and called for more attacks on U.S. interests. During that summer, there were signs that more were on the way. CIA director George Tenet would later tell the 9/11 Commission that the U.S. intelligence system "was blinking red" with credible reports of al Qaeda's plans.[58] Yet even though al Qaeda was clearly plotting, the United States was not taking advantage of these warnings to make plans of its own with respect to al Qaeda's safe haven in Afghanistan. Legendary journalist Bob Woodward notes that while the U.S. military "seemed to have contingency plans for the most inconceivable scenarios," there was "nothing on the shelf that could be pulled down to provide at least an outline" for addressing al Qaeda's safe haven in Afghanistan were a large-scale attack to force America's hand.[59]

In part, this is because top administration officials were firmly ensconced in traditional security paradigms that focused on threats posed by other nation-states to the exclusion of nonstate actors. CIA director Tenet mentioned al Qaeda in his daily briefings to President Bush more than forty times before the 9/11 attacks.[60] Bush famously received an intelligence briefing on August 6, 2001, titled "Bin Laden Determined to Strike in U.S." The briefing warned of "patterns of suspicious activity in this country consistent with preparations for hijackings or other types of attacks" and claimed, using a figure that proved to be exaggerated, that seventy Federal Bureau of Investigation field investigations were considered related to bin Laden.[61] Yet despite these and other warnings, Bush did not publicly mention al Qaeda between August 6 and September 11.

National Security Adviser Condoleezza Rice was in fact scheduled to deliver a major address on September 11, 2001, that in the White House's own words was designed to examine "the threats and problems of today and the day after, not the world of yesterday." But the focus of this address was on promoting missile defense, and it did not mention Osama bin Laden, al Qaeda, or any other jihadi groups.[62] The intended speech demonstrates the power of a paradigmatic focus on nation-state threats to the exclusion of nonstate actors.

An interesting academic article published in the Massachusetts Institute of Technology Press journal *International Security* in the summer of 2001 provided an indication of what U.S. planners should have been considering before the 9/11 attacks. Written by Ivan Arreguín-Toft, a postdoctoral fellow in the International Security Program at the Belfer Center for Science and International Affairs at Harvard University's Kennedy School of Government, "How the Weak Win Wars" began with an extended look at the famed "rumble in the jungle" boxing match that Muhammad Ali and George Foreman fought in Kinshasa, Zaire (now the Democratic Republic of the Congo) in October 1974.[63] Foreman had been heavily favored in the fight, for he was "the strongest, hardest hitting boxer of his generation" and had sparred with nimble opponents in preparation for the quick and graceful Ali. But as Arreguín-Toft recounts, the more powerful Foreman's preparation did not ready him for Ali's strategy, which turned Foreman's strength against him:

> In round two, instead of moving into the ring to meet Foreman, Ali appeared to cower against the ropes. Foreman, now confident of victory, pounded him again and again, while Ali whispered hoarse taunts: "George, you're not *hittin'*," "George, you *disappoint* me." Foreman lost his temper, and his punches became a furious blur. To spectators, unaware that the elastic ring ropes were absorbing much of the force of Foreman's blows, it looked as if Ali would

surely fall. By the fifth round, however, Foreman was worn
out. And in round eight, as stunned commentators and a
delirious crowd looked on, Muhammad Ali knocked George
Foreman to the canvas, and the fight was over.[64]

With the right strategy, a weak actor may be able to neutralize a
stronger power's inherent advantage. Indeed, Muhammad Ali's "rope
a dope" would serve as a chilling metaphor for events to come. Could
al Qaeda similarly succeed in making a series of U.S. measures directed at
the militant group exhaust the world's only superpower?

3

September 11, 2001

The subtlest change in New York is something people don't
speak much about but that is in everyone's mind. The city,
for the first time in its long history, is destructible. A single flight of planes no bigger than a wedge of geese can
quickly end this island fantasy, burn the towers, crumble the
bridges, turn the underground passages into lethal cham-
bers, cremate the millions. The intimation of mortality is
part of New York now: in the sound of jets overhead, in the
black headlines of the latest edition.

—E. B. White, Here Is New York, 1949

Despite millions of words that have been written about that shocking day in September 2001, it is difficult to fully express the
impact it had on the American psyche. The world watched in horror
as two hijacked airplanes crashed into and toppled the World Trade
Center's Twin Towers in New York City and another demolished a
large section of the Pentagon in Washington, D.C. After a struggle

between passengers and hijackers, a fourth plane crashed in a field in Shanksville, Pennsylvania, killing everyone on board.

Various rumors and confused reports that surfaced during the day held the damage to be even worse. Officials in Washington, D.C., heard that eleven aircraft may have been hijacked. There were reports of a car bomb at the State Department. Richard Clarke, then a high-ranking counterterrorism official in the Bush administration, recalled mentally tabulating the possible damage: "With the towers collapsed, the death toll could be anywhere from 10,000 to maybe as high as 50,000. No one knew. And it wasn't over."[1]

What so profoundly changed the United States was not just the enormous structural damage and massive death toll incurred by the most vicious surprise attack in U.S. history. There was also the shattering of national myths and assumptions. The 9/11 attacks showed that the United States could no longer rely on the Pacific and Atlantic Oceans for its security. The attacks disproved the rather comforting assumption that terrorist groups were deterred from carrying out mass casualty attacks out of fear that they would lose public sympathy. And September 11, 2001, boldly announced the rise of nonstate actors capable of striking at the heart of the military and economic power of the world's strongest country. As Clarke put it, "They had proven the superpower was vulnerable, that they were smarter, they had killed thousands."[2]

On a warm, tranquil morning, Americans sat glued to their televisions in horror as three separate sites on the East Coast were transformed into unthinkable open-air graves. The new world seemed overwhelmingly unsafe. For many Americans, the attacks were a horrifying introduction to the depths of hatred directed at the United States. Terrorists' lethal capabilities were now clear. And the 9/11 attacks awoke many citizens to the inherent difficulties of defending an open society from attack. Suddenly there seemed to be no shortage of easy targets: shopping malls, amusement parks, pizzerias, trains, buses, and bridges.

Underscoring our vulnerabilities—and ostensibly confirming Americans' worst fears—a number of prominent figures received letters containing anthrax the following month. Five people died, and seventeen others were infected; the figures to whom these letters were addressed included NBC News anchor Tom Brokaw and Senators Tom Daschle and Patrick Leahy. Although it seems that these letters were not mailed by Islamic extremists, they were a sign of the dangerous new environment that Americans were only beginning to understand.[3]

9/11 and the U.S. Economy

I have already noted that the United States has suffered because of its failure to understand al Qaeda. America's lack of knowledge about the jihadi group should have been apparent the moment the 9/11 attacks occurred. After all, the attacks demonstrated a massive underestimation of al Qaeda's ability to strike the continental United States. But even after witnessing the group's deadly competence, U.S. planners likewise underestimated its resilience and made little effort to comprehend its strategy.

This strategy could be known and understood through a nuanced look at bin Laden's personal history and thought. Even at the time of 9/11, it was clear that bin Laden believed it was essential to undermine the economy of his superpower foe and to make the battlefield on which the Americans had to fight as broad as possible. American strategic documents analyzing al Qaeda reveal a lack of awareness of these twin goals.

Bin Laden's attacks on the United States before 9/11 did not have much of an economic impact. Al Qaeda's most successful previous attack on American interests was its near-simultaneous bombings of the U.S. embassies in Kenya and Tanzania in August 1998. Although 247 people died in those attacks (12 of them U.S. citizens) and the attacks forced the United States to expend a decent amount of money upgrading the security of its overseas facilities, these are the kind of losses and expenditures that an economic and military superpower can absorb. In the wake of those attacks, the government took immediate action to upgrade perimeter security at overseas embassies and missions.[4] It reprioritized construction and upgrades in order to bring overseas facilities up to "Inman standards," so named after a report that outlined the standards sufficient to deal with contingencies like terrorist attacks.

The embassy bombings also led the State Department to initiate a $21 billion program to replace 201 different facilities that it regarded as either dilapidated or insecure.[5] America's ability to absorb these security outlays could be seen in the fact that the country continued to run a budget surplus during this period.

But the economic damage caused by 9/11 dwarfed that of previous terrorist attacks, a fact that was not lost on bin Laden. Some observers doubt that bin Laden and al Qaeda were as focused on attacking their enemy's economy in 2001 as they would later be. The reason for this skepticism can be found, for example, in an early fatwa (religious ruling) issued by Sheikh Omar Abdel Rahman, a spiritual guide to two Egyptian jihadi groups, who has been imprisoned in the United States since his October 1995 conviction for taking part in a terrorist conspiracy to attack the United Nations and other New York City landmarks.[6]

The fatwa reads, "Cut off all relations with [the Americans, Christians, and Jews], tear them to pieces, destroy their economies, burn their corporations, destroy their peace, sink their ships, shoot down their planes and kill them on air, sea, and land. And kill them wherever you may find them, ambush them, take them hostage, and destroy their observatories."[7] Peter Bergen assesses this document as significant, writing that the "fatwa to attack the United States economy and American aviation was an important factor in the 9/11 attacks."[8]

The flavor of Abdel Rahman's fatwa, which was typical of early jihadi arguments for striking Western economies, helps to show why some observers have been skeptical that the U.S. economy was a major focus for al Qaeda in 2001. Although economic targets are prominent within the fatwa, the incitement to violence is broad, suggesting to skeptics that while al Qaeda did have America's economy in mind, it was not central to the group's strategy.

Two critical data points shed light on how bin Laden and al Qaeda thought of the connection between 9/11 and the U.S. economy at the time the attacks were executed. The first is a letter bin Laden wrote to Taliban leader Mullah Omar on October 3, 2001, just before the United States began to bomb Afghanistan. (The letter was subsequently recovered from one of al Qaeda's computers.) In the letter, bin Laden claimed that if the United States invaded Afghanistan, the military conflict "will impose great long-term economic burdens, leading to further economic collapse, which will force America, God willing, to resort to the former Soviet Union's only option: withdrawal from Afghanistan, disintegration, and contraction."[9]

He continued that the campaign against the United States should focus on "serving a blow to the American economy," which would in turn shake investors' confidence, causing them "to refrain from investing in America or participating in American companies, thus accelerating the fall of the American economy." The fact that bin Laden explicitly compared the situation the United States would face in Afghanistan to that encountered by the Soviets speaks volumes. So too does the fact that he connected America's coming campaign in Afghanistan to the Soviet campaign exclusively through the impact of invasion and occupation on both countries' economies. Thus, even as a retaliatory U.S. attack on al Qaeda's safe haven was imminent, bin Laden recognized the American economy as the superpower's key vulnerability.

The second data point is an October 21, 2001, television interview that bin Laden gave to Al Jazeera's Taysir Allouni, who is now imprisoned in Spain after a controversial criminal conviction for cooperating with al Qaeda.[10] The wide-ranging interview, conducted shortly after the U.S. military campaign began, is significant contemporaneous evidence of what bin Laden intended to accomplish through the 9/11 attacks. The interview began with bin Laden acknowledging al Qaeda's culpability but insisting that the attacks were a form of self-defense, designed to defend the Palestinian people and religious sites in Saudi Arabia. He continued, "And if inciting for this is terrorism, and if killing the ones who kill our sons is terrorism, then let history witness that we are terrorists."[11]

Allouni pointed out that in the United States, al Qaeda faced an opponent that "dominates the world militarily, politically, and technologically." Since the jihadi group couldn't match America's capabilities, he asked bin Laden, what hope did it have of defeating the United States? It should come as no surprise that bin Laden pointed to the Soviet Union and the Afghan-Soviet war in his answer.

Bin Laden explained that at the beginning of the 1980s, "the Soviet empire was a force that was very, very strong, which scared the whole world, and NATO used to shake in fear in front of the Soviet empire." Yet the Soviet Union dissolved after the war in Afghanistan, its massive empire fracturing into Russia and a number of smaller states. Bin Laden thought that America could likewise be defeated.

When bin Laden was asked to speak of the impact of the 9/11 attacks, his first observation concerned the economic damage they caused. "According to their own admissions," he said in the interview with Allouni, referring to the Americans, "the share of the losses on the Wall Street market reached 16%. They said that this number is a record, which has never happened since the opening of the market more than 230 years ago."

Bin Laden then provided an extended exposition of the economic numbers, as well as associated costs, that shows he had given much thought to the economic implications of 9/11. "The gross amount that is traded in that market reaches $4 trillion," he said. "So if we multiply 16% [by] $4 trillion to find out the loss that affected the stocks, it reaches $640 billion of losses from stocks, with Allah's grace. So this amount, for example, is the budget of Sudan for 640 years."

He knew, though, that the direct damage to America's stock market was not the only economic impact. He factored in lost productivity, but in doing so reached a bizarre conclusion about post-9/11 life in America. Figuring the national daily income to be $20 billion, bin Laden claimed that the country did not work for an entire week after the attacks because of the psychological impact. "So if you multiply $20 billion by one week, it comes out to $140 billion, and it is even bigger than this," he said. One might be inclined to gloss over this inaccuracy, but it is worth dwelling on for one reason: it illustrates that even though the United States often misinterprets and underestimates jihadi militants, they do the same to the United States.

The notion that the entire nation missed a full week of work is preposterous. In September 2001 I was living in New York City, which experienced more death and trauma as a result of the 9/11 attacks than any other city in the country. Although Lower Manhattan was shut down temporarily after the Twin Towers' collapse, the rest of the city was back at work immediately. I remember how New York City seemed dazed as it returned to its daily life. Most noticeable was the change in traffic patterns: New York's aggressive drivers typically honk their horns in anticipation before traffic lights turn green, but now an unexpected politeness gripped the citizenry. Horns were rarely heard for several days, and drivers looking to make a turn through a crosswalk would uncharacteristically wave pedestrians through first.

Equally unexpected was how the movie theater up the street from where I lived, the United Artists Union Square Stadium 14, decided to show free films for a day. Restaurants brought free food to the ground zero workers, and New Yorkers lined the West Side Highway offering support to the rescue crews. The attacks changed the United States and changed New York; but even in the city that absorbed the most damage, people were not just staying home in shock.

After claiming falsely that Americans had missed a full week of work because of the attacks, bin Laden estimated to Allouni that building and construction losses may have amounted to $30 billion. He then gloated about all of the lost American jobs—stating that 170,000 employees were fired from the airline industry and that the InterContinental Hotel chain had been forced to cut 20,000 jobs. So taking into account the second- and third-order economic consequences, bin Laden calculated that the cost to the United States was "no less than $1 trillion by the lowest estimate."

Yet even though some of bin Laden's claims were false, his overall damage estimates were accurate and may in fact have been conservative. As former CIA officer Bruce Riedel has noted, the property damage and lost productivity caused by the 9/11 attacks probably cost more than $100 billion. When factoring in lower profits and economic volatility, Riedel writes that the price tag is even larger, "as high as $2 trillion according to some estimates."[12]

In a video that bin Laden released in October 2004, he amplified this analysis by pointing out how much damage 9/11 inflicted upon the United States, in comparison to the much smaller costs that al Qaeda incurred in executing them. "Al Qaeda spent $500,000 on the event," he said, "while America, in the incident and its aftermath, lost—according to the lowest estimate—more than $500 billion, meaning that every dollar of al Qaeda defeated a million dollars."[13]

To be sure, bin Laden spoke with Allouni in the October 2001 interview about more than just economics. A consummate propagandist, he also discussed how Western civilization itself had lost its appeal with the collapse of the Twin Towers. But the first demonstration of the 9/11 attacks' success that bin Laden pointed to was their economic impact, and he had obviously given a great deal of thought to the precise costs for the United States. The economic aspects of bin Laden's fight with America dominated his interview with Allouni.

Thus, the earliest data points reflecting bin Laden's thinking at the time of the 9/11 attacks—his interview with Allouni and the letter he had written to Mullah Omar—show that he had America's economy in mind from the very outset.

Know Your Enemy?

The United States has not heeded the ancient Chinese military strategist Sun Tzu's famous maxim that to succeed in a military conflict, it is necessary to know your enemy.[14] America gave little thought to al Qaeda's strategy at the time of the 9/11 attacks, and the jihadi group's overarching strategy remains poorly understood today.

To comprehend America's shallow understanding of al Qaeda, one need look no further than the official documents outlining U.S. thinking about this conflict. The "National Military Strategic Plan for the War on Terrorism" (NMSP-WOT), published by the chairman of the Joint Chiefs of Staff, Richard B. Myers, on February 1, 2006, accurately bills itself as "the comprehensive military plan to prosecute the Global War on Terrorism (GWOT) for the Armed Forces of the United States."[15]

Although the NMSP-WOT outlines *America's* ends, ways, and means, it does not perform the same analysis for al Qaeda—which is striking, because understanding an enemy's ends, ways, and means is fundamental to formulating military strategy. Indeed, the NMSP-WOT displays a laserlike focus on a single tactic—terrorism—without asking deeper questions about this tactic. What objectives does the enemy hope to accomplish through the use of terrorism? The NMSP-WOT tries to sidestep this question by stating that "there is no monolithic enemy network with a single set of goals and objectives."[16] But certainly there are *commonalities* among the various groups affiliated with al Qaeda.

The NMSP-WOT does not explore these common goals and strategies, other than making the rather banal observation that such groups possess "extremist ideologies antagonistic to freedom, tolerance, and moderation" and use terrorism "to impede and undermine political progress, economic prosperity, the security and stability of the international state system, and the future of civil society."[17]

The report also examines the enemy's center of gravity—a concept that the Department of Defense describes as "the source of power that provides moral or physical strength, freedom of action, or will to act"— but it does not explain how al Qaeda and affiliated movements understand America's center of gravity.[18] Is their use of terrorism aimed at a particular point of weakness? Reading the NMSP-WOT, one gets the impression that these groups are striking at random targets, with no overarching plan.

The White House's "National Strategy for Combating Terrorism," published in September 2006, does more to explain the common goals of America's jihadi foes. It notes that although the transnational jihadi movement isn't monolithic and is not controlled by one leader, "what unites the movement is a common vision, a common set of ideas about the nature and destiny of the world, and a common goal of ushering in totalitarian rule." The document continues by noting that these groups "seek to expel Western power and influence from the Muslim world and establish regimes that rule according to a violent and intolerant distortion of Islam."[19]

But even though the National Strategy for Combating Terrorism discusses the end state that these groups desire, it doesn't even try to assess how they intend to get there. Do they have an envisioned path to victory that seeks to exploit certain U.S. vulnerabilities? Or have they embraced the tactic of terrorism and the goal of creating totalitarian religious regimes without any conception of how the tactic might connect to the goal?

Even the *9/11 Commission Report* fails to provide any kind of strategic assessment of bin Laden and al Qaeda. It notes that "for those yearning for a lost sense of order in an older, more tranquil world, [bin Laden] offers his 'caliphate' as an imagined alternative to today's uncertainty."[20] But the report provides no assessment of how al Qaeda intends to bring about the caliphate. There is yet again an unresolved disconnect between al Qaeda's tactics and goals. It is, of course, possible that al Qaeda *doesn't* think strategically: that its desired end state is a pie-in-the-sky dream, and this adversary has no concept of how its dream can be turned into a reality. But it is dangerous to begin strategic assessments with the *assumption* of an adversary's incompetence, and the idea that al Qaeda does not possess strategic thought is just that, an assumption. Moreover, it is an unfounded assumption. Al Qaeda is in fact rather strategically adept.

Charlie Allen, a forty-year veteran of the intelligence community who also served as a high-ranking official in the fledgling Department of Homeland Security (DHS), has been described by *U.S. News & World Report* as "more of a legend than a man around the CIA."[21] When I asked him about the lack of an assessment of al Qaeda's strategy, he said, "I think it was a frenetic period where everyone was pushed to the limit as we expanded on the intelligence and military side. First DHS was setting up, and we didn't have any analysts. Then came the planning for the Iraq War, and we had to wield a great deal of resources to deal with that." Sitting in his office near Washington, D.C.'s Dupont Circle, Allen concluded, "But there's no excuse for not taking a cold eye to al Qaeda's strategies and capabilities."[22]

Brian Michael Jenkins, senior adviser to the president at the RAND Corporation, is a well-regarded terrorism expert, a Vietnam veteran, and a former Green Beret. He also agreed that the lack of assessment of al Qaeda's strategy is a significant problem. "We have to do a better job of understanding our foe," he told me. "At the governmental level, we need to have a better understanding of our foe's approach to warfare and strategy. One of the reasons we haven't done so is that we're trapped by the word *terrorism* itself."

Jenkins compared the current shallow strategic assessments of al Qaeda to those performed during World War II and the Cold War, when America's understanding of Soviet strategy and means was sophisticated, and American planners carefully examined the writings and thinking of the German generals. In contrast, Jenkins said, in the view of U.S. planners, terrorists "were not worthy foes; they didn't measure up."[23]

To return to Ivan Arreguín-Toft's metaphor of Muhammad Ali's rope-a-dope strategy (see chapter 2), this lack of strategic awareness made it difficult for American planners to discern whether al Qaeda had adopted a plan designed to neutralize America's inherent advantages. This lack of strategic awareness made it difficult to avoid being sucked into a fight where the harder the United States hit, the more worn out and vulnerable it became.

High Hopes

After the 9/11 attacks, it seemed that American politics had fundamentally changed. The United States had been through a divisive election in 2000, with the outcome of Florida's critical recount ultimately being determined by the Supreme Court. Partisan wounds remained from the court's controversial decision in *Bush v. Gore*, which held that a constitutionally valid recount could not be completed in Florida by the relevant deadline.[24] That decision in effect handed the election to George W. Bush, and as a result many Americans saw Bush as an illegitimate president. Beyond this, as one newspaper noted in August 2001, President Bush faced "a nation skeptical of his policies."[25] Yet despite this political antagonism, the shock of 9/11 brought people together.

The public rallied behind President Bush, and his approval rating soared to over 90 percent in the days after the attack.[26] This represented the highest public approval that had been recorded for a serving president; Americans clearly wanted to "rally 'round the flag" in a time of crisis. As one analyst put it, conventional wisdom holds that "a foreign crisis plays into the hands of a sitting president" because "people look to their leaders for reassurance."[27]

Democrats expressed their support for the Republican president. As Senator Joe Biden said, 9/11 represented "the most god-awful wake-up call we've ever had."[28] The change in political dynamics—with the public standing behind President Bush and the Democratic Party offering its support—prompted Cornell University government professor Theodore J. Lowi to tell the *New York Times* that the United States would likely be "operating as if we have a national unity party."[29]

The media agreed that a vigorous response to the attacks was justified and necessary. The government, in turn, promised that its response would be overwhelming. Secretary of State Colin Powell encapsulated widely held views of how the administration would respond when he said of al Qaeda, "We will go after that group, that network, and those who have harbored, supported and aided that network." Representing the scope of the administration's ambitions, Powell then said that "when we're through with that network, we will continue with a global assault against terrorism in general."[30]

It appeared to all observers that al Qaeda had awoken a sleeping dragon: the powerful United States of America had finally been hit by a provocation that it could not ignore. All elements of national power were trained on al Qaeda. The United States was determined to deprive it of its safe haven and its flow of money, and to capture or kill its leaders and operatives.

It was natural for Americans to rally around their country and their government after the attack. But this moment of national consensus makes all the more tragic what would follow. Colin Powell's hubristic and laughably overoptimistic statement—in which he anticipated finishing off al Qaeda quickly and then moving on to other, unrelated terrorist groups—was indicative of official thinking. The statement was representative in failing to account for the enemy's strategic logic, massively underestimating al Qaeda's resilience, and possessing a startlingly ambitious scope.

The decisions the government made at the very outset of the fight against al Qaeda and associated movements would have long-lasting ramifications. If the government established the right systems for addressing the challenge, capabilities could build over time. Expertise could be developed internally, and counterterrorism efforts could become more competent and more efficient. If the wrong system were put in place—a bloated, disconnected bureaucracy that has trouble keeping up with a small, nimble foe—the costs would only mount.

If we invaded the wrong country, anti-American passions could be inflamed and the United States could become insolubly bogged down. Every decision by a person or a country is made in light of all previous decisions, and it can be exceedingly difficult to turn back after making the wrong move in the fight against terrorism.

There is even a political science concept explaining how early decisions in a sequence matter more than later ones: *path dependence*. As University of California at Berkeley political science professor Paul Pierson puts it, path dependency is the idea that in any political system, "once a particular path gets established . . . self-reinforcing processes make reversals very difficult."[31] This is true, because interested parties make investments around the initial decisions, and institutions are organized around them. These investments and institutional arrangements function as "positive feedbacks" that make it difficult to turn back from one's first choices.[32]

America's initial response to the 9/11 attacks, unfortunately, contained the paradigmatic failures that would drive up costs, present the enemy with openings it never expected, and ultimately play into al Qaeda's hands.

4

Our Politicized Fight
against Terrorism

Here is the thing that the Democrats do not get. . . . They do
not seem to get the fact that there are people, terrorists in
this world, really dangerous people that want to come here
and kill us. That in fact they did come here and kill us twice and
they got away with it because we were on defense.

—*Rudy Giuliani, 2007*

It was perhaps inevitable that the fight against al Qaeda and other
jihadi groups would become politicized, but it has nonetheless been
extremely harmful to the United States. The fact that being seen as
tough and effective in the fight against terrorism could help one's
political fortunes was evident almost immediately, for the standing of
two politicians—George W. Bush and Rudy Giuliani—and that of the
entire Republican Party dramatically changed because of the events
of September 11, 2001.

President Bush's initial reaction to the attacks was in fact rather confused and unimpressive. Just before he sat down with a class of second graders at Emma E. Booker Elementary School in Sarasota, Florida, he learned that a jumbo jet had hit the World Trade Center's North Tower. Bush thought at the time—as did many Americans—that the incident had been a tragic accident. But at 9:03 a.m., when United Airlines flight 175 struck the South Tower, there could be no further doubt. As Bush interacted with the second graders, his chief of staff, Andy Card, whispered to him, "A second plane has hit the second tower. America is under attack."[1]

Bush tried to remain stoic, but the look on his face conveyed the gravity of the news. One of the students in that class still recalled the president's expression ten years later, after bin Laden was killed. "In a heartbeat, he leaned back and he looked flabbergasted, shocked, horrified," Lazaro Dubrocq, now seventeen, told *Time*. "I was baffled. I mean, did we read something wrong? Was he mad or disappointed in us?"[2] One of Dubrocq's classmates, Mariah Williams, told *Time* that she would "always remember watching his face turn red." She added, "I'm just glad he didn't get up and leave, because then I would have been more scared and confused."

Bush's facial reaction and delayed response after hearing this news (in other words, his decision to stay with the children rather than immediately spring into action) were famously lampooned by leftist documentarian Michael Moore in his film *Fahrenheit 9/11*, but this is not the reason I say that Bush's initial reaction was unimpressive. There would be critics of virtually anything President Bush did just after learning that the country had been attacked, but his decision not to leave the classroom in emergency mode was imminently defensible. "The President told us his instinct was to project calm," the *9/11 Commission Report* noted, "not to have the country see an excited reaction at a moment of crisis." Noticing that members of the press were learning about the attack through their cell phones and pagers, Bush reasonably decided that the best course was to "project strength and calm until he could better understand what was happening."[3]

After concluding his time with the students, Bush went to a classroom where a secure phone had been set up. He spoke briefly to Vice

President Dick Cheney, then gave his first address to the nation after the attacks. "Ladies and gentlemen," President Bush said, "this is a difficult moment for America. Today, we've had a national tragedy. Two airplanes have crashed into the World Trade Center in an apparent terrorist attack on our country." Bush was then rushed to Air Force One. Concerned that the president could be a target, his security detail wanted to keep him on the move until they had a better understanding of the threat. As Bush flew around the country, he clearly became frustrated by the situation. The TV signal on board Air Force One kept breaking up, and his calls to Vice President Cheney would lose reception.[4] In the thick fog of war, Bush heard reports that Camp David and the State Department had been attacked, that there was a fire in the White House, and that his own ranch in Texas may have been targeted. Most critical were the fears that Air Force One could be a target.

The president's plane checked its internal security and also received two F-16s to escort it. Air Force One was cautious in the transmissions it sent, out of fear that they could be heard by the attackers. Although the concern that Air Force One could be targeted was understandable, these fears helped make President Bush's reaction to the attacks less than impressive. He was generally invisible throughout the day, a situation that made strong leadership basically impossible.

Bush touched down just before noon at Louisiana's Barksdale Air Force Base to issue another brief statement to the nation. He then took off again, landing at Nebraska's Offutt Air Force Base around 3 p.m. Bush stayed there for some time before finally being flown back to Washington. As 60 Minutes noted, the fact that Bush was largely out of touch for most of that fateful day raised doubts in the public's mind. "Some wondered," it said, "with the president out of sight, was he still running the government?"[5]

Fortunately, President Bush hit his stride rapidly. That night, back in Washington, he declared in an address to the country, "Today, our fellow citizens, our way of life, our very freedom came under attack in a series of deliberate and deadly terrorist acts." Bush invoked the victims of 9/11, who were just going about their lives and their work when they were struck. The speech outlined several themes that would become his administration's staples: al Qaeda's targeting of the United

States "because we're the brightest beacon for freedom and opportunity in the world," America's resilience in the face of terrorism, the need to bring the full weight of the country's resources to bear against those responsible, and his refusal to distinguish between the terrorists attacking America and the regimes harboring them. After quoting from Psalm 23—"Even though I walk through the valley of the shadow of death, I fear no evil, for You are with me"—President Bush declared that "none of us will ever forget this day, yet we go forward to defend freedom and all that is good and just in our world."[6]

The speech was well received. As one British commentator said, it "was not the Gettysburg address, but it summed up admirably the trauma of his countrymen."[7]

President Bush's growing confidence was obvious later in the week, when he visited rescue workers digging through the rubble at ground zero. Grabbing a bullhorn to speak to them, he said, "I can hear you. And the rest of the world can hear you. And the people who knocked these buildings down will hear all of us soon!" He was greeted by chants of "USA! USA! USA!" Karen Hughes, who at the time served as an adviser on Bush's public statements, told the *New York Times*, "At that moment, I thought America is seeing the President Bush that I know, his ability to relate to people."[8]

Bush would give several more increasingly forceful speeches that month. The public's connection with him was obvious; Bush's approval ratings rose from 55 percent to over 90 percent within two weeks of the attack. His ratings would not stay at that level, and Bush would leave office a controversial and highly unpopular figure. But the remarkable rise in his ratings just after 9/11 showed the public's fear, concern, and desire for action. It also showed why politicians would be so tempted to politicize terrorism.

America's Mayor

New York City mayor Rudy Giuliani also found his fortunes dramatically changed by the 9/11 attacks. A former prosecutor known for his toughness, Giuliani had won two mayoral terms because of his ability to return good governance to the city, in particular for tackling its seemingly intractable crime problem. A profile of Giuliani published in *Time* in December 2001 noted that "he had restored New York's spirit, cutting crime by two-thirds, moving 691,000 people off the welfare rolls, boosting property values and incomes in neighborhoods rich and poor, redeveloping great swaths of the city."[9] Despite these accomplishments, Giuliani's popularity had eroded, and he was viewed as a divisive figure at the time of the 9/11 attacks.

The controversy surrounding Giuliani was a result of his double-edged personality. On the one hand, his ego, tenaciousness, and combativeness actually served him well, leading him to believe he could govern the city that mayor after mayor had failed to fix. He exceeded all expectations when he proved to be right. On the other hand, even though crime had plunged, New Yorkers thought that this problem had been supplanted by police heavy-handedness, a perception that was bolstered by such incidents as the racially charged shooting of twenty-three-year-old Guinean immigrant Amadou Diallo by four New York City Police Department (NYPD) officers. There were multiple ways that Giuliani's finicky, angry personality created further problems. *Time* explains:

> New York City was getting better, but the mayor seemed to be getting worse. When *New York* magazine launched an ad campaign calling itself "Possibly the only good thing in New York Rudy hasn't taken credit for," Giuliani had the ads yanked from the sides of city buses. The magazine sued and won. . . . Giuliani launched a "civility campaign" against jaywalkers, street vendors and noisy car alarms and a crusade against publicly funded art that offended his moral sensibilities. But the pose seemed hypocritical at best when Giuliani, whose wife had not been seen at City Hall in years, began making the rounds with Judi Nathan, a stylish New Yorker with wide, liquid eyes. The clash between the mayor's lifestyle and his policies became a pop-culture target, deftly skewered by *Saturday Night Live* comedian Tina Fey. "New York Mayor Rudy Giuliani is once again expressing his outrage at an art exhibit, this time at a painting in which Jesus

is depicted as a naked woman," Fey deadpanned. "Said the mayor: 'This trash is not the sort of thing that I want to look at when I go to the museum with my mistress.'"[10]

As Giuliani's biographer, Fred Siegel, noted, it is impossible to separate Giuliani's ego and intransigence from his success in running "ungovernable" New York City: these characteristics allowed him to stand up to entrenched interests and boldly act in ways that flouted the conventional wisdom. As Siegel writes, "You couldn't pick and choose from among his virtues and vices. You had to take him whole."[11]

But the mayor's inspiring response to the 9/11 attacks caused these critical perceptions to recede. Giuliani projected not only leadership and toughness but also compassion. "Mayor Giuliani survived his own scrape with death," the *New York Daily News* noted, referring to a close call with the collapse of the World Trade Center's Building 7. "Consoled grieving families. Marshaled selfless rescue workers of the nation's largest city. Worked tirelessly, almost around the clock."[12]

The mayor took time to condemn the racial and religious hatred that might be directed at New York City's Muslim community, a move that New Yorkers, and Americans as a whole, saw as genuine and laudable. Encapsulating the changing perceptions of the mayor, one scenic artist who was not a Giuliani supporter told the *New York Times*, "I have new-found love for him, for what he said about how we are a multicultural city, we can't begin to single out cultures, harbor ill feelings. He sounded like a real leader. I didn't feel that way about President Bush."[13]

Giuliani became known as "America's mayor," an iconic figure who was instantly recognizable countrywide. He was named *Time*'s Person of the Year, and he became regarded as a viable presidential candidate.

He did run for president in 2008, and early polls put Giuliani at the forefront of the Republican contenders. A January 2007 *Washington Post*–ABC News survey showed Giuliani leading Senator John McCain 34 percent to 27 percent among Republican-leaning voters.[14] The following month, a Gallup poll showed Giuliani continuing to lead eventual nominee McCain, and the poll's issue-by-issue breakdown made clear that the coolness and resolve that Giuliani had displayed on September 11 was his key political strength.

Although McCain had some significant foreign-policy advantages over Giuliani in Republican eyes, Gallup noted that Giuliani enjoyed a clear edge over McCain on terrorism. "Giuliani's widely praised response to the Sept. 11 terror attacks while serving as mayor of New York City is likely the reason for this," Gallup stated, "and is enough to overcome the perhaps more general sense that McCain is better on international matters."[15]

By May 2007, polls showed Giuliani handily beating the Democratic frontrunner, Senator Hillary Clinton, in a general election, and tying Senator Barack Obama. Britain's *Economist* described these numbers as "extraordinary," since the United States then had a "snarlingly anti-Republican mood."[16] A July 2007 Gallup poll inquiring about what voters perceived as the best and worst aspects of a Giuliani presidency found that Americans, by an overwhelming margin, identified "good on terrorism/security/handling of Sept. 11" as the most positive thing about having Giuliani in the White House.[17]

Giuliani ultimately did not receive the Republican nomination. There were multiple reasons for his loss, including his blemished personal life and a bizarre campaign strategy that involved skipping the Iowa caucuses, running halfhearted campaigns in both New Hampshire and South Carolina, and placing all his bets on winning the Florida primary.[18] (Giuliani finished third in that critical contest.)

Even though he was dealt a strong hand on terrorism issues, he may have overplayed it. Joe Biden famously commented in an October 2007 debate that Giuliani only mentions three things in a sentence: "a noun, and a verb, and 9/11." But if Giuliani did overemphasize his response to those attacks, it was because he realized that it was such a political asset. Although Giuliani didn't win the presidency, his experience confirms the political benefits of being seen as strong on terrorism.

The Republicans Capitalize

The fact that there were clear political benefits to being seen as strong on terrorism wouldn't inevitably create a problem. After all, it could be *healthy* to motivate politicians to perform admirably under intense pressure, as Rudy Giuliani did. Rather, the problem was that terrorism became politicized as an issue within a year of the attacks in an incredibly divisive manner. A climate was created that has harmed rather than helped America's effectiveness.

The Republicans were able to capitalize in the 2002 midterm election on the fact that their party was identified as tougher on terrorism. Before the attacks, it seemed that the Republicans could face significant midterm losses. Layoffs and rising unemployment, projected to hit 5 percent by the beginning of 2002, created the risk that voters would punish the party.[19] (The fact that 5 percent unemployment was considered a major political liability seems quaint today.)

Moreover, Vermont senator James Jeffords's sudden defection from the party after the 2000 election deprived Republicans of their control of the Senate. Prominent Republicans feared that this change could have a ripple effect, dampening donations and discouraging grassroots activism. Furthermore, they were concerned that being relegated to minority status in the Senate could discourage some Republicans from seeking reelection and make the recruitment of strong candidates more difficult.[20]

The 9/11 attacks, however, transformed the political landscape. Although the economy had been the voters' predominant concern until terrorists struck the United States, Gallup polling from January to June 2002 consistently found that terrorism and national security had eclipsed the economy as the issue voters cared about most. (In July 2002, the economy again surpassed terrorism and national security, 40 percent to 30 percent.) And if terrorism was on voters' minds, this was good for the Republicans. An August 2002 Gallup analysis noted that although Democrats had a six-point edge among all voters (48 percent to 42 percent), Republicans enjoyed a commanding nine-point lead among registered voters who considered terrorism to be the most important electoral issue.[21]

The Republicans exploited this national security advantage. Karl Rove, a senior adviser to President Bush whom the president would later refer to as "the Architect" of his 2004 electoral victory, said in January 2002 that the fight against terrorism would help the Republicans because voters "trust the Republican Party to do a better job of protecting and strengthening America's military might and thereby protecting America." During the campaign, Rove misplaced a computer disk that contained his PowerPoint presentations about the upcoming midterm election. One piece of advice to candidates in the presentations was that they should "focus on the war" in their campaigns.[22]

Rove's advice proved controversial once the public learned of it, but the issue resonated with voters, as did President Bush's focus on selling the coming Iraq War during the campaign. *Time* reported that in private, "Republicans concede that Bush's focus on Iraq has vastly improved their chances in November and bless Rove for his efforts."[23]

The Democrats complained loudly. In September 2002, the *Washington Post* quoted President Bush as saying at a GOP fundraiser in New Jersey, "Democrats are not interested in the security of the American people." When Senate Majority Leader Tom Daschle demanded an apology, the White House argued that the quote was not as incendiary as it initially appeared when understood in its context. The White House claimed that Bush had in fact criticized the Senate for slowing down the creation of a Cabinet-level Department of Homeland Security. Rather than saying that the Democrats were uninterested in national security, he had said that "the Senate is more interested in special interests in Washington and not interested in the security of the American people."[24]

Daschle would hear none of this. Saying that the White House's explanations about context were "not worth the paper they are printed on," he continued to demand an apology. "We ought not to politicize this war," Daschle said. "We ought not to politicize the rhetoric about war and life and death." (Senate Minority Leader Trent Lott responded to Daschle with a bizarre non sequitur: "Who is the enemy here, the president of the United States or Saddam Hussein?")

The bottom line is that Daschle was right: politicizing national security when there was general agreement between the Republicans and the Democrats on how to combat terrorism was bad for the country. After all, the actual point of contention that had caused Bush to claim that the Senate was "not interested in the security of the American people" was whether civil service protections should be preserved for employees of the new Department of Homeland Security.

I do not want to diminish the significance of this issue: the dispute was legitimate, representing a genuine philosophical disagreement between the two parties. But the Republicans and the Democrats agreed on the need to create the department and were capable of forging ahead without the kind of incendiary accusations that Bush made. Rather than taking advantage of the opportunity to try to create a consensus paradigm on national security issues (albeit one that would feature inevitable differences between the parties), the Republicans helped to create an environment where national security was a constant point of contention. In this environment, safeguarding the country often took a backseat to opportunities for partisan gain.

But even though Daschle was right philosophically, the Republicans read national politics correctly. They regained control of the Senate in the 2002 election, picked up five seats in the House, outperformed expectations in the gubernatorial races, and even gained in state legislatures. In general, the president's party averages a loss of 350 state legislature seats in a midterm election, but in this one the Republicans actually gained 200 seats.[25] The GOP's overwhelming victory was not just unexpected but also historic: not since Franklin D. Roosevelt in 1934 had a president's party made gains in both the House and the Senate during the midterm election of his first term in office.[26] Terrorism was the key to this victory.

Afterward, Democratic Party chairman Terry McAuliffe commented that the Republicans derived significant political advantages from the war on terrorism as well as the looming war with Iraq. "You put all that together with the President out there actively campaigning," he said, and it added up to a Democratic defeat.[27]

McAuliffe's perception of why the Democrats lost squared precisely with the Republican game plan. A *Newsweek* investigative report published in mid-November 2002 concluded that Bush and his advisers had formulated a three-part plan for electoral victory by August: "to raise the stakes and lengthen the debate on our dealings with Iraq, to press the Democrats to accept the White House version of a Department of Homeland Security (and hammer them if they opposed it) and to deploy both issues to burnish the president's popularity with the GOP faithful, to whom Bush would appeal in coast-to-coast campaigning in the final weeks of the 2002 campaign."[28]

Summarizing what many commentators had come to realize after the midterm election, conservative columnist Charles Krauthammer wrote, "Why did the Democrats lose? Forget the tactics. Forget the fundraising. Forget even the President's popularity. This election was about Sept. 11."[29]

The 2004 Election

Terrorism and national security would continue to be a critical, divisive issue for the next few election cycles. It was clear from the outset that terrorism would factor heavily in the 2004 campaign. The Republicans' choice of New York City as the location for that year's Republican National Convention and their decision to hold it in September were obvious references. As Brookings Institution government scholar Stephen Hess told CNN, "Terrorism is why they're in New York and why they're doing it at the beginning of September. It's not very subtle."[30]

Terrorism was invoked almost constantly throughout the convention. In a speech that mentioned *terror* or *terrorism* forty-four times, and *9/11* eleven times, Rudy Giuliani said, "President Bush sees world terrorism for the evil that it is. John Kerry has no such clear, precise and consistent vision."[31] Arnold Schwarzenegger claimed in his convention speech, "If you believe we must be fierce and relentless and terminate terrorism, then you are a Republican!"[32] (Though not as ubiquitous as Giuliani's invocations of 9/11, Schwarzenegger's references to the *Terminator* movie series have been every bit as consistent when he has spoken publicly and privately.)[33]

Although the Iraq War clearly helped the Republicans in the 2002 election, by 2004 the public perception was mixed. The death toll, both American and Iraqi, was mounting. So too were the economic costs of the war. And an intensive search had failed to unearth evidence that Saddam Hussein had rebuilt his nuclear weapons program—which was the central claim the Bush administration had used to justify its invasion. Kerry, Bush's rival in the general election, campaigned on the idea that the invasion had been "the wrong war, in the wrong place, at the wrong time." [34]

President Bush's campaign would not—in all likelihood, could not—back down from its claim that the Iraq War had been good for America. Instead, it linked that war to the broader fight against terrorism and positioned Bush as the only candidate Americans could trust with keeping the country safe.

One line of attack for the Bush campaign was the so-called Kerry Doctrine. Speaking of Bush's decision to undertake preemptive warfare against Iraq, Senator Kerry had said he would preemptively attack another country only when doing so "passes the global test where your countrymen, your people understand fully why you're doing what you're doing, and you can prove to the world that you did it for legitimate reasons."[35]

Labeling this idea of a "global test" the Kerry Doctrine, President Bush insisted that it was radical and dangerous. "Think about this," Bush said during an Ohio campaign stop less than a month before the election. "Senator Kerry's approach to foreign policy would give foreign governments veto power over our national security decisions." In contrast, Bush said that in his administration, "our national security decisions will be made in the Oval Office, not in foreign capitals."[36] Naturally, Senator Kerry took issue with the way the Bush campaign had portrayed the Kerry Doctrine.

In addition to criticizing Senator Kerry's "global test," President Bush argued that the invasion of Iraq made America safer—period. In the first of three presidential debates, he argued that one critical lesson of 9/11 was to "take threats seriously, before they fully materialize." Because of the U.S. invasion of Iraq, he said, "Saddam Hussein now sits in a prison cell. America and the world are safer for it." Later in the debate, Bush said that Kerry's criticism of the Iraq War reflected a "pre–September 11th mentality, the hope that somehow resolutions and failed inspections would make this world a more peaceful place."[37]

Similarly, in the vice presidential debate, Dick Cheney said that if he had to decide whether to recommend war with Iraq all over again, he would take the same course. "The world is far safer today because Saddam Hussein is in jail," Cheney said. "His government is no longer in power. And we did exactly the right thing." He said that in contrast, he didn't think Kerry "would pursue the kind of aggressive policies that need to be pursued if we're going to defeat these terrorists." Invoking one of the antiterrorism paradigms that the government adopted in the immediate wake of the 9/11 attacks, Cheney concluded that "we need to battle them overseas so we don't have to battle them here at home."[38]

For his own part, Kerry did himself few favors on these issues. For example, the Democrats were eager to capitalize on the popularity of Michael Moore's *Fahrenheit 9/11*, a documentary critiquing the Iraq War. Moore spoke at several events at the Democratic National Convention in Boston, and the cameras caught him sitting next to former president Jimmy Carter during part of the convention.

The problem is that Moore was more than just an antiwar filmmaker. In one statement on his personal website, posted about three months before the convention, he wrote: "The Iraqis who have risen up against the occupation are not 'insurgents' or 'terrorists' or 'The Enemy.' They are the REVOLUTION, the Minutemen, and their numbers will grow—and they will win. Get it, Mr. Bush?"[39] Rather than simply disagreeing with the war, this post celebrated the insurgents who were killing American forces—and it generated justifiable controversy.

Predictably, the image of Moore sitting next to Carter featured prominently on conservative cable news shows, making the concerns that the Bush campaign raised about Kerry's seriousness on national security issues seem credible to many voters.

As election day neared, the Bush campaign continued to emphasize its national security bona fides. Typical of the campaign's rhetoric, President Bush clearly framed the issue during one stop in Pennsylvania: "A crucial difference between my opponent and me is the most important question for voters this election: Who can lead this war against terror to victory? Which candidate can best protect America's families and our national security?"[40]

Then on October 29, mere days before the election, Osama bin Laden appeared in a video address that was broadcast on the Al Jazeera Arabic-language satellite station. Obviously timed to coincide with the U.S. election, bin Laden addressed the American people directly. In the speech, he boasted that al Qaeda was winning its war against the United States. The primary reason he gave was the economics of the fight and his group's strategy of "bleeding America to the point of bankruptcy." Explaining that al Qaeda alone could not be credited with the coming victory, bin Laden said that the Bush administration's decision to open multiple war fronts was also bringing about America's downfall. "And so it has appeared to some analysts and diplomats," bin Laden said, "that the White House and us are playing as one team towards the economic goals of the United States, even if the intentions differ."[41]

The voting public was largely uninterested in the substance of bin Laden's speech. Rather, the most significant aspect to Americans was that the video showed that bin Laden was still alive. Before that, bin Laden featured infrequently in al Qaeda's propaganda, and it had been years since he'd appeared in a video, leading many commentators to believe that he had been killed. (Baseless rumors that bin Laden was in ill health, forced onto a dialysis machine by kidney problems, further bolstered these conclusions.)[42] Bin Laden's video dominated the news cycle in the days leading up to the election, again putting national security at the forefront of voters' minds.

President Bush won the election in 2004, and the GOP again made gains in both the House and the Senate. Party insiders correctly pointed to national security as a critical issue.

The Democrats Capitalize, Too

By 2006, national security issues had been transformed from a significant Republican advantage into a thorn in the party's side. The overarching reason was the Iraq War. Bloodshed markedly increased in that country during the course of the year, and many observers thought it was mired in civil war. Certainly anything resembling a victory appeared implausible.

An event that had a major impact on the war was the February 22, 2006, destruction of the Golden Dome Mosque in Samarra, a major holy site for Iraq's Shia community and for Shiites throughout the world, in a bombing ordered by the leader of al Qaeda in Iraq (AQI), Abu Musab al Zarqawi. The Golden Dome Mosque's importance to the Shia community was underscored by Iraqi vice president Adel Abdul

Mahdi, who likened the attack to 9/11.[43] Some observers believe that this attack dramatically reshaped the war, whereas others think that it was an indicator of an already existing instability rather than a trigger. Taking the latter position, Pulitzer Prize–winning journalist Thomas Ricks noted that "according to the United States military's database of 'significant acts,' violence had increased at a steady pace since March 2005 and would continue to increase at about the same pace after the mosque bombing until peaking in June 2007."[44]

Regardless, it's clear that the mosque attack did produce a ripple effect. Shiite reprisals against Sunnis were swift, devastating, and largely indiscriminate. The Sunnis struck back, often with AQI taking the lead. Some Sunnis found allegiance with al Qaeda to be advantageous in protecting them from sectarian bloodshed. For other Sunni insurgents, bloody attacks orchestrated by Shiite militias made some of al Qaeda's sectarian arguments seem sensible for the first time. (Zarqawi referred to the Shia as "the insurmountable obstacle, the lurking snake, the crafty and malicious scorpion, the spying enemy, and the penetrating venom.")[45] The fact that AQI came to the fore of the Sunni insurgency during this period has been verified by insurgents who later changed sides.[46]

By the time Americans turned out to vote in the 2006 midterm election, the cycle of violence in Iraq was clearly spiraling out of control, and the damage seemed irreparable. AQI had been able to take and hold territory. It became the dominant player in Iraq's expansive Anbar province and was able to erect a governing structure in the city of Mosul.[47]

As the situation deteriorated, the Democrats realized that this time, unlike in the last two elections, the Republicans were vulnerable on the issue of terrorism and national security. Democratic senator Evan Bayh of Indiana said in February 2006 that "for both substantive and political reasons," the Democrats should take the Republicans on over terrorism and national security.[48] Indeed, Senate Democrats took advantage of the anniversaries of 9/11 and the Hurricane Katrina disaster to argue that Bush and the Republicans hadn't done enough to safeguard Americans from terrorism and from other threats they faced.[49]

The Republicans were viewed as vulnerable on national security in general, but Democratic strategists saw Iraq as their Achilles' heel. Key Democratic politicians promised to push for immediate withdrawal. Indicative of the mood within the party was Connecticut's senatorial race, where long-serving Democratic senator and former vice presidential candidate Joe Lieberman—who supported the U.S. efforts in Iraq— lost a primary challenge to Ned Lamont, who campaigned on his opposition to the Iraq War. Lamont wanted to withdraw American troops within a year.

Lieberman, a popular and powerful figure in Connecticut politics, decided to run in the general election as an independent, and he was expected to caucus with the Democrats if he prevailed. Yet despite Lieberman's long service to the party and his vice presidential nomination just six years earlier, key colleagues threw their support behind Lamont. John Kerry sent a fundraising appeal to millions of supporters on behalf of Lamont, as well as on behalf of Senate candidates in New Jersey and Hawaii, making clear that Iraq and defense issues were the reason. "Each of these candidates is making the mess in Iraq a central issue in their campaigns for the Senate," he wrote.[50] Other Democratic politicians, including Representative Jack Murtha of Pennsylvania and Senator Russell Feingold of Wisconsin, likewise called for a quick withdrawal.

Campaigning on national security issues again paid off in 2006, this time for the Democrats, who took back the House and the Senate. According to late November polling data from the Pew Research Center, 53 percent of Americans considered the Iraq War one of the top two issues in the election.[51] ABC News analyst Gary Langer noted, "Opposition to the war remains the prime issue driving congressional voter preference. And the war's critics include not just eight in 10 Democrats but 64 percent of independents, 40 percent of conservatives, 35 percent of evangelical white Protestants and a quarter of Republicans."[52]

Although Iraq had been central to the GOP's defeat, President Bush did not hasten to withdraw after the election. Instead, he announced a "surge," an increase in the presence of American soldiers in an attempt to clear out al Qaeda's strongholds and diminish sectarian violence. There was nothing wrong with the Democrats campaigning on national security issues: the Iraq War was incredibly costly, and there was a strong argument for political accountability. But many Democrats went beyond this, arguing that Bush's surge ignored the "mandate" provided by the American people to get the U.S. military out of Iraq as soon as possible. They first registered this disapproval by passing House Resolution 157, which condemned Bush's decision to send more soldiers to Iraq.

Speaking in favor of the resolution, Representative Dale Kildee of Michigan said, "President Bush either did not get or did not understand the message the American people sent last November. Before the end of this year, United States troops should be redeployed and their efforts focused on support and training the Iraqi Security Forces."[53]

Representative Kirsten Gillibrand of New York mentioned her own constituency's vote, saying, "Last November the voters in upstate New York spoke loudly and clearly in demanding a change in direction in Iraq, and I will cast my vote in favor of this resolution to fulfill my duty to represent their will."

Representative Joe Courtney of Connecticut also referred to the 2006 vote: "Today we are here, exactly 100 days after a historic watershed election in this country, in which the American people spoke loudly and clearly that they wanted a new Congress to rise to its constitutional duty and hold this administration accountable for its war policy in Iraq. The day I was sworn in as a new Member of Congress, I accepted this responsibility, and I rise today in opposition to the President's escalation of the war."

Although it passed, House Resolution 157 was nonbinding. However, the dispute over the surge between the White House and Congress produced funding battles, raising the question of whether the legislature would use its power of the purse to deprive the White House of the funds it required to execute the surge.

One of the surge's most consistent critics was Illinois senator Barack Obama. On January 10, 2007, as the surge was announced, Obama said, "I am not persuaded that 20,000 additional troops in Iraq is going to solve the sectarian violence there. In fact, I think it will do the reverse." Obama swore that he would "actively oppose the president's proposal."[54] In May 2007, Obama introduced a plan to begin redeploying troops out of Iraq, with all combat troops to be removed by March 31, 2008.

Ultimately, the surge was given the funding that it needed, and—as will be discussed in detail later—it worked. Although serious questions remain as the United States draws down its troops, President Bush made the right decision by undertaking a surge rather than a withdrawal. This is particularly true when one recalls the dark days of 2007, when Iraq was wracked by sectarian violence and ethnic cleansing and AQI was able to carve out geographic safe havens. Obama himself conceded in a September 2008 interview with Fox News Channel host Bill O'Reilly, "I think that the surge has succeeded in ways that nobody anticipated. . . . It's succeeded beyond our wildest dreams."[55]

But in the highly politicized context in which debates over national security issues take place, the results of the 2006 midterm election were used to argue that President Bush should have chosen a course of action that would have been worse for the country. And it was not just Democrats who employed the election results in this manner. "By stepping up the American military presence in Iraq, President Bush is not only inviting an epic clash with the Democrats who run Capitol Hill," Sheryl Gay Stolberg wrote in a news analysis column for the *New York Times*. "He is ignoring the results of the November elections, rejecting the central thrust of the bipartisan Iraq Study Group and flouting the advice of some of his own generals, as well as Prime Minister Nuri Kamal al Maliki of Iraq."[56]

The 2008 and 2010 Elections

National security and terrorism was not the key election issue in either 2008 or 2010 that it had been previously; the September 2008 financial crisis caused economic issues to overshadow everything. This does not mean, however, that the issue was entirely absent.

By 2008, Bush's approval rating was microscopic, and he was considered politically toxic. The Republican nominee, Senator John McCain, found himself in the unique position of running a general-election presidential campaign that took aim at *his own party's* incumbent. The Democratic nominee, Senator Barack Obama, ran against the Bush administration virtually across the board, including on national security.

When the Obama administration took office after a resounding electoral victory, the new president trumpeted the new direction he would take on terrorism and foreign affairs. His efforts appeared so derogatory toward the Bush administration's approach that they prompted Juan Zarate, President Bush's counterterrorism advisor, to tell NPR, "I don't think the administration has helped themselves, or frankly helped the country, by trying so hard to paint their policies as being so radically different from the past. They're not, and for the sake of the country they shouldn't be."[57]

Zarate was right. Although Obama swore on the campaign trail that his national security efforts would differ markedly from those of his predecessor, and although he made considerable efforts during his first year in office to show the public that substantive differences existed, Obama's counterterrorism policies have largely been a continuation of those forged during the last two years of the Bush administration. Some conservative pundits still attempt to show Obama's overarching weakness on national security, and a select few portray him as dangerous, but there is a growing awareness among analysts of the continuity between Bush and Obama on counterterrorism policy.[58]

Indeed, national security was marginal as an issue in the 2010 midterm election. One Republican pollster noted during that campaign that the economy "dwarfs everything. It's sort of like looking at a house and there's all these things that need repair, but if the roof's on fire, all these things are secondary. Jobs and the economy are the equivalent of the fire on the roof."[59] An ABC News analysis of the election results found that the economy, health care, and illegal immigration were the top three issues for voters. The Afghanistan War came in a distant fourth, with only 7 percent of voters citing it as their top concern.[60]

From 2002 through 2008, the politicians and parties that benefited from their politicization of terrorism and national security got a number of significant substantive points wrong. In 2002, the Republicans were wrong to politicize the issue in the first place. Moreover, the midterm results were viewed by many as a mandate for the disastrous invasion of Iraq. In 2004, President Bush's winning campaign insisted that the country was safer due to this invasion and that the administration would change neither its decision to go to war nor its execution of the conflict if given the opportunity. Not only did the invasion not make the United States safer, but the situation in Iraq would not improve until the administration dramatically changed its approach.

The Democrats finally gained some advantage from Bush's foreign policy failures in the 2006 election, but they promptly interpreted the vote as a mandate to get out of Iraq while it was mired in civil war and al Qaeda enjoyed a significant foothold. They used the 2006 results as a bludgeon with which to attack the surge that would help to reverse that dangerous situation. And in 2008, Obama exaggerated the aspects of Bush's counterterrorism policies that should be changed, even making campaign promises that he couldn't keep in an attempt to capitalize on the issue.

The good news is that because of the continuity between the Bush and Obama administrations on terrorism and national security, as well as waning voter interest, it may be possible to eliminate some of the harmful partisanship that has produced a suboptimal policy. Later I will address how this can be done. For now, what matters is that after the 9/11 attacks, politicians immediately realized how terrorism could benefit them and their parties as a campaign issue. This politicization in turn contributed to the misallocation of resources designed to serve counterterrorism purposes and to the inefficiency of efforts that were actually important to public safety. This book now turns to these twin problems.

5

Our Inefficient Fight against Terrorism

> It is no exaggeration to say that the fate of our nation depends upon the degree to which the department succeeds in accomplishing its mission. And, in seeking to accomplish a mission such as this, the department cannot afford to waste one minute or one dollar.
>
> —*Clark Kent Ervin, February 27, 2003, as he was sworn in as the Department of Homeland Security's first inspector general*

Osama bin Laden's ideas about how to defeat a superpower were forged in the anti-Soviet jihad on the battlefields of Afghanistan in the 1980s. After the Soviet Union launched its ill-considered invasion, bin Laden not only saw it withdraw from Afghanistan in defeat but also watched its empire collapse. Bin Laden thought, incorrectly, that his own actions were significant in the eventual dissolution of the Soviet empire. However, he also perceived, accurately, that the Soviet Union's economic woes ultimately undermined it. He brought this paradigm, the centrality of economics, to his fight against the United States.

Bin Laden was not the only jihadi thinker to see economics as the key to defeating the United States. Fouad Hussein's book *Al Zarqawi: The Second Generation of al Qaeda*, draws on the insights of such thinkers as al Qaeda security chief Saif al Adel and outlines seven stages in al Qaeda's strategic plan. Attacks on the U.S. economy figure prominently throughout. The means of hitting the economy envisioned in this master plan include exhausting the U.S. economy "by means of the escalating battle," attacking the oil supply in Arab countries, an "electronic jihad," and collapsing the U.S. dollar through the Islamists' promotion of gold as the new international medium of exchange. The destruction of the U.S. economy, in this vision, will leave the Americans "weak, exhausted, and unable to shoulder the responsibilities of the current world order."[1]

Abu Bakr Naji, whom two prominent analysts describe as "a rising star in the jihadi movement," wrote in his influential text *The Management of Savagery* that economic strength (and access to oil in particular) is central to the movement's foes.[2] He stated, "As for attacking economic targets from which the enemy benefits, particularly petrol, the reason for doing so is that this is the core—or at least the prime mover—of the enemy, and its great leaders will only be cut down by this means."[3] A number of other jihadi intellectuals, as well as rank-and-file jihadis, have also noted the importance of the U.S. economy as a target.[4]

When a relatively small nonstate actor's strategy for combating you is focused on your economy, it is critical to counter with a strategy designed to conserve your resources. Any other approach risks playing into the enemy's hands. This is where political scientist Ivan Arreguín-Toft's analogy to Muhammad Ali's rope-a-dope strategy (see chapter 2) is so prescient. Ali's opponent, George Foreman, was the stronger, more powerful fighter, so he thought he had the smaller Ali beaten when Ali spent several rounds cowering against the ropes rather than going toe-to-toe with him. Rather than conserving his energy, Foreman unleashed flurry after flurry of blows. All these punches and all this effort did nothing to defeat Ali; instead, the effect was to tire Foreman. In the end, Foreman's frenetic efforts allowed Ali to knock out his exhausted adversary and pull off a stunning upset.

A terrorist or insurgent group that is engaged in asymmetric warfare focused on its more powerful opponent's economy can be likened to Muhammad Ali in that famed boxing match. The overarching goal is to grind the foe down not only through attacks but also by ensuring that the opponent's offensive and defensive measures are as costly and exhausting as possible. Under these conditions, creating an expensive security apparatus to counter a group like al Qaeda can be a recipe for defeat rather than a strength. If security measures are extraordinarily costly, and if expenses mount each time a terrorist attack is executed (whether or not the attack succeeds), then the smaller nonstate actor may be able to put its foe in a position where it crumbles under its own weight.

Unfortunately, the United States created a bloated, expensive, and inefficient system to combat terrorism. There are multiple reasons we ended up with such a system, but the politicization of the fight against terrorism (see chapter 4) did not help; it only ensured that politicians of both parties would consistently boast of their commitment to expending resources in the fight. Considerations related to *conserving* resources received short shrift because they did not make powerful sound bites.

For example, President George W. Bush noted in July 2005, shortly after suicide terrorists struck London's mass transit system, that "we're spending unprecedented resources to protect our nation." This unprecedented spending wasn't portrayed as cause for concern, nor was it a clarion call to increase the efficiency of our efforts. Rather, it was meant as proof of how seriously the United States took the problem: given the difficulty of demonstrating a concrete enhancement in security, one of the few ways politicians can demonstrate action is by citing spending increases, regardless of their effectiveness. The president concluded, "We will not let down our guard."[5]

In August 2004, notes came to light after the capture of al Qaeda operatives in Iraq suggesting that they were "casing" New York City's stock exchange, the Citigroup building, and other financial centers for possible attack. In response, the federal government raised the color-coded threat level to orange for five targets. New York City mayor Michael Bloomberg emphasized his willingness to incur great expenses in response. "We are deploying our full array of counterterrorism resources," he said. "We will spare no expense and we will take no chances."[6] In actuality, the information suggesting that these attacks were possible was awfully thin. Michael Sheehan, then in charge of counterterrorism efforts for the NYPD, recalled the reaction that he and the NYPD's head of intelligence, David Cohen, shared:

> We're like, "Holy shit, this is the real deal." Then we went back and reread it, and the more I looked at it, the more I looked at Cohen and said, "Wait a second. This *sounds* really ominous. But this could be done by any jackass having a cup of coffee at a Starbucks across from the Citigroup building, and on the Internet." . . . Within an hour after reading it, I knew this was one guy, educated, who did a pre-9/11 reconnaissance of these buildings, and the information was five years old.[7]

Bloomberg used a similar rhetorical formulation in October 2005, after Department of Homeland Security (DHS) officials noted a "specific yet non-credible" threat to New York City. As commuters witnessed security staff in chemical hazard suits responding to a false alarm in Penn Station, Bloomberg said, "We have done and will continue to do everything we can to protect this city. We will spare no resource, we will spare no expense."[8] Bloomberg's decision was second-guessed that time around, as the NYPD scaled back its heightened security measures just four days after the threat was announced.[9]

Senator Chuck Schumer of New York publicly noted that although the threat was specific in terms of locations to be struck, it lacked credibility and corroboration. Despite this, he did not question the "spare no expense" paradigm that Bloomberg outlined. Instead, Schumer said, "In a post-9/11 world, you cannot be too careful."[10]

Around the same time, Baltimore officials decided to temporarily shut one of the tunnels underneath the city's harbor in response to a threat that the FBI described as "of undetermined credibility."[11] Although Baltimore officials' decision to take this action was similarly questioned, they presented an almost identical defense to Bloomberg: it's best to err on the side of caution.

In other words, mistakenly raising the terror alert or taking preventive action only wastes resources, whereas mistakenly deciding not to raise it can cost lives. As a political calculation, this was clearly correct. Taking action when threats prove to be false can be wasteful but won't really hurt a politician's career. On the other hand, if a politician fails to act when there is a terrorist plot in progress and he or she has caught even a whiff of it, the result can be politically fatal.

Nevertheless, the costs of inefficiency are greater than this calculation concedes. The point is not to second-guess any politician's decision to take action in response to past threats; these choices are related to specific intelligence and indicators that are available to decision makers at the time, and critics can later unfairly attack them with the benefit of more complete information when there is no "fog of war" effect. Rather, my point is that in the present political climate, taking action and even expending "unprecedented" resources can bolster one's credibility on the terrorism and national security issue. Overspending has generally been seen as a political virtue and not a vice. This paradigm helps to produce highly inefficient counterterrorism efforts.

The Misallocation of Resources

Former DHS inspector general Clark Kent Ervin has observed that "in Washington, D.C., where some degree of wasteful spending is accepted as par for the course, the Department of Homeland Security has become notorious for it."[12] There are multiple ways that this wasteful spending occurs.

Some of the problems lie in DHS's inception itself, and Ervin's 2006 book *Open Target* is an invaluable guide to the problems that existed at the outset. After having served admirably as the State Department's inspector general, Ervin was tapped to serve as the first inspector general of DHS. He served competently and vigilantly in that role as well. Danielle Brian, the executive director of the Project on Government Oversight, rightly praised him as "the citizens' last chance of ensuring that vitally important money was being spent well."[13] Ervin took his job seriously, pointing to what he saw as the country's critical vulnerabilities as well as procedures that the new department needed to implement to make sure that taxpayer money wasn't squandered.

The potential for waste was enormous because of the rush to get DHS up and running. The department was created in President Bush's first term, on January 24, 2003, and getting it into operation was seen as an urgent national priority. DHS merged such disparate agencies as the Transportation Security Administration (TSA), the Federal Emergency Management Agency (FEMA), the Immigration and Naturalization Service (INS), and the Secret Service. A new bureaucracy was created for DHS, and a large number of positions had to be filled. Contractors and subcontractors were brought in to expedite the process.

Despite the competence and sense of mission Ervin brought to the job, his book is an infuriating read, because he never received adequate support from the top levels of DHS. Rather than viewing Ervin as an ally in protecting the country, DHS's first secretary, Tom Ridge, saw him as an adversary. At one point, Ridge asked him in a private meeting, "Are you *my* inspector general? When I was Governor of Pennsylvania, I had an inspector general, but he wasn't out there like you constantly criticizing and embarrassing us."

Ervin replied that Ridge had put his finger on the problem between them. "The fact is I'm not *your* inspector general," he said. "I'm the American people's inspector general. By law, I report to you and to Congress, but I work for the American people."[14]

Ervin, unfortunately for us, did not last long in the job. His penchant for pointing out inefficiencies and perceived security gaps—which was exactly what he was hired to do—made him a pariah within DHS. He was excluded from key meetings and reprimanded and derided for sharing information with Congress (again, something the job obligated him to do). He found himself with few allies. When his recess appointment lapsed on December 8, 2004, Ervin was out of a job—all because he took seriously the responsibilities of his position.

In *Open Target*, Ervin outlines the inefficiencies produced in the rush to get DHS going. He correctly foresaw that the department, "with billions of dollars to spend, under tight congressional deadlines and immense political pressure to do something as quickly as possible to make the homeland more secure, would be targeted by rapacious contractors like buzzards homing in on carrion."[15] He found himself at

loggerheads with his DHS colleagues over controls he recommended
to stem this problem: Undersecretary for Management Janet Hale
insisted that his recommendations not be passed along to Ridge
because she didn't want to draw attention to the fact that these controls weren't already in place. Ervin had his assistant personally make
sure that Ridge received his memorandum, but this early encounter
set the tone for the fights that were to come.

The most wasteful agency at DHS during Ervin's tenure was TSA,
which was created in a rush after the 9/11 attacks. Previously, the
airlines had been responsible for paying private contractors to serve as
airport security screeners. There were many critics of the contractors'
performance, and a remarkable 105 percent average annual attrition
rate—that is, attrition that over the course of a year was equivalent to
all the workers in the force plus 5 percent of those hired to replace
them—was testament to low job satisfaction.[16] This illustrates why
policy makers decided to transfer responsibility for aviation security to
the federal government.

The rushed hiring of sixty thousand screeners (along with the
precertification of an additional sixty-six thousand) was handled by
the Minnesota-based contractor NCS Pearson, and it was a financial
disaster. The contract that NCS Pearson received provided it no incentive to keep costs low, and the volume of work required it to bring in
168 subcontractors. Ervin explains some of the most egregious mis-
uses of money:

> A travel and event coordination firm was hired without a
> written contract to book hotels around the country, taking
> a 10 percent profit on each room it booked. So, the more
> rooms it booked and the higher the room costs, the greater
> the firm's take. There are ordinary hotels, and there are
> luxury hotels. In high-rent Manhattan, relatively high-end
> hotels like the Waldorf Astoria were booked. TSA was billed
> $129,621.82 for long-distance phone charges, with no sup-
> porting documentation, at two other Manhattan hotels,
> including almost $3,500 for calls to foreign countries. Pier
> 94, a Manhattan convention and trade show center, was

rented for nearly $700,000, or about $39,000 a day for two
weeks. . . . The president of one firm [that was] awarded a
no-bid contract to book hotels paid herself a salary of $5.4
million for nine months of work. The firm wasn't even incorporated until it received the subcontract.[17]

The cost of hiring the TSA screeners, originally budgeted at $104
million in the contract with NCS Pearson, ballooned to $867 million.
(Not all of this was the contractor's fault, however. TSA contributed
to the inefficiency by more than doubling the number of screeners
required and accelerating the deadline for delivery three months into
the contract.) The lack of oversight and accountability in this process
can be seen in the finger-pointing that occurred after the disastrous
performance became public knowledge.

One NCS Pearson employee who ran assessment centers complained to the *Washington Post* that the waste was "unbelievable"
because of a lack of checks and balances, with "zero government people involved" in the process. In contrast, a TSA contracting officer
insisted that keeping an eye out for such waste was not the agency's
responsibility because "I paid the contractor to do that."[18]

TSA's inefficiencies did not end with the hiring of screeners; the
waste of money extended to other contracts that the agency awarded.[19]
It was inefficient and wasteful even in its self-congratulation. The
bonuses that the agency doled out to its employees were far out of proportion to government-wide cash performance awards, and its awards-
ceremony spending was so lavish that it became a news item inside the
Beltway.[20] As recently as 2010, TSA's oversight of its support-service
contracts remained inadequate.[21]

TSA was the worst offender within DHS, but the inefficient and
wasteful spending did not end there. A first-year audit found that
seven problems within DHS could be considered "material" because
of their ability to have a negative effect on the department's overall
financial health.[22] By the end of fiscal year 2004, when the next audit
was performed, these material weaknesses had actually grown from
seven to ten.[23]

Ervin notes, "Wasteful spending and chaotic accounting are themselves security gaps. Unless the department can account for every

dollar it spends, and every dollar it spends makes the homeland more secure in some way, it is needlessly exposing the nation to additional risk."[24] Although this observation is correct, Ervin actually *understates* the case. Not only does wasteful spending expose the country to greater risk, it also directly enhances al Qaeda's strategy, which aims to drive up its adversaries' security costs.

The Explosive Growth of the National Security Apparatus

Even though TSA was the most wasteful agency that Ervin encountered at DHS, the phenomena that produced TSA's excessive spending were being replicated elsewhere in the government. TSA was forced to rapidly bring in a massive workforce after 9/11, and an expansive counterterrorism and national security apparatus was likewise being hastily erected beyond the context of TSA.

One of the best windows into this is a two-year investigation by *Washington Post* reporters Dana Priest and William Arkin, published under the name "Top Secret America" in the summer of 2010. Their investigation concludes that the security bureaucracy erected after the 9/11 attacks "has become so large, so unwieldy and so secretive that no one knows how much money it costs, how many people it employs, how many programs exist within it or exactly how many agencies do the same work." This investigation of Top Secret America was quite literal: the newspaper examined only the top-secret part of this massive infrastructure, because the work "classified at the secret level is too large to accurately track."[25]

The growth of the security infrastructure in the wake of 9/11 that is described in the *Post's* report is startling in its scope. The U.S. intelligence budget—publicly announced at $75 billion in 2009—is now two and a half times larger than it was on September 10, 2001, but that monetary figure "excludes many military activities or domestic counterterrorism programs." More than 20 percent of the governmental organizations devoted to counterterrorism "were established or refashioned in the wake of 9/11," and preexisting agencies were given "more money than they were capable of responsibly spending" to address the

terrorist threat. Examples of this mushrooming of the security apparatus include the growth of the Pentagon's Defense Intelligence Agency
from 7,500 employees in 2002 to 16,500 by 2010; the doubling of the
budget of the National Security Agency (NSA); and the growth in
the FBI's Joint Terrorism Task Force offices from 35 to 106.

The *Post* notes that the number of intelligence agencies also mul-
tiplied. "Twenty-four organizations were created by the end of 2001,
including the Office of Homeland Security and the Foreign Terrorist
Asset Tracking Task Force," it reports. "In 2002, 37 more were created
to track weapons of mass destruction, collect threat tips and coordinate the new focus on counterterrorism. That was followed the next
year by 36 new organizations; and 26 after that; and 31 more; and 32
more; and 20 or more each in 2007, 2008 and 2009."[26]

As of 2010, the *Post* found, 1,271 government organizations and
1,931 private companies were working on counterterrorism, homeland
security, and intelligence within the United States. A terrorist or insurgent group that seeks to bankrupt its foe derives an advantage when it's
up against a massive, uncoordinated, expensive security apparatus—
and that is precisely what the United States erected. Even unsuccessful
attacks can send shock waves through the system, causing the nation
to spend more and more money inefficiently in its quest for security.

Indeed, the size of the security bureaucracy *ensures* that redundant
work is performed and that wasteful spending occurs. Some work that
appears redundant to outsiders is, however, a function of creating more
consumers of intelligence within the government. It simply wouldn't
be possible for the CIA, the NSA, and the various Department of Defense
components to write for and brief all the consumers of intelligence.

"Nobody at CIA will rely on DHS's analysis for anything," a senior
U.S. intelligence analyst told me. "DHS's analytical shop serves Janet
Napolitano, and nobody out of the department relies on DHS analysis.
If you're going to have a DHS secretary, and she is given the president's
daily brief every morning, that's only one part of her morning. To get daily
intelligence, you need your own staff to keep you updated on various
threats. The more people you determine are going to be consumers
of intelligence, the more I and A [intelligence and analysis] shops
you need." Although he felt that some of the allegedly redundant

functions were more rational than some observers perceive, the analyst conceded that they were part of a generally harmful "ballooning of government."[27]

Indeed, one key problem is lack of accountability, since it is difficult to get a sufficient handle on the overall system. For example, retired army lieutenant general John Vines, who was asked in 2009 to review methods for tracking sensitive Defense Department programs, has said, "I'm not aware of any agency with the authority, responsibility or a process in place to coordinate all these interagency and commercial activities. The complexity of this system defies description." Because of this lack of synchronization, Vines said, "it inevitably results in message dissonance, reduced effectiveness and waste. We consequently can't effectively assess whether it is making us more safe."[28]

Sometimes even supervisors are denied the information they need. The *Washington Post* reports:

> One military officer involved in [an ultrasecret Special Access Program] said he was ordered to sign a document prohibiting him from disclosing it to his four-star commander, with whom he worked closely every day, because the commander was not authorized to know about it. Another senior defense official recalls the day he tried to find out about a program in his budget, only to be rebuffed by a peer. "What do you mean you can't tell me? I pay for the program," he recalled saying in a heated exchange.[29]

Some officials charge that this secrecy is used not just to safeguard critical information but also to protect ineffective programs from scrutiny. In fact, top intelligence officials concede that there's tremendous waste in the current system and that the current resource-intensiveness of our counterterrorism efforts is not sustainable. CIA Director Leon Panetta told the *Washington Post* that he has been mapping out a five-year plan to address this problem. "Particularly with these deficits, we're going to hit the wall. I want to be prepared for that," Panetta said. "Frankly, I think everyone in intelligence ought to be doing that."[30]

Too frequently, when the enemy's attempted attacks expose vulnerabilities—such as the incident in which Umar Farouk Abdulmutallab boarded a Detroit-bound flight with a bomb sewn into his underwear—the proposed fixes involve further increasing the size of the security bureaucracy. Officials such as White House counterterrorism adviser John Brennan acknowledged that an intelligence failure was part of the reason that Abdulmutallab was able to board that flight: his own father had warned of his radicalization.[31]

Nevertheless, Director of National Intelligence Dennis Blair used that failure as a call for more resources, asking Congress for more analysts and funding as a hedge against future mistakes. Similarly, the National Counterterrorism Center's director, Michael Leiter, asked for more analysts. "The Department of Homeland Security asked for more air marshals," the Washington Post notes, "more body scanners and more analysts, too, even though it can't find nearly enough qualified people to fill its intelligence unit now."[32]

The Use of Private Contractors

The cost of this security apparatus is further driven up by its extensive use of private contractors rather than government employees to undertake top-secret work. There was clearly a good reason for the use of contractors in the immediate wake of 9/11. Charlie Allen, a forty-year intelligence community veteran and former DHS official, told me, "Contractors were extraordinarily valuable as we ramped up in the first year. We couldn't have done what we needed to do without them: we couldn't have taken the war to Afghanistan and eventually to the tribal areas of Pakistan without strong contractor capabilities, bringing in retired CIA officers and technology from the private sector. We of course, on September 12, 2001, didn't anticipate a U.S. invasion of Iraq, which accelerated greatly the number of contractors who needed to continue taking the lead as the tip of the spear in Pakistan's Federally Administered Tribal Areas (FATA) and other areas where al Qaeda and affiliate networks were active."[33]

The Bush administration's post-9/11 reliance on private contractors was originally intended to be temporary—necessitated by the massive expansion in counterterrorism responsibilities. Ronald Sanders, the associate director of national intelligence for human capital, noted in 2008, "It takes a fair amount of time to take a raw recruit off the street and develop him or her into a seasoned intelligence professional. . . . And in the meantime, we've had to use contract personnel to augment our U.S. government military and civilian personnel in order to perform the mission."[34]

Increasingly, however, contractors look not like a temporary measure but like a permanent part of the national security apparatus. The *Washington Post* estimates that 265,000 of the country's 854,000 individuals holding top-secret clearances are contractors.[35] In February 2010, Senators Joseph Lieberman and Susan Collins, the chairman and ranking member of the U.S. Senate's Homeland Security and Governmental Affairs Committee, were "astounded" when their committee learned that there were more contractors than civilian employees working for DHS.[36] (I should mention, in the interest of full disclosure, that I have done consulting work for several national security contractors. Although I am confident of the value I provided for the money that I received, this does not alter my view of the inefficiency of the current system.)

The Bush administration made it easier for agencies charged with national security functions to hire private contractors rather than new civil servants. This was done for a variety of reasons, including limiting the size of the federal government's permanent workforce and escaping the bureaucracy of the federal hiring process. The administration also mistakenly believed that contractors were more cost-effective.[37] The fact that this belief was inaccurate is now entirely clear. A report submitted by the Senate Select Committee on Intelligence noted in 2007 that "the average annual cost of a U.S. government civilian employee is $126,500, while the average annual cost of a 'fully loaded' (including overhead) core contractor is $250,000."[38] Thus, as of 2008, contractors comprised about 29 percent of the workforce in the Office of the Director of National Intelligence's agencies, but they received pay equal to 49 percent of the agencies' personnel budgets.

Vice Admiral David Dorsett, the director of the Office of Naval Intelligence, said that he "could save millions each year by converting 20 percent of the contractor jobs" in his workforce into civil service jobs. But even though he has received authorization to do so, he has found the process sluggish: as of mid-2010, only one contractor job had been converted and one eliminated—out of a total of 589.[39]

The process of replacing contractors with regular employees is made even more difficult by the fact that the government cannot keep track of the number of contractors on the federal payroll. "This is a terrible confession," said Secretary of Defense Robert Gates. "I can't get a number on how many contractors work for the Office of the Secretary of Defense."[40] Perhaps the intelligence community needs to create a new agency tasked with keeping track of all the contractors working for it.

Pork Barrel Politics

The wasteful spending on national security has also been driven by pork barrel politics. DHS grants that at their inception went to the states were subject to a nonsensical formula ensuring that sparsely populated states with low risks of terrorism still received generous sums. Each state would receive a minimum of .75 percent of this state-grant program, which was quite high in comparison to other federal programs.[41] Thus, this formula inherently advantaged small states in the allocation of money. The results were predictable: cash-starved localities that received homeland security grants used them for purposes entirely unrelated to counterterrorism. This was compounded by a lack of reporting back to DHS about how the money was spent.

A 2007 report issued by Representatives Anthony Weiner of New York and Jeff Flake of Arizona relied on publicly available information to outline some of the more egregious ways that this infusion of money was spent.[42] For example, in Dillingham, Alaska, a town of twenty-four hundred people that has no roads linking it to anywhere else, a homeland security grant of $202,000 paid for seventy "downtown" surveillance cameras. Madisonville, Texas, used a $30,000 grant to buy a customized trailer for its annual October Mushroom Festival, for use by people who become overheated or get lost. Lake County, Indiana, spent $30,000 of its grant money on a truck intended to tow a hazmat disposal trailer. Later, however, it was discovered that a county employee used the truck to commute to and from work.

In Modoc County, California, $3,500 from DHS's State Homeland Security Grant Program paid for crates and kennels for holding stray animals. Converse, Texas, spent $3,000 of DHS money to buy a secure trailer for transporting riding lawn mowers. In Crawfordsville, Indiana, the city's fire department received $55,000 from DHS's Assistance to Firefighters Grant Program and used the money to purchase gym equipment, hold puppet and clown shows, and help the firefighters become fitness trainers. The Kentucky Office of Charitable Gambling received more than $36,000 to stop terrorists from raising money at the state's bingo halls. One official told a reporter that even though he didn't know of any terrorists raising money that way, "the potential there, to me, is huge."

Because the state-grant formula was designed to help smaller and less populous states, some of the most obvious resource misalloca-tions occurred in such jurisdictions. In April 2005, the chief of West Virginia's homeland security agency resigned in the midst of an inves-tigation into such questionable purchases as a $3.4 million fleet of emergency-response vehicles that were never used.[43] Another bizarre use of homeland security funds in West Virginia was the purchase of equipment for the Fairmont Fire Department that could suck up 412 gallons of water a minute. This was odd because, as one West Virginia commentator noted, Fairmont is not particularly flood-prone— although, like any place, it does have "basements that are vulnerable to flooding."[44] Thus, Fairmont's homeowners can sleep easier at night knowing that the state's homeland security spending will safeguard the dryness of their basements.

Obviously, the examples detailed here constitute only a small per-centage of DHS's budget. But this is just a partial snapshot and does not represent the full extent of woefully misspent money that was doled out to states and localities. Moreover, it represents an utterly foreseeable problem. In 2003 Sean Moulton, a senior analyst for OMB Watch, a policy institute that monitors the White House Office of Management and Budget, noted that the lack of a clear governmental picture pri-oritizing needs created a "troubling" potential for the misallocation of resources.[45] It should have been clear that a systemic design that does not prioritize the areas at greater risk of terrorist attack will result in the areas at lesser risk spending the superfluous money to fulfill their mundane needs. This is precisely what Clark Kent Ervin warned of when he spoke of the need for controls at DHS to guard against waste.

In the summer of 2007, President Bush signed the Implementing Recommendations of the 9/11 Commission Act into law. This law was designed to address the problem that states with a low risk of terrorism were receiving a disproportionate share of the funds. However, some observers have questioned whether these changes really moved the country away from a pork barrel system that favors small states without much terrorism risk.[46]

Policing Inefficiencies

Even policing efforts that are clearly necessary for public safety have often been carried out in an inefficient manner that ensured unnecessary expenditures. TSA again provides an example. As I have already mentioned (see chapter 1), just after 9/11, every effort was made to ensure that no group felt unfairly singled out by intensified aviation security procedures. Thus, the opportunity to implement a system of terrorist profiling at the outset was lost. I have noted some of the most visible manifestations of this policy: Al Gore being singled out for extra screening twice during a 2002 trip to Wisconsin and seventy-five-year-old Representative John Dingell of Michigan being forced to strip down to his underwear to prove that his artificial hip, and not a weapon, had set off a metal detector. Although there was a noble goal underlying the desire to avoid terrorist profiling, this policy resulted in wasted resources and less effective policing.

Terrorist profiling does, of course, have its critics. For example, in October 2005, New York City implemented a system of random bag searches in its subways in response to a terrorism scare. (Some sources have told me that the searches were not really as "random" as advertised, but this is how they were explained to the public.) The following morning, the *San Francisco Chronicle* published an op-ed by

Mike German, a former FBI agent who now works for the American Civil Liberties Union, defending the use of purely random searches rather than terrorist profiling.[47] (His op-ed concerned bag searches on subways, but the arguments he employed typify debates over terrorist profiling in aviation security and other contexts.)

German's op-ed is indicative of the overall weaknesses in the case against profiling. Specifically—and this happens time and again in the profiling debate—the piece formulates the most crude and inefficient system of profiling that could possibly be erected and then argues against it. Central to German's argument about what profiling constitutes, German notes that "otherwise intelligent people suggest that it's perfectly reasonable to racially profile all Asian, black and Arab Americans who might be Muslim in the hope of catching the very tiny percentage of Muslim extremists who might actually be a problem."

Obviously, profiling "*all* Asian, black and Arab Americans" would be highly inefficient—and problematic for other, deeper reasons. German correctly points out the potential for increasing resentment and bolstering al Qaeda's narrative through a system that makes all Muslims (or Asians, blacks, and Arabs) feel stigmatized. But those who argue against straw men should be aware that their concocted argument does not fairly represent the other side.

The argument for profiling is simple. If our last line of defense is an airport checkpoint or a search of bags before riders enter the subway, we should maximize the chance that the searches succeed by focusing on the passengers who are most likely to be terrorists. This is the way to conserve resources and to improve public safety. There are, in reality, a large number of choices that lie between completely random searches at one extreme and heavy-handed profiling of all members of at least three different minority groups at the other.

A truly effective system of terrorist profiling would not look solely, or even *primarily*, at a person's race in determining whether extra scrutiny is justified. Rather, a range of factors—including sex, age, dress, and, most critically, behavior—can be used to identify the most likely terrorists. (By dress, I don't mean "Muslim garb," but rather bulky clothing or a coat worn in warm weather that could be used to conceal a bomb.) Although Americans tend to bristle at the idea that race could be used as a proxy for determining whether an individual may be involved in illegal activities, there is no compelling moral or practical argument against considering these nonracial factors.

Security officers can make good use of statistical profiles that encompass the above factors to focus their searches on the most likely terrorists. German's column, on the other hand, makes bad use of statistics in an attempt to prove otherwise. He homes in, for example, on the fact that Arabs are not the largest group of American Muslims. "If you wanted to stop Muslims here in America you'd have better luck targeting South Asians (such as Pakistanis, Indians, Bangladeshis and Afghans), who make up the largest percentage (33 percent) of the American Muslim population," he writes. "Southeast Asians make up an additional 1.3 percent."

But this is one non sequitur heaped atop another: terrorist profiling is not synonymous with "Arab profiling," nor should it be synonymous with "Muslim profiling." For one thing, there are plenty of non-Muslim terrorists—such as Joseph Stack, the fifty-three-year-old software consultant who crashed a Piper Dakota airplane into the IRS building in Austin, Texas, in February 2010. But even if we limit the sample to al Qaeda and affiliated jihadi movements, the purpose of targeted searches is not to single out *Muslims* but rather to find *terrorists.* So the relevant question is not the demographics of the American Muslim community as a whole, which German outlines at length, but rather the *specific subset likely to engage in terrorist acts.*

German argues that racial profiling would "miss Muslims of European descent (2.1 percent) and white American Muslims (1.6 percent) such as Adam Gadahn." It's true that al Qaeda has managed to recruit operatives outside what one might think of as the group's general racial profile, and its ability to do so has seemingly increased over time. But it is only the straw-man profiling system that German sets up and argues against that would focus on *all* Asian, black, and Arab Americans while *completely ignoring* Europeans and Caucasian Americans.

Leaving aside the reality that factors other than race would be incorporated into an effective terrorist profile, an efficacious means of utilizing race would concentrate policing resources on races that are statistically most likely to be jihadi terrorists, but it would not simply ignore other races. Thus, if German's statistics correctly represented the threat emanating from various racial groups (which they *don't*, since they account for Muslim demographics and not terrorist demographics), one could expect Europeans and white Americans to be searched as well— but in a smaller proportion. Moreover, if the intelligence suggested that al Qaeda was recruiting more white people, the applicable profile could be adjusted, and searches of white people could be increased.

Many commentators, German included, make the perfect the enemy of the good. There is no doubt that profiling isn't perfect; as every serious commentator acknowledges (but the public may not fully comprehend), there is no such thing as perfect security. The relevant question is not whether terrorist profiling would be 100 percent effective. Rather, it's whether trying to concentrate policing resources on individuals who are likely to pose greater terrorism risks is superior to a system that makes no such attempt at risk assessment.

TSA's "Passenger Revolt"

Ultimately, DHS decided—correctly—that a more efficient policing system was warranted at airports. For example, it has begun to use behavior detection officers at some checkpoints. I spoke with Erroll Southers, who had been President Barack Obama's first nominee to head TSA, in January 2011 at his office at the University of Southern California's Center for Risk and Economic Analysis of Terrorism Events (CREATE). A former bodybuilder and a serious law enforcement professional who had been assistant chief of homeland security and intelligence at the Los Angeles World Airports Police Department, Southers described TSA as crawling toward more efficient policing. "The government did what it's good at doing," he said. "After 9/11 they threw a lot of money at the problem, they threw a lot of people at it, and they threw a blanket at the challenge, thinking that it would smother the flame—without knowing what the flame was, or where it would come from."[48]

Despite this slow adoption of behavior detection officers, terrorist attempts are still able to impose large burdens on the entire traveling public, and the public is growing tired. After Umar Farouk Abdulmutallab snuck a PETN-based bomb past airport security in his underpants in December 2009, the system adapted in a typically cumbersome fashion, asking passengers to submit to either electronic full-body scans or highly intrusive manual pat-down searches at airport checkpoints.

The public's weariness can be seen in the reaction to the video of software engineer John Tyner, thirty-one, that went viral in November 2010. Tyner left his mobile phone's video recorder on as he placed his carry-on items and shoes on the X-ray belt at a San Diego airport checkpoint. When he refused to submit to a full-body scan, he was given the option of a pat-down instead. Tyner's mobile phone captured the encounter.

A TSA officer explained the pat-down that Tyner would receive and said that it could be done in private if he was more comfortable with that. Tyner replied in an agitated voice, "We can do that out here, but if you touch my junk I'm gonna have you arrested."

The officer called his supervisor and explained Tyner's response. The supervisor (a woman) said to Tyner, "You have a couple of choices here. Someone is going to pat you down, and they will be raising their hand up your inner thigh until they reach the bottom of your torso. If you're not comfortable with that, we can escort you back out and you don't have to fly today."

An increasingly belligerent Tyner replied, "Okay, I don't understand how a sexual assault can be made a condition of my flying."

The supervisor stammered, "This is not—this is not considered a sexual assault."

"It *would* be if you weren't the government," Tyner snapped.

The video goes on like this at length, for about fifteen minutes. The supervisor told Tyner that everybody who goes through the checkpoint has submitted himself or herself to such a search simply by entering, and Tyner replied, "If you enjoy being touched by other people, that's fine. I'd like only my wife and maybe my doctor to touch me there."

In conversation with the guard, after the supervisor had walked away, Tyner explained, "There are plenty of people walking through a metal detector who aren't being felt up, and I'm happy to submit to that level of screening." Tyner's ticket was refunded at the end and he left, but he was confronted by security officials on his way out after being highly argumentative each step of the way. One official suggested that Tyner should be more cooperative because "it would look better for you when we bring the case against you that we're going to bring."

In the wake of the incident and Tyner's video going viral, "Don't touch my junk" became a national punchline—or, some might say, battle cry. Tyner became a folk hero of sorts, albeit an undeserving one. His story was featured on every major news and late-night comedy program. A T-shirt with the saying "Don't Touch My Junk . . . and Don't Touch My Kid's Junk Either" sold briskly on the Internet, as did other products making use of Tyner's line.[49]

But even a cursory review of the incident shows that Tyner immediately became belligerent, before anybody laid a finger on him. Moreover, his assessment of what level of search is justified is nonsensical. Tyner said that he was willing to submit to a metal detector, but body scans or touching his "junk" was unreasonable.

The manifest problem with this position is that less than a year earlier, a terrorist had actually smuggled explosives aboard a plane inside his underwear—and that terrorist was able to do so *despite* passing through a metal detector. Metal detectors do not protect us from that method of attack when the bomb doesn't contain metal components: only a body scan or a pat-down that includes the groin area would do so. In Tyner's view, then, the only reasonable course of action is for checkpoints to include *no* search procedures designed to detect the underpants bomb, thus allowing it to permanently remain an effective method of bringing bombs onto planes.

Nonetheless, one can see why the video went viral and why Tyner received so much adulation. Travelers are frustrated with being subjected to intrusive searches every time they go through an airport checkpoint. Their concerns are met not with satisfactory explanations for why these measures have been implemented—only bureaucratic justifications. Tyner himself was met with bureaucrat-speak when he insisted that his "junk" not be touched. As the supervisor told him, "This is considered an administrative search, and we are authorized to do it. You have submitted yourself to it by coming through the checkpoint."

This is an explanation of how the security bureaucracy is able to *exercise power* over travelers: It is not an explanation of why passengers

should feel comfortable with such measures. Thus Tyner's stand resonated with the public. It was one man saying that the government had
gone too far, and he was refusing to submit.

Showing that others share these concerns, the same month that
"don't touch my junk" entered the national lexicon, there was an
Internet campaign designed to persuade air passengers to opt out of
full-body scanners on November 24, the day before Thanksgiving—
one of the busiest travel days of the year—and instead insist on the
more time-intensive pat-downs. Very few air travelers chose pat-downs
rather than full-body scans on National Opt-Out Day.[50] Despite that,
like Tyner, the idea of National Opt-Out Day captured the public
imagination, and TSA chief John Pistole even felt the need to publicly
warn against participation, saying that delaying actions could "tie up
people who want to go home and see their loved ones."[51] Thus, the
organizer of National Opt-Out Day, Brian Sodergren, wasn't wrong to
laud its results despite the lackluster participation. "We're finally having a debate about how far we are willing to go in terms of privacy and
security," he told ABC News.[52]

When I spoke with Erroll Southers, he told me that he believed
that if TSA implemented a robust system of profiling, it could reduce
some of the generalized intrusiveness that passengers face, particularly
if coupled with a "trusted traveler" program. Under such a program,
frequent air travelers can agree to submit to background checks that
will establish they do not pose a terrorism risk. In return, they would
face streamlined security procedures at checkpoints.

Illustrating how such a program could work in conjunction with
a system of profiling, Southers said, "If I have ten people, and four of
them are in the trusted traveler program, now I only have six people
I have to worry about who aren't vetted. Three are over seventy years
of age. One of the other three is four years old. Now I only have to
worry about two people. Now my resources are used effectively."[53] The
U.S. Travel Association, a group that represents the travel and tourism
industry, has endorsed a trusted traveler program.[54]

Increased profiling in aviation would reduce the generalized intrusiveness that passengers feel because it would shift the system from
searching primarily for *weapons*—which could potentially be anywhere,

thus requiring extensive searches of any nook or cranny that could contain them—to trying to identify which *passengers* may pose threats. Not all passengers pose an equivalent risk. If searches can be better prioritized, that would lessen the generalized burden on the traveling public.

Israeli aviation security is often mentioned in this context, and justifiably so. As Malcolm Gladwell observed in the *New Yorker* shortly after the 9/11 attacks, the difference between American and Israeli aviation security is "that the American system focuses on technological examination of the baggage while the Israeli system focuses on personal interrogation and assessment of the passenger." He noted that this focus on the passenger has resulted in El Al, the Israeli airline, "having an almost unblemished record against bombings and hijackings."[55] And that record has had no blemishes in the days since 9/11.

In Israel's Ben Gurion International Airport, rather than finding sophisticated full-body scanners and intrusive searches that inconvenience everyone equally, you encounter security officers who ask a series of often unpredictable questions of everyone in line, trying to determine whether some passengers' stories don't fit. As independent foreign correspondent Michael Totten put it, "If they pull you aside, you had better tell them the truth. They'll ask you so many wildly unpredictable questions so quickly, you couldn't possibly invent a fake story and keep it all straight. Don't even try."[56]

This is not to say that America's aviation security should, or even could, be like Israel's. There are significant differences between the two countries, not the least of which is that the United States has many more airports than Israel, a country the size of New Jersey. However, there is an applicable lesson: the choices the United States faces are (1) to keep the current full-body scanners and intrusive pat-downs, (2) to repeal these measures but allow a permanent vulnerability to bombs hidden in a terrorist's underpants, or (3) to use a system of profiling that can maintain sufficient security without inconveniencing all travelers.

At present, the public has an inconsistent morass of ideas about aviation security. Travelers want to be completely safe when they fly, yet they hate being inconvenienced. At the same time, various lobbying groups vociferously oppose attempts at profiling—the only thing that can break this impasse—as discriminatory. This is where the country's political leadership, under both Presidents Bush and Obama, has failed. If an administration wants everyone to submit to full-body scans and intrusive searches, it should explain why this is necessary for protecting the public from attack. The case for these intrusive measures is rather obvious, since they are designed to deal directly with an actual method that terrorists have used to get a bomb aboard an international flight—but the public needs a more persuasive explanation than "this is considered an administrative search, and you have submitted yourself to it." On the other hand, if the administration does not want to generally inconvenience the public, it should make the case for a more aggressive profiling regime.

Instead we get the worst of all worlds. Full-body scans and intrusive pat-downs are implemented with minimum explanation. Behavioral profiling is slowly and quietly implemented, as though the politicians are trying to sneak it past us. Meanwhile, these limited profiling efforts do precious little to prevent the generalized inconvenience that passengers experience.

The inefficiency of our counterterrorism efforts is different from the politicization of terrorism. I previously noted that because terrorism has receded as a campaign issue, now is an opportune time to work to depoliticize it. But when it comes to the efficiency of our counterterrorism efforts, the risk runs the other way: because we haven't experienced a major terrorist attack for a while, some people will push for measures, ostensibly designed to protect civil liberties, that will make our counterterrorism policing even less efficient.

An example can be seen in a report published in January 2011 by the Brennan Center for Justice at the New York University School of Law. Written by Emily Berman, *Domestic Intelligence: New Powers, New Risks* advocates restricting the availability of the FBI's investigative techniques. In particular, it calls for a prohibition on the FBI's use of what it describes as "improper consideration of race, religion, ethnicity, national origin, or First-Amendment-protected activity."[57] Essentially, Berman's report constitutes a brief against profiling.

It should be obvious that making it more difficult for the FBI to examine factors that it can use to differentiate terrorists from others will reduce the efficiency of counterterrorism policing. But Berman's report improbably argues that it would actually *improve* policing, because "profiling can waste resources by allocating money and manpower inefficiently."[58] Thus, Berman argues that her recommendations to deprive the FBI of investigatory authority actually make policing efforts more efficient by reducing the deluge of information that confronts intelligence analysts. Although it's true that analysts have trouble keeping up with the current volume of threat reporting, that obviously doesn't mean that depriving them of information therefore automatically improves analytic efforts—as Berman's report absurdly claims.

Rather, the question is whether the report's recommendations take away only information that is truly unnecessary or if they in fact deprive law enforcement of information that it needs. The sheer arrogance of Berman's assertion—that an attorney with no investigatory background, who didn't even consult with law enforcement in producing the report, somehow stumbled upon the magic formula to make the FBI more effective *by limiting its authority*—is truly astounding.

Berman's claim that her recommendations take away only the investigatory authority that wastes the FBI's time and resources, but no powers that are needed, is premised on the total inefficacy of terrorist profiling. She writes, for example, of an alleged "general consensus that profiling is ineffective." But like Mike German's previously explored arguments about profiling, this "consensus" is based on a false view that conceptualizes profiling in its broadest and most offensive form. Berman writes, "In the past, law enforcement organizations have successfully policed groups engaged in organized violence—like the mafia or the KKK—without trenching on the civil liberties of the entire Italian-American or Southern Christian communities."[59] But focusing on the *entire* Muslim community is not an effective way to profile, is something that no serious analyst recommends (although unfortunately there are fringe commentators who argue for just that), and is not what is occurring in the status quo.

My point is not to refute Berman's report, even though its conclusions are dubious. Rather, it is to show that the report represents a current risk: because there has not been another large-scale attack in the United States since 9/11, there will be similar calls to remove some of the law enforcement tools that currently exist, and this could make us less safe. It is a virtual certainty that removing these tools would result in our counterterrorism efforts being even less efficient, further driving up costs.

6

The Consequences of the Invasion of Iraq

The people of England have been led in Mesopotamia into a trap from which it will be hard to escape with dignity and honour. They have been tricked into it by a steady withholding of information. . . . Things have been far worse than we have been told, our administration more bloody and inefficient than the public knows. It is a disgrace to our imperial record, and may soon be too inflamed for any ordinary cure.

—T. E. *Lawrence, Aug. 2, 1920*

Although it is hard for many of us to remember this now, in 2000 George W. Bush and Dick Cheney campaigned on the idea that their predecessors were too eager to use the military as a tool of foreign policy. In one debate with Democratic candidate Al Gore, Bush claimed that because of the Clinton administration's policies, the country was now "overextended in too many places."

Cheney also had strong words about America's role in the Middle East when he defended the George H. W. Bush administration's decision not to attack Baghdad at the end of the Persian Gulf War, when Cheney was the secretary of defense. On a *Meet the Press* appearance during the 2000 campaign, he said that the United States should not act as if it were "an imperialist power, willy-nilly moving into capitals in that part of the world, taking down governments."[1]

Many of the foreign policy advisers who dominated the Bush campaign, and who would later play high-level roles in the administration, likewise believed that America should be very hesitant to use military force. (This, of course, was not a universal belief among Bush campaign advisers, whose ranks also included notable Iraq hawks.)

A *New York Times* profile of future national security adviser Condoleezza Rice written during the campaign noted that she "takes a dim view of American military intervention." The article concluded that both Bush and Rice shared a "balance-of-power, realist Republican approach" to foreign affairs that favored strengthening the U.S. military but at the same time scaling back the country's military commitments overseas in order to focus on big nation-state competitors, such as China and Russia.[2]

For example, during the campaign Rice said that the United States should cease its peacekeeping role in the Balkans, instead letting its European allies bear the costs.[3] One may agree or disagree with this policy prescription, but it evinced clear systemic thought: the United States was spending too much on its overseas commitments, and both the treasury and the military were suffering. Under this paradigm, the United States shouldn't bear the brunt of the costs in military operations that primarily benefit other nations. Other countries should be made to shoulder a fair portion of the costs as well as the responsibilities.

During one of his last campaign stops before Americans turned out to vote in November 2000, George W. Bush reiterated his critique of how Bill Clinton and Al Gore had abused the U.S. armed forces. He charged that they had "used our military too much and supported it too little." Bush said that although defense spending at this time was a lower share of the U.S. economy than it had been since 1940, the military had rarely "been used so freely . . . more commitments, less resources." He gravely intoned that the Clinton administration's use of the military was "a short-sighted policy with long-term consequences."[4]

It seems that this belief that the military should be used infrequently was intended as anything but an empty promise. Indeed, after winning the election, the Bush administration's earliest actions toward Saddam Hussein's regime left the Iraq hawks who had supported the Bush-Cheney campaign dissatisfied and apprehensive.

The administration's major policy initiative toward Iraq was to replace the extant sanctions—which were criticized on humanitarian grounds—with what Secretary of State Colin Powell dubbed "smart sanctions."[5] This new sanctions policy was designed to continue to contain Saddam Hussein and prevent him from developing nuclear weapons while lessening the impact on average Iraqis.

Influential hawks were suspicious. Richard Perle, who had advised the Bush campaign on foreign policy, told the media, "Re-energizing sanctions is a mistake. Ten years later, they're an obvious failure."[6] Senator Sam Brownback of Kansas complained, "It seems that with Saddam Hussein, we're saying we don't like this man in power, but we're then not willing to go ahead and take steps to remove him."[7]

By the time Powell testified before the House and Senate Foreign Relations Committees in March 2001, a key purpose of his testimony had become allaying conservative fears that the administration was too soft on Iraq. He did not receive the aggressive grilling that many observers expected from Republicans, perhaps because they didn't want to be too tough on an ideologically aligned administration that was still struggling to get on its feet after a contentious election. But Representative Benjamin Gilman of New York did warn that "loosening sanctions against Iraq could provide Saddam Hussein with a greater ability to increase his weapon account." The *Washington Post* noted that Powell "showed little enthusiasm for a policy widely advocated on Capitol Hill: removing the Iraqi leader from power."[8]

Washington Post columnist Jim Hoagland argued in May 2001 that Bush's Iraq policy was doomed before it even began. He wrote that the administration needed to instead embrace "a clear American commitment to supporting the establishment of democracy in Iraq, through a long-term program of material and political support for Iraqis who share that goal and will work for it."[9] Summarizing this period in the Bush presidency, Patrick Clawson, a Middle East expert at the Washington Institute for Near East Policy, has said that those who argued that the administration came into office determined to attack Iraq—such as former Treasury secretary Paul O'Neill—failed to grasp the actual thrust of Bush's early policies. "What O'Neill doesn't notice is that those who wanted to go to war lost, and those who supported 'smart sanctions' won," Clawson said.[10]

But, to use a phrase that has long since become cliché, 9/11 changed everything.

The Afghanistan War

Within hours of the devastating surprise attack on the United States, top thinkers in the administration had already begun to fixate on Iraq. In his 2011 book *The Longest War*, Peter Bergen details the numerous early references to Iraq among administration insiders, even before a single American soldier set foot in Afghanistan. According to a deputy's notes, Secretary of Defense Donald Rumsfeld considered whether "to hit S.H. [Saddam Hussein] same time—not only UBL [Osama bin Laden]" at 2:40 p.m. on September 11, 2001. The same day, the number three official at the Pentagon, Douglas Feith, raised the idea of overthrowing Saddam Hussein to the Arabic-speaking General John Abizaid while the two were flying back to the United States from Europe. Abizaid cut Feith off: "Not Iraq. There is not a connection with al Qaeda."

But the exploration of military options against Iraq continued. On September 12, President Bush asked Richard Clarke to see if there was evidence of Iraqi involvement in the 9/11 attacks. At a September 13 meeting in the White House Situation Room, Rumsfeld outlined the basic arguments that would later justify the Iraq War, stating that Iraq supported terrorists and that Saddam Hussein might even be willing to provide them with weapons of mass destruction (WMDs).[11]

The early search for evidence of Iraqi involvement in the 9/11 attacks was perhaps defensible. After all, the United States had just been blindsided by a massive surprise attack, and it made sense to examine all possibilities. But this inquiry was not entirely impartial.

Rather, there was a palpable desire among some of the key players in the administration to unearth reasons that Saddam Hussein posed a threat to America, thus making a war against him justified.

Nonetheless, cooler heads prevailed in the initial U.S. response to the 9/11 attacks. Rather than lashing out at Iraq, which hadn't attacked America, the United States invaded Afghanistan and toppled the Taliban regime that sheltered al Qaeda. The invasion of Afghanistan was necessary to deprive al Qaeda of a safe haven where it could plan, train, and communicate freely, thus posing a continual risk of having another catastrophic attack like 9/11 inflicted on the United States.

There are different views about how bin Laden expected the United States to respond to the 9/11 attacks. On the one hand, some commentators believe that he expected a minimal response. After all, America's response to the August 1998 bombing of two of its embassies in East Africa was limited to cruise missile strikes against a few targets in Afghanistan and Sudan. The United States did not retaliate at all for the bombing of the USS *Cole* in October 2000. But on the other hand, some commentators think that bin Laden actually wanted to provoke a massive military response. Former CIA officer Bruce Riedel argues that one overarching goal of the attacks was to draw the United States into Afghanistan in order to produce a quagmire, similar to the situation the Soviet Union faced there in the 1980s.[12] Consonant with this view, the letter that bin Laden wrote to Mullah Omar just before the U.S. bombing began (see chapter 3) envisions a quagmire in Afghanistan that would undermine the American economy.[13]

The United States began a bombing campaign against the Taliban on October 7, 2001. When it inserted troops later in the month, America did not enter Afghanistan with a "heavy footprint." Rather, the United States attacked with a light force, consisting of about 300 Special Forces soldiers and 110 CIA officers who established a liaison with tens of thousands of fighters from the Northern Alliance, a group based in northern Afghanistan that opposed the Taliban. (The name *Northern Alliance*, it is worth noting, was not preferred by that group's leaders. They thought that it was created by their adversaries to highlight the fact that the alliance was composed primarily of northern leaders who did not come from Afghanistan's dominant Pashtun ethnic group.)[14] Al Qaeda operatives had assassinated Ahmad Shah Masud, the Northern Alliance's leader, just before the September 11 attacks.

The Taliban had no response to American airpower, which proved devastating to their ranks. The accuracy of the U.S. airstrikes made some Northern Alliance commanders think that the United States had "death rays"—an idea that American soldiers made little effort to debunk. The combination of U.S. airpower and the light counterattack toppled the Taliban from power within weeks.

The Northern Alliance captured the key city of Mazar-e Sharif, which sits about a hundred miles from the border with Uzbekistan, on November 10. It was a significant loss for the Taliban, because the city was critical to the Taliban's supply routes. Losing it had the potential to damage the Taliban's access to food, ammunition, and other supplies. The Northern Alliance then captured Kabul on November 13.

The United States missed the opportunity to kill or capture Osama bin Laden and other top al Qaeda leaders when it failed to dedicate additional troops to an operation in the Tora Bora mountains. CIA veteran Hank Crumpton, who oversaw the intelligence agency's operations in Afghanistan, was convinced that bin Laden was holed up in Tora Bora, but General Tommy Franks rebuffed his request for additional troops. Because General Franks didn't want to deviate from the light-footprint approach that began the Afghanistan War, at this critical juncture Pakistani forces were largely given the responsibility of intercepting al Qaeda operatives as they fled across the border into Pakistan.

Unfortunately, around that time—on December 13—Pakistani militants launched a dramatic attack on India's parliament. Five militants armed with guns and grenades burst into that complex around noon and opened fire. One of the attackers managed to fire at the door to Vice President Krishan Kant's office before being chased away by a security official who was subsequently shot dead. In all, six police officers, a gardener, and all five attackers were killed in the hour-long battle. This attack ratcheted up tensions between India and Pakistan, thereby causing the Pakistanis to redeploy troops to the border with India—and leaving them with fewer men to intercept fleeing al Qaeda and Taliban leaders.

Although Pakistani leader General Pervez Musharraf claimed that his forces arrested 240 fleeing militants, much of al Qaeda's leadership, including bin Laden, escaped.

Despite this, the Afghanistan conflict seemed to be going well to the public at large and military officials alike. This view was justifiable even after Tora Bora, for the Taliban was out of power and al Qaeda had been significantly degraded. Bergen writes, "Bin Laden retreated from the Tora Bora battlefield demoralized, wounded, and contemplating his own death, while the organization he had so carefully nurtured for more than a decade was now on life support."[15]

In November 2001 the Pentagon began the formal consideration of plans to attack Iraq, and by 2003 the military described the Taliban as a "spent force" to American officials.[16] As the United States prepared for an invasion of Iraq, CIA specialists and Special Forces units alike were reassigned from Afghanistan to Iraq.

The Iraq War as Strategy

Before I examine the costs of the Iraq War, one thing should be made clear: if one has a proper understanding of al Qaeda's strategy, something to which the United States has paid insufficient attention, it was foreseeable that invading Iraq was a poor strategic move and could well prove disastrous. Bin Laden had two major ideas about how to defeat America, stemming from his experiences fighting the Soviets in Afghanistan. The first was the necessity of bleeding a superpower adversary's economy, and the second was the importance of making his fight against America as broad as possible.

In terms of al Qaeda's economic strategy, the Iraq War was extremely expensive. It will, when all is said and done, cost the United States more than a trillion dollars in direct budgetary outlays. When you account for second-order economic consequences and opportunity costs, the economic impact on America has been even higher. It is true that prewar projections didn't estimate that the cost would be close to this amount, but part of the problem is that much of the prewar planning was built around *best-case* scenarios, which is no way to prepare for a war.

Deputy defense secretary Paul Wolfowitz, for example, told Congress in 2003 that oil revenues from Iraq "could bring between $50 and $100 billion over the course of the next two or three years." He therefore projected that Iraq "could really finance its own reconstruction, and relatively soon."[17] Dissenting voices that projected higher war costs and a harder road ahead were marginalized.

Army chief of staff General Eric Shinseki had said in Capitol Hill testimony that although he didn't want to question "the combatant commander's exact requirements," in his view several hundred thousand soldiers would be needed for the occupation of Iraq following Saddam Hussein's ouster. Wolfowitz brushed these figures aside in his subsequent testimony, describing them as "wildly off the mark." He asserted that "it is hard to conceive that it would take more forces to provide stability in post-Saddam Iraq than it would take to conduct the war itself." As Pulitzer Prize–winning journalist Thomas Ricks notes, "Wolfowitz's slapdown of Shinseki echoed for months across the military."[18]

So the administration embraced the most favorable cost estimates rather than considering the full range of possibilities. Also known was the potential for Iraq to serve as a magnet for jihadi fighters from elsewhere in the region. Even in 2003, a "flypaper theory" was touted by some as a virtue of the invasion. Under this theory, the war's advocates held that jihadis would flock to Iraq to fight the United States, and they argued that this was a *good* thing. In this view, the United States would be able to kill or capture the jihadis inside Iraq rather than risking a terrorist attack on U.S. soil. This flypaper theory was in many ways an extension of the notion that the United States should fight the terrorists overseas so it doesn't have to fight them at home, a concept often advanced by President Bush and others.

Expressing this view, General Ricardo Sanchez said in a July 2003 interview with CNN that foreign fighters were entering Iraq "from various places. This is what I would call a terrorist magnet, where America, being present here in Iraq, creates a target of opportunity, if you will. But this is exactly where we want to fight them. We want to fight them here. We prepared for them, and this will prevent the American people from having to go through their attacks back in the United States."[19]

Of course, there are multiple problems with the flypaper theory. Like much of the planning for the Iraq War, it represents naive best-case-scenario thinking, downplaying the potential for the war to create *new* enemies while overestimating the military's ability to deal with the foes who would be attracted to Iraq. The war's planners should have wondered whether, by attracting foreign fighters to the battlefield, the costs for the United States might be driven up far beyond the estimates provided by Wolfowitz and others. The planners should have asked whether these foreign fighters could attack targets other than American forces that might significantly undermine the war effort—such as al Qaeda's subsequent attacks on Shiites, which became a major driver of sectarian killing.

In addition to bolstering al Qaeda's economic strategy, the Iraq invasion helped the other major element of al Qaeda strategy by feeding its overarching narrative. This narrative held that Islam itself was under attack by the United States and other forces of nonbelief. The invasion made this narrative more powerful to its intended audience; after all, Iraq had nothing to do with the 9/11 attacks. Saddam Hussein had provided aid and comfort to Palestinian terrorist groups, but his relationship with al Qaeda was limited.

The decision to invade Iraq thus fueled the perception that the United States was engaged in some kind of anti-Islam crusade and that countries all across the Muslim world could be targeted next. These perceptions were only enhanced when it turned out that the primary justification for the invasion—that Saddam Hussein was developing nuclear weapons—proved to be false. In the Arab world, many of the domestic niceties about how "intelligence failures" rather than malicious intent were responsible were simply not convincing.

Essentially, the United States responded to 9/11 in a similar manner to how George Foreman approached the "rumble in the jungle" fight against Muhammad Ali (see chapter 2): using all its strength to unleash a furious series of blows. The U.S. response broadened the fight rather than keeping it narrow, which is exactly the wrong approach to defeating a smaller adversary like al Qaeda. For some inexplicable reason, most strategists gave little consideration to the fact that the only way a large power like the United States can be defeated by a weaker foe like al Qaeda is if it overreacts, creating more enemies while also exhausting itself.

Nevertheless, broadening the fight beyond Afghanistan to include Iraq was sold to the public as a way to defeat terrorism and undermine al Qaeda. Instead this decision would erode American power and provide al Qaeda with a remarkable opportunity to reconstitute.

The Failed Justifications for the Iraq War

In addition to being a poor strategic decision, the justifications provided to the public for invading Iraq did not hold up. Saddam Hussein had neither WMDs nor an active program to develop them, contrary to what the Bush administration claimed. The administration put its credibility on the line in making that case and never adjusted after it was definitively shown that Saddam Hussein hadn't restarted his nuclear weapons program. In 2004, both David Kay and Charles Duelfer, successive heads of the Iraq Survey Group—an official U.S. body designed to search for Iraqi WMDs—concluded that Saddam Hussein had eliminated his stockpiles in the early 1990s. Both investigators concluded that the nuclear weapons program had never resumed.

I say that the Bush administration never adjusted, because the absence of WMDs was an obvious blow to its credibility. It never explained to the world why its future claims and intelligence should be believed despite this spectacular failure. Thus, U.S. credibility suffered.

Compounding the problem, President Bush made light of the lack of WMDs at the annual Radio and Television Correspondents Dinner in 2004. When he presented a slideshow of humorous photos documenting life inside the White House, one of them showed Bush looking under Oval Office furniture. The president joked, "Those weapons of mass destruction have got to be somewhere. Nope, no weapons over there . . . maybe under here?" Although I have decried the politicized environment that has surrounded our counterterrorism policies, the Democratic outrage at this attempt at humor was justified. "This is a very serious issue. We've lost hundreds of troops, as you know, over there. Let's not be laughing about not being able to find weapons of mass destruction," Democratic National Committee chairman Terry McAuliffe said.[20]

A second overarching justification for the war, an alleged connection between Iraq and al Qaeda, likewise proved to be overstated. The administration clearly tried to create the perception that there was a working relationship between the two, with President Bush arguing in his January 29, 2003, State of the Union address that "Saddam Hussein aids and protects terrorists, including members of al Qaeda."[21] Donald Rumsfeld similarly claimed that America had "bulletproof" evidence connecting Saddam Hussein's Iraq to al Qaeda.[22]

I should note that the idea put forward by many war critics that there was *no* connection between Saddam Hussein's Iraq and al Qaeda is untrue. But there was no working relationship that could justify the invasion as a strategic matter. Despite limited contacts between Saddam Hussein's regime and al Qaeda members, toppling his government was not a blow to the jihadi group. In fact, al Qaeda indisputably attained a far greater presence in Iraq after the invasion than it had had before.

These two reasons—Iraqi WMDs and an alleged connection between Saddam Hussein and al Qaeda—were the primary justifications for America's war in Iraq. There were other, secondary and tertiary justifications as well. Foremost among these was the idea that after toppling Saddam Hussein, the United States could establish a democratic regime, which would be a model for the region. This argument holds that one critical cause of radicalization in the Muslim world is the absence of democracy: disenfranchised citizens turn to hard-line religious practice and to violence because of a lack of societal alternatives.

However, this is obviously an insufficient reason for America to go to war without either an Iraqi WMD program or a connection to al Qaeda. The Middle East, and the Muslim world in general, is filled with nondemocratic states, so holding that it is legitimate to topple an authoritarian regime if it's replaced by a democracy is a particularly perilous justification for war. It could create many more enemies for the United States of people who fear they could be next.

Moreover, spreading democracy is a poor primary justification for the Iraq War because of the uncertainties embedded in the process: it was unclear that invading Iraq would actually result in a sustainable democracy. Finally, there are other means to spread democracy than by invading a country. War should be a last resort rather than a dominant tool of democracy promotion.

A few commentators have claimed that the "Arab spring" of 2011—including the toppling of Zine El Abidine Ben Ali's regime in Tunisia and Hosni Mubarak's regime in Egypt by popular protests—vindicates President Bush's "freedom agenda" and perhaps even the invasion of Iraq. The idea that this "hidden benefit" justifies the Iraq War is absurd. There are still questions about whether these revolts will actually result in democratic governments or a safer region; neither outcome is by any means self-evident. More to the point, it is highly unlikely that these revolts were enabled by Saddam Hussein being deposed. Certainly none of the evidence that has emerged from these protests points to the invasion of Iraq as a proximate cause.

More direct contributions include the development of social media technology (such as Twitter, Facebook, and even dating websites), which was used as an organizing tool; Al Jazeera's coverage, which heavily promoted the revolutionary cause; and the social conditions on the ground in early 2011, including unemployment, rising food and fuel prices, and ineffective and corrupt governance.[23] As a senior U.S. intelligence analyst told me, "I think that the claim that the Iraq war caused the Arab spring is just as absurd as the point of view that Obama's Cairo speech caused it. In both cases, you have U.S. pundits who assume that we are the uncaused cause behind everything that happens anywhere in the world."[24]

This is not to say that nothing good came from Saddam Hussein's fall. But any benefit derived from his ouster must be balanced against the costs of invading Iraq. And those costs are substantial.

Damaging the War Effort in Afghanistan

We can begin to evaluate the cost of invading Iraq with a look at the effect the invasion had on the war the United States was already fighting in Afghanistan. Unlike the Iraq War, the war in Afghanistan was not a war against a target of choice, since the 9/11 attacks were executed by a jihadi group that found safe haven with Afghanistan's Taliban regime. Since Iraq was a war of choice, it is particularly problematic that it undermined another conflict that was clearly tied to real U.S. interests.

As I noted previously, a perception existed among many Iraq War advocates and planners that the war in Afghanistan had already been won. This proved to be tragically wrong. Dick Cheney, speaking at the Air National Guard Senior Leadership Conference in December 2002, described the Afghanistan War as "America's most dramatic victory in the war against terrorism" and claimed that "the Taliban regime and the al Qaeda terrorists have met the fate that they chose for themselves."[25]

Kenneth Pollack, a former CIA intelligence analyst and the director of the Saban Center for Middle East Policy at the Brookings Institution, wrote an article in Foreign Affairs in early 2002 in which he claimed that "the key to victory in Afghanistan was a U.S. air campaign that routed the Taliban combat forces." Advancing the theme that the Afghanistan War had been won, he warned that "too much delay" in invading Iraq "could be as problematic as too little, because it would risk the momentum gained from the victory over Afghanistan."[26]

As a result of this flawed perception, significant military and intelligence assets were diverted from Afghanistan to Iraq. Robert Grenier, a former director of the CIA's counterintelligence center, noted that from late 2002 to early 2003, "the best experienced, most qualified people who we had been using in Afghanistan shifted over to Iraq," including counterterrorism specialists and paramilitary operatives.[27] This had such second-order effects as diminishing U.S. influence over Afghan warlords.

At the same time, the preparation for Iraq caused such special mission units as Delta Force and Navy SEALs Team Six, as well as aerial surveillance platforms like the Predator, to be shifted into Iraq. A former Central Command official told the New York Times in 2007, "If we were not in Iraq, we would have double or triple the number of Predators across Afghanistan, looking for Taliban and peering into the tribal areas. We'd have the 'black' Special Forces you most need to conduct precision operations. We'd have more CIA."[28]

Indeed, in March 2002, as preparation for the Iraq War was well underway, CIA deputy director John McLaughlin told senior members of Bush's national security team that the CIA's presence in Afghanistan would be scaled back. Thereafter, the CIA closed bases in Herat, Mazar-e Sharif, and Kandahar and delayed an $80 million plan for training the Afghan intelligence service. The *Washington Post* reports that the commando unit Task Force 5, which took the lead in hunting for bin Laden at the time, lost around two-thirds of its personnel.[29]

The result of this drawdown in resources was predictable: it weakened American efforts in Afghanistan and allowed the enemy forces to regain strength. Compounding the problem, insurgent groups expanded their funding sources, including the drug economy.[30] Meanwhile, the ability of the United States and its allies to provide stability on the ground, facilitate reconstruction, and improve the mechanisms of governance suffered.

For this reason, journalist James Fallows argued in the *Atlantic* that the coalition in Afghanistan never really had the opportunity to show whether it could provide order in the country. "The campaign in Afghanistan was warped and limited from the start," he writes, "by a pre-existing desire to save troops for Iraq."[31] Iraq would continue to cause resource diversion from the Afghanistan campaign, not just as America and its allies geared up for the Iraq War but also years later. In 2007–2008, for example, violence grew in Afghanistan even as the U.S. surge in Iraq attempted to salvage a very bad situation there.

In February 2011, I spoke with Andrew Exum, an Arabic-speaking counterinsurgency expert at the Center for a New American Security who served in both Iraq and Afghanistan as an Army Ranger officer. When I asked him why U.S. efforts in Afghanistan have been so uneven, he replied without hesitation, "One word: Iraq. I remember in 2002 coming back from Afghanistan and being immediately forgotten. We had just fought the largest set-piece battle since the Persian Gulf War, Operation Anaconda, and it was the first time our regiment had been in battle since Vietnam. But the focus was on Iraq." The United States had been in Afghanistan for more than nine years at the time I spoke with Exum, but because of the focus on Iraq, he thought that the military hadn't *really* been there for nine years. "It's been an economy-of-force mission, really, since 2002," he said. "The vast majority of our efforts and our resources—not just military but also intelligence assets—have been focused on Iraq."[32]

Angering Allies, Aiding Iran

The Iraq War was largely a unilateral U.S. effort, despite a small "coalition of the willing": countries that at least voiced their support for the campaign. In the process of going to war in Iraq, the United States angered many, including its allies and the "Arab street." Ultimately, the war would prove to be a recruiting boon for al Qaeda and other jihadi groups as well as a major geopolitical victory for Iran.

The controversial nature of the Iraq War can be seen by the street protests it engendered. In February 2003, crowds took to the streets in antiwar demonstrations throughout the world. During the weekend of February 15–16, between six and ten million people marched in as many as sixty countries.[33] This included around 1.3 million people protesting in Barcelona, 750,000 in London, 650,000 in Rome, and 500,000 in the six state capitals of Australia. There were also large protests in the United States that weekend, including a rally of 100,000 outside the U.N. headquarters in New York City.

The Bush administration was unable to secure the U.N. Security Council's support for the invasion. In fact, the process of debate over the war, coupled with such brash remarks as Rumsfeld's derision of Germany and France (both of whom opposed the invasion) as the "old Europe," created deep fissures between the United States and its long-standing allies.[34]

The Arab states were particularly alarmed by the invasion. Indeed, a comprehensive study published in 2010 by the RAND Corporation found that the invasion produced "uncertainty about U.S. intentions and capabilities in the region," resulting in many Arab states becoming increasingly receptive to Chinese and Russian assistance. "Post-invasion disarray in the Arab world was accompanied by a corresponding erosion of confidence in the United States as a security guarantor," the report notes, "stemming from the perception of U.S.

entanglement in Iraq, which some viewed as limiting both U.S. capabilities and willingness to intervene elsewhere."[35]

Indeed, only one Middle Eastern state was significantly empowered by the U.S. invasion of Iraq: the Islamic Republic of Iran, which has an adversarial relationship with the United States. Back in 2001, before the 9/11 attacks, Iran was surrounded by a number of antagonistic or outright hostile Sunni regimes, including Iraq (with whom it had fought a prolonged war), Taliban-run Afghanistan (with which Iran almost went to war in 1998, after the Taliban's murder of nine Iranian diplomats), Saudi Arabia, and Pakistan. America's ouster of the Taliban removed one of these competitors; and after the United States also toppled Iranian archenemy Saddam Hussein and thereby empowered Iraq's Shiite majority, Iran no longer faced a hostile wall of Sunni states.

Iran was able to drive up the cost of the U.S. invasion of Iraq by supporting the full spectrum of insurgent factions. It had a natural affinity for Shiite groups, but Sunnis also received its aid. One signature of Iranian assistance was the explosively formed projectile (EFP), which is uniquely dangerous because, as *Wired* has noted, "when it detonates, the concave end blows outward and melts into a bullet-shaped fragment that slices through armor and flesh."[36]

Captain Greg Hirschey told *Wired* about an EFP that went through a Humvee, taking off both of the driver's legs and also an arm. I reported from Iraq in May and June 2007 as an embedded journalist, and during my time there, Lieutenant Patrick Henson, a West Point graduate, told me of a video he watched in which an EFP went straight through a heavily armored Humvee and left an impression on the curb on the other side of the road.[37] In addition to EFPs and other weapons, Iran also provided insurgents with military training.

But Iran's strategy for addressing the U.S. invasion of Iraq was not solely military. It also fashioned a soft-power approach to expand its influence inside Iraq. The extent to which Iran could gain soft-power influence was overlooked by many U.S. planners before the invasion because they thought that the animosity created by the Iran-Iraq War in the 1980s would serve as a buffer against such gains.

Iran was able to make economic inroads: it became one of Iraq's largest trading partners, with around $10 billion in annual exports to its neighbor. Iran is also predominant in certain business sectors in Iraq, including religious tourism to Najaf, which is the largest competitor within Shia Islam to the theological dominance of the Iranian city Qom. A National Public Radio report noted that Iranian involvement in Najaf extends far beyond that sector:

> It's not just tourism companies here that are controlled by Iran. "This is the hospital—you see it says Islamic Republic of Iran," says Radhwan Kilidar, a former member of parliament from Najaf. He points out Iranian construction projects around the city. Some are public, such as the Iranian consulate. Others, including the office of an Iranian cultural organization in Kilidar's neighborhood, are more discreet.[38]

Iran's economic ties to Iraq are not in themselves nefarious, but given the rivalry between the United States and Iran, they have to be regarded as a loss for the United States.

Moreover, Iran has also been able to expand its social and political influence inside Iraq. Many Iraqi Shiite parties already had connections to Iran because they were based there during Saddam Hussein's oppressive rule. But Iran has reportedly supplemented this influence by funding select candidates in Iraq's 2005 and 2010 parliamentary elections as well as in the 2009 provincial elections.[39] Unlike its economic activities, Iran's involvement in Iraq's politics represents a malign interference. When one country actively buys politicians inside a neighboring state to extend its influence, it has begun to engage in the kind of behavior from which we expect nation-states to refrain in international relations.

In addition to its economic and political activities, Iran launched an Arabic-language television network, Al Alam, on the eve of America's invasion of Iraq. Al Alam's coverage reflects official Iranian thinking on contemporary events.

One commentator, writing in the preeminent foreign policy journal *Foreign Affairs*, noted that America's invasion of Iraq "handed Tehran a priceless strategic gift: the opportunity to promote a friendly Shiite government in Saddam's stead."[40] While the U.S. invasion stirred up angry protests throughout the world and strained America's relations with its trusted allies, Iran was securing a far more advantageous geopolitical position.

Aiding Jihadi Recruitment

Precious few U.S. actions could have promoted al Qaeda's narrative better than invading Iraq. America's invasion of a major Muslim country based on a justification that turned out to be false gave credence to al Qaeda's contention that the United States was attacking and trying to undermine Islam itself.

This perception was inadvertently fed by George W. Bush's rhetoric. His bellicose words, such as the statement that "either you are with us, or you are with the terrorists," lent themselves to the idea that Islam was under attack. After all, what did "with us" mean? Did it mean that those Muslims who don't adopt Western values and morals, or who dislike the United States or Israel, are "with the terrorists"? This is not the meaning Bush intended, but it was how al Qaeda's leaders painted the president's words.

As bin Laden said in the interview he gave to Al Jazeera's Taysir Allouni in October 2001, "Bush has said that the world must make a choice between one of two parties; there is the party that supports him, and that any state that does not join the Bush government and the world Crusade will necessarily be considered with the terrorists."[41] Indeed, many in the Muslim world interpreted Bush's words in that precise, inflammatory way. But in addition to his bellicose rhetoric, some of Bush's verbal gaffes—such as his unthinking description of the fight against al Qaeda and affiliated movements as a "crusade"— helped to create the image of America being at war with Islam.

Indeed, immediately after the U.S. invasion of Iraq, there were some parallels to be drawn between the Arab world's reaction and its response more than twenty years earlier to the Soviet invasion of Afghanistan. Volunteers from the Arab world traveled to Baghdad to fight America. The *New York Times* provided a snapshot of these foreign fighters on April 2, 2003, less than two weeks after combat began:

Adil Omar Abu Shinaf, a 30-year-old Libyan in a flowing khaki robe, strode into a battered phone booth near one of [Damascus's] main bus terminals and dialed long distance to his family home in the coastal hamlet of Barak. "Dad," he said. "I am going to the jihad in Iraq!" After the call, he recounted that his father wished him godspeed and his mother, weeping, chastised him for not telling anyone of his plans before leaving Libya. Mr. Abu Shinaf, a laborer, is one of hundreds of men from across the Arab world and beyond milling around Damascus daily, hoping to cadge a seat to Baghdad on one of the free buses provided by the Iraqi interests section or, if they have the means, paying for a long-haul taxi.[42]

As the *Times* indicates, from the onset of the war there were hundreds of men like Shinaf. This anger toward the invasion was intensified over time by the gruesome video images of the war broadcast on Arabic-language satellite television as well as by the condemnations of the invasion by key religious figures. Yusuf al Qaradawi, whose appearances on Al Jazeera catapulted him to superstar status, repeatedly justified attacks on Americans inside Iraq. Syria's top religious authority, Sheikh Ahmad Kaftaro, called for suicide bombings against coalition forces.[43] Such rhetoric came not just from prominent theologians but also from lesser-known imams during Friday (*juma*) prayers.

As Baghdad fell to American forces, keen observers of the Arab world discerned a growing rage. Diaa Rashwan of Cairo's Ahram Center for Political and Strategic Studies warned, "The American media and people are in a state of euphoria right now, but they are not seeing it the way we are seeing it at all. The Arab street is very frustrated, and to America, I repeat, I repeat, I repeat, the real war hasn't started yet. We have to be careful with such euphoria. It will only increase the feelings of anger in the Arab world. No Arabs want to welcome an occupying power."[44]

Al Qaeda and other extremist groups were able to capitalize on this anger, as top U.S. officials acknowledged in testimony on Capitol Hill in February 2005. CIA Director Porter Goss said, "The Iraq conflict, while not a cause of extremism, has become a cause for extremists." Defense Intelligence Agency director Lowell Jacoby said, "Our policies in the Middle East fuel Islamic resentment. Overwhelming majorities in Morocco, Jordan and Saudi Arabia believe the United States has a negative policy toward the Arab world."[45]

These views were verified by the 2006 National Intelligence Estimate, which described the Iraq conflict as "the cause célèbre for jihadists, breeding a deep resentment of U.S. involvement in the Muslim world and cultivating supporters for the global jihadists."[46]

A 2007 study by Peter Bergen and Paul Cruickshank further supported these conclusions. Bergen and Cruickshank concluded that the Iraq War "has motivated jihadists around the world to see their particular struggle as part of a wider global jihad fought on behalf of the Islamic *umma*." They believed that it served as a catalyst, helping to globalize jihadism by making al Qaeda's "message of global struggle even more persuasive to militants."[47]

The fact that the Iraq War would serve as a prime propaganda piece for al Qaeda, and a recruiting tool, was foreseeable if al Qaeda's strategy had been clearly understood. The war fueled perceptions of an imperialist power rampaging through the Muslim world. It is all the more ironic that the Bush administration ended up on this course, since Bush and Cheney came into office dedicated to using the armed forces more sparingly.

The Human and Economic Costs

Finally, there are the human and economic costs of the invasion. These have been substantial, for both the United States and the Iraqis. The official Department of Defense casualty figures reflected 4,421 U.S. military and defense department civilian deaths in Iraq as of March 11, 2011, and an additional 31,938 wounded in action. At the same point, the Iraq Body Count website found between 99,980 and 109,230 Iraqi civilian deaths as a result of the violence.

Much can be said about these human costs. Each death is a tragedy. Those who are killed leave behind families: mothers and fathers, spouses, children, siblings. The lives of victims' families, American and Iraqi alike, are forever changed. If the victims are Iraqi and the perpetrators American, the United States may have turned the family members into permanent enemies even if the killing was accidental. Many of the injuries suffered, including loss of limbs, are utterly life-changing.

It is no secret that wars, both just and unjust, have significant human costs. Both World Wars and the Vietnam War produced more casualties than Iraq has, a fact that makes the deaths caused by the Iraq War no less tragic. But where the costs of the Iraq War are unrivaled is in the economic expense of the conflict. Thomas Ricks wrote in 2006 that the decision to invade Iraq "ultimately may come to be seen as one of the most profligate actions in the history of American foreign policy."[48] We can now see that this fear was correct.

As of September 2010, a Congressional Research Service report placed the Iraq War's price tag at $751 billion, when taking into account the cost of military operations, base security, reconstruction, foreign aid, and embassies.[49] The total costs will likely run higher, to more than $1 trillion. In fact, in 2008, a $3 trillion overall economic price tag was calculated by Columbia University's Joseph Stiglitz, a Nobel Prize winner in economics, and Harvard University's Linda Bilmes.[50]

They followed up their 2008 book with a September 2010 *Washington Post* column, published as the United States ended what·it dubbed its "combat operations" in Iraq, arguing that their $3 trillion calculation was in fact too low—a notable claim, since the $3 trillion estimate had been markedly higher than previous projections.[51]

In their column, Stiglitz and Bilmes found that the actual cost of the war was higher than they had previously thought for multiple reasons. Some costs, such as "the cost of diagnosing, treating and compensating disabled veterans," were higher than they had expected. Beyond that, Stiglitz and Bilmes stated that their initial estimate did not sufficiently capture opportunity costs, what might have been if not for the invasion. For example, they pointed out that the invasion of Iraq diverted resources from Afghanistan. "It is hard to believe that we would be embroiled in a bloody conflict in Afghanistan today if we had devoted the resources there that we instead deployed in Iraq," they wrote. I agree: the Iraq War made Afghanistan an economy-of-force mission, and if more resources had been devoted at the front end, the course of the conflict would have been different. Stiglitz and Bilmes wrote, "A troop surge in 2003—before the warlords and the Taliban reestablished control—would have been much more effective than a surge in 2010."

Another consequence of the Iraq War was higher oil prices. Stiglitz and Bilmes linked spiraling oil prices to the invasion as a result of the destabilizing effect it had on the Middle East, estimating that the war increased oil prices by at least $10 a barrel. Moreover, the war undoubtedly increased the national debt. "This was the first time in American history that the government cut taxes as it went to war," Stiglitz and Bilmes wrote. "The result: a war completely funded by borrowing. U.S. debt soared from $6.4 trillion in March 2003 to $10 trillion in 2008 (before the financial crisis); at least a quarter of that increase is directly attributable to the war."

Finally, Stiglitz and Bilmes contended that the Iraq War contributed to the global financial crisis. Higher oil prices (to which the invasion contributed) led to more money being sent overseas, while the war itself provided a lesser economic boost than might have been attained through other spending. Thus, "loose monetary policy and lax regulations kept the economy going—right up until the housing bubble burst, bringing on the economic freefall." Although the financial crisis would likely have occurred without the war, Stiglitz and Bilmes noted that "the bubble would have been smaller," and thus so too would have been the consequences when it burst. The Iraq War also left the United States with fewer resources to respond with once the crisis hit. "With the unemployment rate remaining stubbornly high, the country needs a second stimulus," they wrote. "But mounting government debt means support for this is low. The result is that the recession will be longer, output lower, unemployment higher and deficits larger than they would have been absent the war."

It is clear that the true cost of the Iraq War is far, far greater than a simple look at America's budgetary outlays might suggest.

Long before the financial crisis hit, Osama bin Laden recognized that the invasion of Iraq played into his strategy of economic warfare. I previously mentioned that bin Laden delivered a major address that Al Jazeera broadcast on October 29, 2004, just days before the U.S. presidential election. At the time, bin Laden had been presumed dead by many observers. But after Al Jazeera broadcast his new tape, it was picked up by networks the world over and aired endlessly.

Bin Laden stood at a podium in the video, his beard gray, wearing a white turban and a white tunic covered by a gold cloak. In the speech, he referred to current events and also to Western media sources, two signatures of his rhetoric. Purpose and symbolism surrounded both of these choices. Referring to current events proved to his audience that he was still alive. And citing information he could only know through familiarity with the Western media showed that far from being subjugated to a remote cave, bin Laden had access to current streams of information that helped him to know his enemy.

In the video, bin Laden addressed the American people directly. The overarching theme was economic in nature, explaining how al Qaeda was succeeding in its strategy of "bleeding America to the point of bankruptcy." He said that it was easy to bait the United States, that al Qaeda needed only to "send two mujahedin to the furthest point east to raise a piece of cloth on which is written al Qaeda, in order to make the generals race there to cause America to suffer human, economic, and political losses."[52]

But bin Laden said also that al Qaeda alone was not responsible for America's coming defeat. Rather, "the policy of the White House that demands the opening of war fronts to keep busy their various corporations—whether they be working in the field of arms or oil or reconstruction—has helped al Qaeda to achieve these enormous results." Thus, he said, "it has appeared to some analysts and diplomats that the White House and us are playing as one team towards the economic goals of the United States, even if the intentions differ."

He referred to America's astronomical budget deficit but said that "even more dangerous and bitter for America is that the mujahedin recently forced Bush to resort to emergency funds to continue the fight in Afghanistan and Iraq, which is evidence of the success of the bleed-until-bankruptcy plan." So al Qaeda had gained since 9/11, bin Laden said, but the Bush administration had gained too, as can be seen by "the size of the contracts acquired by the shady Bush administration-linked mega-corporations, like Halliburton."

So who has lost? "The real loser," bin Laden said, "is you. It is the American people and their economy."

7

One Step Forward

For many months now, the American people have understood that our present policy is a failure—and they want to
know where we go from here. Last night, like millions of
Americans, I listened to President Bush. They hoped and
prayed as I did that the President would present us with
a plan to make things better in Iraq. Instead, I fear that
what he has proposed will make things worse. They hoped
and prayed they would hear a plan that would start to bring
our troops home while leaving a stable Iraq behind. Instead,
they heard a plan to escalate the war—not only in Iraq, but
possibly into Iran and Syria as well. The President's strategy
is not a solution—it is a tragic mistake.

—*Senator Joe Biden, on the Iraq surge*

By 2006, the strategic damage that had been done to the United
States by the invasion of Iraq, as well as the lackluster planning to
stabilize that country thereafter, was evident to the American public.
Opinion polls found that a majority of Americans believed that the

decision to invade was a mistake, and the idea of quickly withdrawing U.S. troops also polled well. In the face of this public opinion, President George W. Bush's decision not to draw down American soldiers from Iraq but to significantly increase their number, seemed quixotic. Yet even though Bush's choice ran counter to the demands of a Democratic Party fresh off an electoral victory, as well as to the desires of a war-weary public, it was the right thing to do.

Despite that, the resources and attention required to undertake the surge, as well as the lives lost in the process, underscore how costly the decision to invade truly was. The success of the surge did not transform the Iraq War into a strategic success; instead, it helped to bring Iraq back from the brink of outright disaster but into a situation that still remained perilous. The resources channeled into the surge could have been more effectively devoted to other aspects of the fight against al Qaeda and its affiliates—and would even have been put to better use had they simply been conserved.

I begin this discussion of the surge, and other changes to the American approach in Iraq, with a review of how the situation worsened after Saddam Hussein fell.

Iraq's Descent into Chaos

The earliest parts of the war in Iraq were actually a rather stunning success. The initial campaign that overthrew Saddam Hussein was brilliantly executed.[1] But when Baghdad fell on April 9, 2003, less than a month after the invasion, the United States had only a lackluster plan to stabilize and reconstruct the country.

Complaints about insufficient planning for the stabilization and reconstruction of Iraq surfaced soon after Baghdad fell in 2003, at a time when many observers still believed, as President Bush had asserted, that America's mission had been accomplished.[2] One of the first signs of the lack of planning was the massive looting of government buildings that occurred just after the regime fell. Although U.S. officials like Secretary of Defense Donald Rumsfeld were dismissive of the looting—Rumsfeld remarked in an April 2003 press conference that "freedom's untidy" and "stuff happens"—Fred Ikle, the Pentagon's policy chief during the Reagan administration, said, "America lost most of its prestige and respect in that episode. To pacify a conquered country, the victor's prestige and dignity is absolutely critical."[3]

I spoke with retired army colonel Ed McCarthy, who was involved in the Iraq War as an adviser and instructor for the U.S. military. "The first thing that struck me was seeing the looting and watching us do nothing about it," he told me. "I commented at the time, 'What Iraq is going through right now requires different rules of engagement, and the U.S. military isn't getting them.' From a tactical level, one can say that things happened faster than we thought they would. But from a strategic level, that phase requires a hell of a lot more attention and planning than did the actual fighting phase."[4]

Contemporaneous media accounts reveal how the planning that this phase required was lacking. In July 2003, the *Los Angeles Times* quoted a senior defense official as saying, "The military's war planning was light-years ahead of its planning for everything else." In fact, the *Times* published an in-depth investigation about America's preparation for stabilization and reconstruction operations that concluded there were significant planning missteps. There were multiple reasons that the planning was lacking. Consideration of how to stabilize the country had been compressed into too short a period; a former CIA analyst told the *Times* that "the messiah could not have organized a sufficient relief and reconstruction or humanitarian effort in that short a time."

The postwar planning had also been compartmentalized, with the various agencies that would be involved working independently of one another rather than coordinating. This stood in the way of obtaining a holistic picture of how reconstruction efforts would be carried out and what would be needed. With these flaws in the process, the United States found itself unprepared for the problems that it encountered in post-Saddam Iraq. The postwar planning that did occur often addressed problems that never arose, such as oil fires, lethal epidemics, and mass starvation.[5]

Looking back at America's preparations years later, Thomas Ricks found that military historians and senior planners involved in Operation Iraqi Freedom agreed that stabilization and reconstruction planning was either lacking or nonexistent.[6] Like the administration's assessments of the cost of the Iraq War, the plans for this phase were based on best-case assumptions. In part this resulted from the overly compressed process for considering postwar Iraq, as well as from the unjustifiable assumption that the war against Saddam Hussein's military represented the real challenge of the invasion. These best-case assumptions may also have derived from a generally overoptimistic outlook about Iraq that dominated official thinking. It is clear, though, that if it was possible to prevent an insurgency from taking hold in Iraq, the lack of planning for stabilization torpedoed those chances.

The fact that an insurgency had emerged became evident over time, although the top military brass seemed loath to admit it. But, as I mentioned previously (see chapter 4), this insurgency was dramatically reshaped by the destruction of the Golden Dome Mosque in Samarra on February 22, 2006—an attack against a major Shia holy site ordered by al Qaeda in Iraq (AQI) leader Abu Musab al Zarqawi. That mosque had featured a large gilded dome and minarets, and the *Washington Post* reported that the attack blasted them into "naked steel and gaping blue sky."[7] Iraqi leaders immediately scrambled to prevent an outbreak of sectarian violence. Grand Ayatollah Ali Sistani, Iraq's most influential Shiite leader, issued a fatwa prohibiting his followers from retaliating against Sunni sites. The police and other security forces had a heavy presence and increased their searches of vehicles. Loudspeakers blared across Baghdad as leaders of both Sunni and Shia mosques condemned the attack.[8]

Despite these efforts, the attack triggered massive Shiite reprisals against Sunnis. At least 54 Sunnis were killed the day after the bombing, and the number only rose with time.[9] Sectarian violence claimed at least 379 lives by the end of that week, with 458 injured.[10] The death toll continued to climb. As the Sunnis struck back at Shiites, AQI often took the lead, and it became the primary driver of the Sunni side of the insurgency during the course of 2006.

Nowhere was AQI's influence greater than Anbar province. A report about that province written by Colonel Peter Devlin on August 17, 2006, provided a stark assessment, describing AQI as the "dominant organization of influence" there. Colonel Devlin assessed AQI as having surpassed not only nationalist insurgents but also Iraq's government and coalition forces in the day-to-day life of average Sunnis. In fact, Devlin concluded that AQI had "become an integral part of the social fabric of western Iraq." Although most Sunnis in Anbar disliked AQI, many saw it as an inevitable part of their lives, as well as a possible means of protection from the physical threats they faced.[11] By late 2006, al Qaeda was able to control territory inside Iraq that was larger in size than New England.[12] To many observers, the situation—with fighting between Sunnis and Shiites, al Qaeda's rise, powerful Shiite militias, and sophisticated improvised explosive device (IED) technology that took a daily toll on U.S. soldiers—seemed hopeless, and the war lost.

Changes in American Strategy

America made two major changes in its military strategy: increasing the number of soldiers on the ground and dramatically shifting the way the troops were used. Increasing the amount of military personnel in Iraq flew in the face of the conventional wisdom, but rather than succumbing to pressure to draw down U.S. forces, President Bush decided to increase their number through a surge.

In addition to the public souring on the Iraq War, the congressionally mandated Iraq Study Group issued a report that would have provided political cover for pulling back. Co-chaired by James Baker III and Lee Hamilton, the report called for enhanced diplomatic efforts and a drawdown in combat forces.[13] In other words, in the midst of Iraq's darkest and most violent days, the report sought to reduce America's military presence and replace it with a diplomatic push that would have been unable to address such issues as al Qaeda's rise and the sectarian violence gripping the country. Peter Bergen rightly described the report's recommendations as "a muddle," albeit one that was predictable "because a successful strategy to prosecute a complex war was unlikely to be generated by a committee of Democratic and Republican elder statesmen, no matter how wise."[14]

On January 10, 2007, from the White House library, President Bush announced a surge of twenty thousand soldiers. That number would eventually be increased to thirty thousand. The political stage was set thereafter, with Democrats arguing that the 2006 elections had provided them with a mandate to oppose the surge and to get American forces out of Iraq. (Some Republicans likewise argued that the surge was doomed to fail, but this was primarily a Democratic position.)[15] At times, arguments against the surge absurdly devolved into personal attacks on General David Petraeus, who became the commander of U.S. forces in Iraq after the surge announcement.

Prominent examples include Senator Harry Reid of Nevada absurdly claiming that Petraeus "isn't in touch with what's going on in Baghdad" (as though a senator sitting in Washington, D.C., was somehow better attuned to the situation on the ground) and Senator Dick Durbin of Illinois accusing Petraeus of "carefully manipulating the statistics" in order to "persuade us that violence in Iraq is decreasing and thus the surge is working." But despite the often heated debates, there was agreement across party lines that this was almost certainly President Bush's last chance to right the course of the war. Polling conducted in the immediate wake of the surge announcement found that a majority of Americans considered the troop increase to be Bush's "last chance for victory."[16]

As the new troops arrived in Iraq, offensive operations were undertaken in Baghdad and also in insurgent strongholds to the north and south. But an additional thirty thousand soldiers would not have made a great difference to the course of the conflict if there hadn't also been a change in the strategic use of this larger force. Previously the military had been generally disengaged from the Iraqi population, operating under the assumption that its presence was a cause of insurgent violence and thus American soldiers should be seen infrequently. This led to the creation of massive forward-operating bases (sometimes called *super-FOBs*) that were literally walled off from the rest of the country.

When General Petraeus assumed command, he had different ideas about U.S. strategy. While he had been posted at Fort Leavenworth beginning in 2005, Petraeus had taken it upon himself to create a new manual on counterinsurgency for the army and the marines. At the end of the process, in February 2006, he convened a group of 135 experts on irregular warfare at Leavenworth to "murder board" the document: that is, outside experts who were not involved in writing the new manual were asked to critique it. This group was diverse, composed not just of officers but also of human rights advocates, journalists, academics, and members of the intelligence and diplomatic communities.

Steven Metz, chairman of the regional strategy and planning department at the U.S. Army War College's Strategic Studies Institute, participated in this process. He told me that the February 2006 session "was one of the more creative and ambitious examples of this because of the diversity of people involved." However, it was not without its issues and frustrations. "There was a major gap in understanding between the counterinsurgency experts in the group, some of whom had been involved with it for decades," Metz explained, "and representatives of the NGO and human rights communities, who were just beginning to grapple with it. This sometimes made it difficult to reach any sort of agreement."[17] With this experience shaping his outlook, Petraeus brought to Iraq a very different approach from isolating the military personnel on super-FOBs.

Rather than keeping U.S. soldiers away from Iraqi civilians, Petraeus's strategy called for engaging in more frequent foot patrols, interacting with Iraqis, and thus putting a more recognizable "face" on the American presence. This new approach correctly recognized the Iraqi population as the "center of gravity" in the conflict. America's focus shifted toward protecting Iraqi civilians from insurgents and other dangers. American forces were better integrated with the Iraqi population through the use of outposts in the districts they patrolled. These outposts had U.S. soldiers living and sleeping in the same districts they were working to secure, rather than being confined to their FOBs. ABC News reported in January 2007 that military planners had said "there will eventually be about 30 mini bases, called joint security stations, scattered around Baghdad, housing both U.S. and Iraqi troops."[18]

When I was in Baghdad in 2007 as an embedded journalist, I was able to see a snapshot of the conflict that reflected the changes occurring throughout Iraq. The 2nd Brigade of the 32nd Field Artillery (2-32), with which I was embedded, was a field artillery unit that had been converted to infantry for its deployment. Its areas of operation were primarily Yarmuk and Hateen in central Baghdad. The unit that

2-32 replaced had had a minimal presence in these areas; as was typical of the conflict, it had primarily been confined to a FOB.

Consonant with Petraeus's new strategy, 2-32 played a much more active role than its predecessor, first beginning to establish itself in these areas through *presence patrols*. People living in Yarmuk and Hateen had only rarely seen Americans since the initial invasion. "In the beginning, we were a novelty," Vincent Passero, who was a sergeant at the time of his deployment, later told me. "A lot of people would come out to see us. Kids would come out to look at our Humvees."[19]

These presence patrols were followed by more intensive engagement, such as performing a census of the area. The census, which was necessarily carried out by foot patrols (rather than in armored vehicles zipping through the neighborhood, without any human interaction), served multiple purposes. The first was mapping the district to learn who the inhabitants were, discovering their complaints and needs while also getting a sense of where "bad actors" might be.

The second purpose was creating the opportunity for interaction between American soldiers and the residents. In his 2009 book *The Gamble*, Thomas Ricks describes how a unit in the 2nd Infantry Division would carry out the census in its area of operation in Baghdad. He wrote that Captain Jim Keirsey "ordered that the soldier doing the talking should sit down, take off his helmet and sunglasses, accept any drink offered, and speak respectfully. The other members of the patrol should stay in uniform and quietly focus outward on security, rather than join the conversation. In this way, they learned about suspected bomb planters and about Iraqi police abuses."[20]

The tactics in the census patrols that I witnessed mirrored those described by Ricks. I saw how putting a human face on the Americans could shift Iraqis' perceptions. At the end of one interview, an old man who had been a general in Saddam Hussein's army told the lieutenant he was speaking with that he had heard that when Americans knock on Iraqis' doors, the soldiers steal valuables, that the Americans take any possessions they want and leave the Iraqis with nothing. The lieutenant, smiling respectfully yet reassuringly, said, "No, we're not here to take anything. We just want to get a sense of what your needs are so that we can help." The look of relief on the old man's face was clearly no act.

This is not to say that being exposed to Americans universally improved Iraqis' perceptions. Some U.S. soldiers acted boorishly, and in rare instances some committed outright atrocities. But General Petraeus's strategic thinking was vindicated, because increased contact with the Americans largely left Iraqis with a more favorable view of U.S. soldiers and of the American presence.

During the course of 2-32's deployment, the soldiers were able to identify key players in their area of operation: who was providing the electricity and who provided links to other neighborhoods. As they gained the population's confidence, they began to receive actionable intelligence from Iraqis who finally believed that the Americans could be trusted.

The soldiers in 2-32 were able to turn a couple of *mulhullas* (neighborhoods) over to Iraqi security forces before the end of the summer. The unit's last action before turning over these *mulhullas* was to remove some Iraqi national police who were aligned with the Jaish al Mahdi militia, a Shiite group affiliated with populist anti-American cleric Muqtada al Sadr that had been responsible for a significant amount of sectarian bloodshed. The intelligence that led to this raid came from the local police, who complained that this national police unit had set up a compound in which the local police were not allowed.

Like most raids, the raid removing the militia members occurred in the dead of night. There are tactical reasons for conducting raids at that time: many of the targets are asleep, and most adversaries the United States faces do not possess night-vision technology. The operation was pretty straightforward, and the Americans didn't have to fire a shot. "They didn't put up too much of a fight," Sergeant Passero told me. "They were actually a larger force than we were; we just had the element of surprise on our side, and we had better technology."

By the time 2-32 finished its deployment, the security situation in its area of operation had markedly improved. When the soldiers first arrived, they regularly found IEDs and the bodies of dead civilians. "But by the end, I felt as safe in *mulhalla* 608 as I do at this table," Sergeant Passero told me, as he downed a Guinness in Washington, D.C.'s Columbia Heights neighborhood.[21]

The Awakening

Al Qaeda brutalized the population in those areas of Iraq where it became a dominant force, and in that way it overplayed its hand. In Anbar, where Colonel Devlin assessed AQI as the "dominant organization of influence," attacks on civilians increased by 57 percent between February and August 2006. A retrospective on improvements in Anbar published in the *Military Review* described AQI as carrying out a "heavy-handed, indiscriminate murder and intimidation campaign" in Anbar's capital of Ramadi during this period, a situation that the Sunni tribes grew tired of soon enough.[22]

In the U.S. Marine Corps official history of the Anbar Awakening, which compiles oral testimony from American and Iraqi perspectives, the head of an Iraqi women's NGO known pseudonymously as "Miriam" recalls al Qaeda committing "the ugliest torture" to intimidate the population. If that didn't work, AQI would slaughter people, sometimes decapitating them.[23]

Al Qaeda also alienated the population through its totalitarian religious governance. In May 2008, military operations caused AQI to melt away from a Sunni area of Mosul, the capital of the Ninawa governorate and al Qaeda's last major urban stronghold in the country. What U.S. forces found there illustrates the brutal and bizarre governance that the jihadi group imposed. It had banned the side-by-side display of tomatoes and cucumbers by food vendors, because AQI regarded the arrangement as sexually provocative. AQI banned a local Iraqi bread known as *sammoun* on the grounds that it did not exist during the Prophet Muhammad's time. The use of ice was banned because Muhammad did not have ice. Barbers were not allowed to use electric razors. All these restrictions might be humorous were it not for the fact that Iraqis died for flouting them. As al Qaeda retreated from Mosul, one barber told the press that AQI had killed several of his colleagues.[24]

It is against this backdrop that Iraq's Sunni tribes rebelled against al Qaeda's excesses. There are multiple points in time that one can claim as the genesis of this tribal uprising. The aforementioned Marine Corps history notes that in 2005, Colonel Stephen W. Davis, commander of Regimental Combat Team 2 (RCT-2), found that al Qaeda fighters in the Qaim area of Anbar were interested only in killing Americans and were doing nothing for Iraq. This stood in contrast to nationalist insurgents, who were fighting for themselves, their families, and their tribes. RCT-2 exploited that schism and began to think about the serious engagement of local leaders. The Marine Corps history states that "commanders during 2006 were able to look back on the actions of their predecessors in 2005 and see the foundations that had been built."[25] The same year, 2005, also saw the first large-scale tribal push-back against al Qaeda in Anbar, in the form of around twelve tribal leaders. Al Qaeda, however, responded rapidly and lethally. Within a month, half of those leaders had been killed, and the survivors fled.[26]

When the army's 1st Brigade of the 1st Armored Division (commanded by Colonel Sean MacFarland) moved into Anbar's capital, Ramadi, in 2006, the desperate situation they faced spurred further interest in tribal engagement. Colonel MacFarland chose Captain Travis Patriquin, an Arabic speaker, as his first liaison to the tribal sheikhs. Those who knew Patriquin described him to me as energetic and proactive—someone who was smart, engaging, and mission-focused. On September 9, 2006, a number of sheikhs publicly announced their plan to fight al Qaeda, calling their movement *Sahwa*, or "Awakening." Though the genesis of the Awakening came before September 2006, it was on that date that the movement was finally ready to go public.[27]

One of the key Awakening leaders was Abdul Sattar Abu Risha. Sterling Jensen worked as an army contract linguist from 2006 to 2007 before returning to Anbar in February 2008 as the first-ever Marine Corps civilian foreign area officer, a regional specialist position that is typically reserved for uniformed officers. He told me that Abdul Sattar was "charismatic, very social, funny." However, Jensen added that Abdul Sattar also blurred his words, didn't enunciate well, and was difficult to understand. "He was very colloquial," Jensen said, "and that endeared him to people."[28]

Abdul Sattar was ecumenical in outlook. When he learned that Jensen was Mormon, he apparently looked the faith up online and later told Jensen, "You need to get me an American wife. Mormons have more than one wife. I have a Shiite wife, I have a Sunni wife, and now I need an American wife." From Abdul Sattar's perspective, the fact that he had wives from different Islamic sects and wanted an American wife next showed how balanced he was.

Abdul Sattar was startlingly frank, giving voice to ideas that other Iraqis might be afraid to articulate. He argued that the Iranians were the real occupiers of Iraq and the Americans should be seen as guests. He spoke against the anti-U.S. resistance, saying that it helped Iran. Dr. Thamer Ibrahim Tahir al Assafi, of the Muslim Ulema Council for al Anbar, explained that Abdul Sattar was instrumental in promoting the idea of the Awakening. "Frankly, we all disliked Sheikh Abdul Sattar Abu Risha," Assafi said. "This being because he was not a religious person, so there was a distance between us." However, when Abdul Sattar advocated for the Awakening, Assafi said that other prominent leaders in Anbar examined the idea and believed it to be the best course.[29]

When the Awakening was announced in September 2006, it issued an eleven-point communiqué. Colonel MacFarland said, "Ten of them I would have written for them almost exactly the same way they wrote them."[30] The other point, suggesting that the Awakening would have to kill the governor of Anbar, was more problematic. After this initial meeting, more sheikhs proved willing to come forward and speak to or work with the Americans.

Captain Patriquin created an unusual PowerPoint presentation explaining the strategy of engaging the Awakening. Far from the typical military PowerPoint, "How to Win in Al Anbar" was illustrated with stick figures and narrated in the tone of a children's tale. The first slide, showing a smiling stick man, was captioned, "This is an American Soldier. We'll call him Joe. Joe wants to win in Al Anbar. But sometimes it seems that other people don't share that idea." It asked, "How can Joe win in Al Anbar? By fighting the insurgents?"

The next slides outlined the problem with simply fighting our way to victory. Not only does Joe have to fight in heavy gear weighing eighty pounds, he also cannot tell the difference between insurgents and regular Iraqis. Both just look like smiling stick figures. How to address this problem? Captain Patriquin introduced the idea of tribal engagement. "This is a Sheikh," the presentation said, the accompanying graphic depicting a turbaned stick figure with a black bar as a mustache.

"They've been leading the people of this area for approximately 14,000 years. In spite of many, many conquering Armies trying to remove him, this man and his family have been involved in the politics here since recorded time began."

Joe sits down with this stick-man sheikh to drink tea. "Mmm," the presentation says, "good Chai." Joe tells the sheikh that although militias are bad, the Iraqi police are good. Thus, "would the Sheikh let his men join the Iraqi Police?" The sheikh says yes. Half of his men go to police school while the other half stay back to protect their families. When the first half return, the other half go to police school. Captain Patriquin's presentation asks, "Now can you tell the difference between the insurgent, the normal Iraqis, and the Iraqi Policeman? Kind of?"

Indeed, the illustration depicts a smiling stick man wearing a police badge, three smiling Iraqis, and one frowning stick figure. "Don't worry, because the Iraqi Policeman can tell the difference. And the insurgent knows that. See, that's why he's sad." The insurgent is captured, after which Patriquin foresaw the program snowballing. "The Sheikh brings more Sheikhs," the presentation says, "more sheikhs bring more men. Joe realizes that if he'd done this three years ago, maybe his wife would be happier, and he'd have been home more." In the end, everyone wins. "Except for the terrorists," the presentation notes, adding parenthetically, "which is OK because terrorists suck!"[31]

Despite the unconventional narrative style, it was a rather prescient prediction of things to come. Sadly, Captain Patriquin would not live to see the ultimate fruits of his efforts; he was killed in an IED attack on December 6, 2006. Today Anbar boasts a police station that the Anbaris chose to name after Patriquin, and he is remembered fondly in the province.[32]

The turning of tribes, as well as former insurgents, to cooperation with coalition forces made a significant difference on the ground in Anbar, and it was expanded beyond that province through a program known as the "Sons of Iraq." At its height, more than a hundred thousand predominantly Sunni Iraqis took part in this program.

General Petraeus and Ambassador Ryan Crocker presented the changes on the ground to Congress in two separate sets of testimony, in September 2007 and April 2008. By the initial testimony in September

2007, the Awakening movement had already helped to significantly improve Anbar, transforming it from the days in which al Qaeda was the dominant actor. General Petraeus said that Anbar had become "a model of what happens when local leaders and citizens decide to oppose al Qaeda and reject its Taliban-like ideology."[33]

Just days after the September testimony, the Awakening was dealt a significant blow when Abdul Sattar Abu Risha was assassinated. Although this could have been devastating for the group, Abdul Sattar's brother Ahmed Abu Risha proved to be a strikingly effective leader. Thus, in his April 2008 testimony, General Petraeus continued to tout the Awakening's success. In that testimony, Petraeus noted that the Awakening continued to root out al Qaeda and establish local security and that it had been broadened to other parts of the country through the Sons of Iraq program. Even the much-maligned Iraqi security forces had increased in number and capability. General Petraeus noted that more than a hundred Iraqi combat battalions had become "capable of taking the lead in operations."[34]

Iraq continues to face significant challenges. As of this writing in mid 2011, Iranian influence within the country remains disturbingly strong. Muqtada al Sadr's movement—once believed to be near death when Sadr fled Iraq during the height of the surge—has found new life as a political party. Iraq's March 2010 national elections resulted in months of political deadlock that were resolved only when Sadr decided to support Prime Minister Nuri al Maliki, a move that resolved the election in Maliki's favor.[35] This makes American planners nervous, both because of Sadr's longstanding opposition to the United States and also his links to Iran.

There remain dangerous militias and jihadi groups, such as Asaib Ahl al Haq and al Qaeda in Iraq. And there are the challenges associated with incorporating the former Sons of Iraq into governmental service; this incorporation has been slow and smaller than expected, with many participants in the program receiving only menial jobs and many more out of work (see chapter 11).

Despite that, Iraq has come a long way since 2006–2007. During those dark days, the country was mired in sectarian violence and civil war, and al Qaeda in Iraq was able to control broad swaths of territory.

Most of the proffered alternatives—a diplomatic push coupled with drawing down U.S. troops, accelerating the training of Iraqi security forces, or splitting the country into three separate regions—would have done nothing to remedy the problems.[36] The turnaround should be regarded as a remarkable achievement.

There were multiple changes in the country during this period, including the tribal awakening, evolving counterinsurgency tactics and operations, Sadr's decision to stay on the sidelines in 2007, and an influx of new U.S. forces. The surge was certainly not the only causal phenomenon that reduced ethnosectarian violence. Nonetheless, having more U.S. soldiers on the ground employing new tactics was a powerful force for quelling violence, especially because the surge worked synergistically with other positive forces, helping to empower the tribal awakening and making Sadr realize that there could be a heavy price for continuing to support violence.

Indeed, some academic work on the matter, such as that of Dr. Bernard Stancati of Colorado Technical University, has found the increased number of American soldiers as one causal factor driving tribal dynamics.[37] President Bush's decision to surge rather than withdraw improved the U.S. strategic position.

Yet the American position was improved only relative to where it had stood in 2006—not relative to where it had stood before the ill-fated invasion itself. Thus, although the surge succeeded, what it achieved underscores the cost and the folly of the war. And even as the United States focused on pulling Iraq back from the brink of disaster, events were spiraling out of control in two other locations.

8

Two Steps Back

The U.S.-led war on terrorism has left in its wake a far
more unstable world than existed on that momentous day
in 2001. Rather than diminishing, the threat from al Qaeda
and its affiliates has grown, engulfing new regions of Africa,
Asia and Europe and creating fear among people and governments from Australia to Zanzibar.

—*Ahmed Rashid*, Descent into Chaos

Although Osama bin Laden left Tora Bora in December 2001
demoralized and injured, he didn't stay that way for long. As
America's attention turned to Iraq, al Qaeda's senior leadership experienced a remarkable regeneration in Pakistan.

It is clear in retrospect that General Tommy Franks's decision not
to commit additional troops to the Tora Bora operation in order to capture bin Laden and his top lieutenants was a costly mistake. As Peter
Bergen notes, the American and allied presence in that battle was
limited to "forty Delta operators from 'black' Special Forces, fourteen
Green Berets from the less secretive 'white' Special Forces, six CIA

operatives, a few Air Force signals operators, and a dozen British commandos from the Special Boat Service."[1]

Because U.S. and allied soldiers were unavailable to intercept al Qaeda's leaders as they fled across the border into Pakistan, the job fell to Pakistani forces. There were two major problems with this. First, after Pakistani militants attacked India's parliament on December 13, tension between the two countries caused Pakistan to redeploy troops to the Indian border and left fewer military resources for intercepting al Qaeda's fleeing leaders.

The second and more important concern was that perhaps the Pakistani military shouldn't have been trusted with intercepting al Qaeda leaders at all. Although Pakistan's military was secular and elitist in orientation at its founding, sympathy for Islamic militants eventually became a strong force within the institution.[2] One reason is its long history of supporting religious militants who fought Pakistan's rivals.

In the 1970s, Zulfiqar Ali Bhutto's government adopted a "forward policy" of sponsoring violent Islamist groups in Afghanistan in response to that government's support for Pashtun and Baloch separatist groups in Pakistan. (Afghanistan aided these groups because of a border dispute between the two countries.)

In the 1980s, Pakistan's support for stateless militants intensified after the Soviet invasion of Afghanistan. In supporting the Afghan mujahedin, Pakistan's military intelligence, the Inter-Services Intelligence agency (ISI), showed a distinct preference for fundamentalists. The major reason was strategic: the ISI perceived Islamists as fearless anti-Soviet fighters and thought they could be more easily transformed into a Pakistani proxy.

In the 1990s, the ISI sponsored Afghanistan's Taliban for similar reasons, understanding that the Taliban were naturally hostile to Pakistan's archrival India. As Pakistan's military sponsored armed Islamist groups, personal bonds developed between Pakistani officers and the people they supported.

But Pakistan's military also underwent a reorientation in organizational culture during these decades. General Muhammad Zia ul Haq, who executed a coup that toppled Bhutto in July 1977, embarked on an ambitious plan for the Islamization of Pakistan, including its military. Zia's reforms included requiring standard military training to include

Islamic teachings such as S. K. Malik's *The Qur'anic Concept of War*, incorporating religious criteria into officers' promotion requirements and exams (so that many skilled officers with secular outlooks were passed over for promotion while religious conservatives reached top levels), and mandating formal obedience to Islamic rules within the military.[3]

Zia required not only that soldiers attend Friday prayers at regimental mosques but also that units bring mullahs to the front lines of combat. At the same time that Zia implemented these policies, the demographics of the officer corps were shifting. The first generation of officers from the country's urban elites was being replaced by junior officers from poorer northern districts who had more conservative religious views and were more prone to fundamentalist practice.[4]

Thus, because of a strategic doctrine embracing the sponsorship of Islamist militants, the personal relationships between Pakistani officers and these militants, and the Pakistani military's evolving organizational culture, there were good reasons to question the choice to rely on Pakistan's military as the last line of defense against fleeing al Qaeda leaders.

The U.S. invasion of Afghanistan devastated al Qaeda's safe haven and a significant portion of its military capabilities.[5] But the group's leadership survived. Although a few—such as Saif al Adel, Saad bin Laden (Osama's son), and Sulaiman Abu Ghaith—fled to Iran, most relocated to Pakistan. During the flight into Pakistan, some Pakistani soldiers sympathetic to the militants' cause allegedly looked the other way, thus allowing them to pass—and others may even have assisted them.[6] In addition, journalist Ahmed Rashid reports that many Arabs who had been hunkered down in the mountains "were escorted out of Tora Bora by Pashtun guides from the Pakistani side of the border, at an average cost of $1,200 each."[7]

Al Qaeda's relocation to Pakistan was reported in the American media even before 2001 had ended. In a December 19 MSNBC broadcast, Chris Matthews said that although the Taliban had been battered in Afghanistan, "it looks increasingly like Osama bin Laden may have crossed the border to Pakistan." He continued, "If bin Laden is in Pakistan, he could find haven with members of Pakistan's intelligence service, which has long ties with al Qaeda."[8] Once in Pakistan, al Qaeda's leadership set about rebuilding the organization.

Al Qaeda's Rebound

With al Qaeda's central leadership in disarray after the escape from Afghanistan, the organization's regional nodes, and other more localized jihadi groups, took the lead in operations. For example, on October 8, 2002, two gunmen linked to al Qaeda opened fire on U.S. Marines on the island of Failaka off Kuwait's coast while they were in the midst of a training exercise, killing one. Four days later, Indonesia's Jemaah Islamiyya was responsible for a series of bomb blasts in the tourist district of Kuta on Indonesia's Bali island, killing 202. On October 23, Chechen terrorists seized a Moscow theater packed with 850 people. The siege ended only after Russian special forces (*spetsnaz*) pumped a fast-acting sleeping gas through holes that had been bored into the theater's auditorium in order to knock out the hostage takers. All fifty Chechen rebels were killed, along with more than ninety hostages.[9]

The United States continued to try to kill or capture top al Qaeda leaders during this period. But because the regional nodes took the lead, many observers concluded that al Qaeda's central leadership must be dead. This conclusion was highly flawed. "For too long, we wanted to believe we had really killed off al Qaeda's central leadership," Bruce Hoffman, the director of the Center for Peace and Security Studies at Georgetown University and one of America's most distinguished scholars of terrorism, told me. "We believed that al Qaeda had progressed downward to clones and imitators. We deluded ourselves into thinking that al Qaeda had been weakened and diluted and the major threat now came from self-starters."[10]

Partly because of the perception that al Qaeda was already beaten, the United States drew its military resources away from Afghanistan and Pakistan for use in Iraq. I have already detailed the impact this diversion of resources had on the war in Afghanistan, but it also helped to enable al Qaeda's regeneration. "If we hadn't gone into Iraq, we wouldn't have so gleefully subcontracted the struggle in Pakistan to Pervez Musharraf," Hoffman told me, referring to Pakistan's former president. "We gave it to him and walked away. This was also the time when all of a sudden bin Laden went from being public enemy number one to 'he doesn't run things, he's just a symbol.' It was a complete

180, and all of it breathed new life into al Qaeda, giving al Qaeda the breathing space that it needed."

Over time, al Qaeda's central leadership began to again play a significant role in terrorist attacks. For example, on July 7, 2005, four British-born suicide bombers blew themselves up on London's public transit system during rush hour, killing fifty-two. The authorities were hesitant to acknowledge that al Qaeda had played a role: two official British reports released the following year described the cell as autonomous and self-actuating rather than tied to al Qaeda.[11]

Even at the time of the reports' release, there was reason to question this conclusion.[12] There were, for example, connections between cell leader Mohammad Sidique Khan and Riduan Isamuddin, mastermind of the Bali bombings. Mohammed Junaid Babar, a Pakistani native living in Queens, New York, who pled guilty in U.S. federal court to smuggling military supplies to al Qaeda and assisting the London bombers, identified Khan as someone he'd met at one of al Qaeda's training camps in Pakistan. And Haroon Rashid Aswat, who helped set up a training camp in Oregon, had contacted the London bombers by telephone hours before the attack.[13]

But the idea that the London bombings were completely unrelated to al Qaeda was definitively refuted by a commemorative video that the jihadi group released in July 2006. That video included not only praise for the attacks from bin Laden and Ayman al Zawahiri but also footage of a martyrdom tape recorded by Mohammad Sidique Khan. Al Qaeda's leadership simply could not have obtained this footage had the plot proceeded completely independently of them.

Underscoring this point, Zawahiri claimed that Khan and fellow plotter Shehzad Tanweer had visited one of al Qaeda's camps "seeking martyrdom," an account that has been corroborated by Western intelligence agencies. Bob Ayers, a security expert at London's Chatham House think tank, commented when the new video was released, "It makes the police look pretty bad. It means the investigation was either wrong, or they identified links but were reluctant to reveal them."[14]

Bruce Hoffman told me that there were definitive reasons that officials were hesitant to link such attacks to al Qaeda. "One of the main rationales for the Iraq War was that we're fighting them over there so we don't have to fight them here," he said. "So there was a built-in desire to say this was something different: this wasn't al Qaeda, because we had killed al Qaeda. It was also an attempt to cover up an enormous security lapse. Thus the reports said these were radicalized individuals, self-starters, who were hard to detect, rather than terrorists connected to a major network."[15]

Furthermore, the plot that was disrupted on August 10, 2006, which was designed to blow up with liquid explosives seven planes bound for the United States from Britain, served as a powerful sign that al Qaeda was back. Although some initial reports hesitated to link the plot to the jihadi group's senior leadership, the evidence soon left little doubt. Pakistani security sources confirmed that the attack was conceived by al Qaeda's "top hierarchy."[16] Published reports stated that high-level al Qaeda operative Matiur Rehman had directed the plot from Pakistan.[17] Officials believe that two suspects identified in the plot met with him there and later received a wire transfer from Pakistan to buy airline tickets for the would-be suicide bombers.[18]

Al Qaeda's Internal Dynamics

There were at least four significant aspects of the strategy that al Qaeda's senior leaders adopted to create a safe sphere for themselves in Pakistan's tribal areas. (Even though Western intelligence services mistakenly believed that bin Laden remained in the tribal areas long after he had left, a fact that became obvious after his death, al Qaeda's regeneration did begin there.)

First, al Qaeda took advantage of the hospitality offered under the Pashtunwali tribal code, which mandates protection for those who seek shelter in Pashtun territory, and the jihadis also benefited from relationships they had developed with local tribes during the Afghan-Soviet war.[19] The combination of these factors impeded efforts by American special forces and CIA paramilitary officers to conduct cross-border raids into Pakistan targeting leaders of the jihadi group.

The second aspect of the strategy was intermarriage. Journalist Hamid Mir, who interviewed bin Laden multiple times, learned from one of bin Laden's guards that "al Qaeda fighters married local women and by so doing ensured undying protection from the tribes they married into."[20] Indeed, Ayman al Zawahiri married a woman from Bajaur's Mohmand tribe after the flight from Afghanistan, and al Qaeda leader Abu Ikhlas al Misri also married locally.[21] Within South Asian tribal culture, not just in the Pashtun areas but also in the Punjab regions, intermarriage is an established way to resolve conflicts and to forge relationships. Hassan Abbas, a professor associated with the South Asia Institute at Columbia University and a leading scholar of Pakistan, told me that he thought this intermarriage may have been initiated at the urging of the Pashtuns rather than by al Qaeda's leadership.[22] Either way, the result was the same: it helped to build bonds and embed al Qaeda into the local tribal structure.

Third, Hassan Abbas told me that in his opinion, al Qaeda developed a better understanding of tribal politics than either Pakistan's military or the Americans. The leaders of the jihadi group knew which tribes were most powerful in the various districts and agencies, which tribes were more influential historically, and which controlled important strategic locations.

Fourth, al Qaeda's ideology, worldview, and objectives became popularized during this period. There were multiple reasons for this, including a backlash against U.S. military operations in Afghanistan. Because of this, Abbas said, "al Qaeda leaders never needed strong communications tools or a media network to explain their position. They jumped on the bandwagon."

In 2002, Pakistani forces launched Operation Meezan ("Balance") into the Federally Administered Tribal Areas (FATA). The operation, which targeted militants, was reportedly motivated by American pressure. Meezan was rather limited, with few forces on the ground.

There was more of a push against foreign jihadis after two assassination attempts targeted President Musharraf in December 2003. Although the subsequent investigation focused initially on junior air force officers, it soon homed in on a Rawalpindi mosque; the mullah preaching there came from the tribal belt and had met with Zawahiri. After statements from Zawahiri calling for Musharraf to be killed came to light, Musharraf became convinced of al Qaeda's complicity in the assassination attempts and gave his military the green light to take action against al Qaeda.

A retired Pakistani army chief once commented that Musharraf "has brilliant tactics but no strategy."[23] This is a perfect description of how Musharraf led a series of assaults aimed at the religious militancy that had festered in Pakistan's tribal areas. These actions were characterized by costly tactical successes, followed by ill-advised peace agreements that occurred when the Pakistani military did not enjoy the upper hand, in contravention of standard warfare principles.

The first of these was the Shakai Agreement in South Waziristan, in which Pakistan agreed to release 163 militants, pay compensation for those who were "martyred" or injured during the operation, and allow foreign fighters to remain in Waziristan.[24] Such terms, unfavorable as they were to the government, allowed militancy to grow.

More flawed treaties followed. Pakistan signed a deal with militant leader Baitullah Mehsud in Sararogha, South Waziristan, on February 7, 2005. In an attempt to remedy the Shakai Agreement's problems, it imposed more restrictions on Mehsud, but it also stated that the government would not take action against him and his followers for their previous transgressions and included a fifty-million rupee payment to the militants. The result was that this deal also strengthened the militants.[25]

After the Uthmani Wazirs revolted in North Waziristan, the government decided to cut a deal with them as well. Even the circumstances under which that agreement was made signaled Pakistan's weakness in the face of a determined adversary. Taliban fighters searched government negotiators and military officers for weapons before allowing them to enter the meeting, which took place in a soccer stadium in the North Waziristan capital of Miranshah. Heavily armed Taliban were posted as guards around the ceremony, and the militants' black flag (*al rayah*) hung over the scoreboard.

It was not just the circumstances of the signing that suggested Pakistani impotence. The accord itself was highly unfavorable to the government. It provided that Pakistan's army would abandon outposts and border crossings throughout Waziristan, as well as cease military actions in the region. Pakistan agreed to return weapons and other equipment seized from militants during army operations, and as in previous peace deals, agreed to pay compensation for property destroyed during combat. Of particular concern to Western analysts was a provision allowing non-Pakistani militants to continue to reside in Waziristan as long as they made the unenforceable promise to "keep the peace."[26]

Immediately after the Pakistani delegation left the stadium, the same black flag of the militants was run up the flagpole of abandoned military checkpoints. The Taliban began looting leftover small arms and held a parade in the streets of Miranshah. The militants clearly viewed this "truce" as a victory and were not inclined to respect its terms. Indeed, the Taliban used the ceasefire as an opportunity to erect a parallel system of government complete with sharia courts, taxation, recruiting offices, and its own police force. Al Qaeda in turn benefited from the Taliban's expansion, building what U.S. intelligence analysts estimated to be twenty-nine training camps in North and South Waziristan alone.

Other peace deals followed, including in Swat and Mohmand. The net effect, one Pakistani writer noted, was to give "much-needed respite to the militants, enabling them to re-group and re-organize themselves."[27]

As al Qaeda gained more of a foothold in Pakistan's tribal areas and was definitively linked to plots against the West, it became difficult to deny the group's recovery, even at an official level. Thus, although the April 2006 National Intelligence Estimate assessed that "the global jihadist movement is decentralized, lacks a coherent strategy, and is becoming more diffuse," the July 2007 National Intelligence Estimate took a very different view, concluding that al Qaeda "has protected or regenerated key elements of its Homeland attack capability."[28]

Bruce Hoffman told me that this official acknowledgement of al Qaeda's regeneration was "a very important document." He added, "It was a very brave document too, because it pushed back against the conventional wisdom."[29]

Al Qaeda's growth in Pakistan occurred while the surge in Iraq was at full force, so few American resources could be devoted to the problem. Near the end of President George W. Bush's second term, the New York Times noted that even though Bush had made al Qaeda's destruction his top priority, "it is increasingly clear that the Bush administration will leave office with al Qaeda having successfully relocated its base from Afghanistan to Pakistan's tribal areas, where it has rebuilt much of its ability to attack from the region and broadcast its messages to militants across the world."[30]

Meanwhile, some two thousand miles away, further strategic problems were growing in the Horn of Africa.

The Case of the Disappearing Somalis

A curious piece of news from Minneapolis–St. Paul garnered national attention in December 2008. The authorities had discovered that more than a dozen young Somali men from the Twin Cities area had disappeared in recent months, and both community members and U.S. intelligence officials feared that they had left the country to join jihadi groups in Somalia. Like al Qaeda's regeneration in Pakistan, the situation in Somalia markedly worsened while the United States was inexorably focused on Iraq.

Lending drama to the disappearances was a string of suicide bombings in Somalia on October 29, 2008, targeting U.N. offices, the Ethiopian consulate, and a presidential palace in Somaliland's capital of Hargeisa. (Somaliland, an autonomous region of Somalia, has declared its independence but has received no international recognition.) These audacious attacks killed at least twenty-five people, including several U.N. employees. At the same time the Hargeisa attacks occurred, suicide bombers also hit police officers charged with a counterterrorism mission in the port city of Bosaso in Somalia's autonomous Puntland region, resulting in at least six fatalities.[31]

The strikes were noteworthy because coordinated blasts were rare in the relatively stable regions of Somaliland and Puntland. They were also noteworthy because one of the suicide attackers, Shirwa Ahmed, was a naturalized American citizen and a graduate of Minneapolis's Roosevelt High School.

Ahmed thus became the first known American suicide bomber. The authorities were alarmed to learn that he was not the only member of Somalia's diaspora to leave the United States to take part in combat in Somalia. By December 2008, the media in Minneapolis–St. Paul reported that a number of other young Somali men—estimates were as high as forty—had disappeared from the area. Members of the local Somali community and U.S. government analysts feared that these men had returned to Somalia to participate in combat against the country's secular transitional federal government (TFG), or else to undertake training with al Shabaab ("the youth"), a jihadi group linked to al Qaeda.

Nor was this phenomenon confined to Minneapolis–St. Paul, which boasts the largest Somali population in the United States, at around seventy thousand. Federal investigations of similar disappearances have occurred in places ranging from the Pacific Northwest to Southern California, from Ohio to New England.[32] Members of the Somali diaspora had also disappeared from other countries—that is, had suddenly and unexpectedly left those countries to return to Somalia—with similar intentions. This phenomenon has been noted in Australia, Britain, Canada, Sweden, and elsewhere. Even some non-Somalis have traveled to Somalia to join its jihadi groups.

As the authorities and analysts looked at the situation, they were concerned about what these young men might do while in Somalia: they could fight the TFG or else, like Shirwa Ahmed, become suicide bombers. But of greater concern was the possibility that they could take part in terrorist plots after returning to the countries in which they had been living.

Why was this happening? Why had jihadism grown in Somalia, and why were members of the diaspora returning to augment it?

Although the United States was successfully pursuing a surge strategy in Iraq, its bungled support of Ethiopia's invasion of Somalia in December 2006 to topple an Islamist-dominated movement that had gained power there only magnified jihadism in Somalia. It also resulted in resentment and a growth in nationalist sentiment within the Somali diaspora, which greatly contributed to drawing members of the diaspora back. In turn, the fact that members of the Somali diaspora were returning to join jihadi groups increased the terrorist threat that Western countries faced, while bolstering al Qaeda's goal of making the battlefield on which the United States had to fight as broad as possible.

I will now examine how this situation arose.

A Brief History of Islamism in Somalia

Since emerging from an era of colonialism under Italy and Britain, Somalia has passed through military dictatorship, famine, and civil war. The practice of Islam in Somalia has traditionally been dominated by apolitical Sufi orders.[33] Islamist movements did not emerge until the late 1960s, when the Somalis gained greater exposure to less moderate currents of Islam. Saudi Arabia was central to these changes, but Egypt's Muslim Brotherhood also played a role.

In 1969, General Mohamed Siad Barre executed a military coup that made him president of the young state, which had won its independence nine years earlier. Some of Barre's draconian tactics for dealing with Somalia's fledgling Islamist movements caused the groups to consolidate and gave them momentum. When Muslim religious scholars denounced his reforms of Somali family law, for example, Barre executed ten of them and prosecuted hundreds more. Underground religious organizations opposing Barre's regime proliferated in response.[34] Although Barre ruled for more than twenty years, by the early 1990s he faced widespread opposition. His opponents forced him to flee the country, which collapsed into civil war and prolonged anarchy.

In these lawless conditions, an Islamist group called al Ittihad al Islamiya (the Islamic Union) became prominent. Although there is no firm date for al Ittihad's birth, most credible accounts date it to around 1983. Ken Menkhaus, an associate professor of political science at Davidson College (North Carolina) and one of the top American experts on Islamism's growth in Somalia, notes that al Ittihad was originally composed "mainly of educated, young men who had studied or worked in the Middle East."[35] It received significant funding and support from—and was in turn influenced by—the salafi movement and its Saudi-sponsored charity organizations.

At the group's founding, al Ittihad members concluded that political Islam (Islamism) was the only way to rid their country of its corrupt leadership. Al Ittihad had two goals. First, it sought to defeat Barre's regime and replace it with a theocratic state. Second, it wanted to incorporate what it regarded as Greater Somalia—including the majority-Somali areas of northeastern Kenya, Ethiopia's Ogaden region, and Djibouti—into the existing Somali state.

In 1991, after warlords drove Barre into exile, al Ittihad attempted to take control of strategic sites throughout the country, including seaports and roads that were vital for commerce.[36] It managed to hold the ports of Kismayo and Merka for almost a year but was quickly expelled from Bosaso. Al Ittihad did, however, manage to control one location for a sustained period: the town of Luuq near the border with Ethiopia. Consonant with its original aspirations, al Ittihad implemented a harsh version of sharia there, meting out punishments that included amputations.

Moreover, Luuq's proximity to Ethiopia allowed al Ittihad to use violent means to agitate for Greater Somalia. The Islamist group stirred up separatist unrest in Ethiopia's Ogaden region and carried out bombings and assassination attempts in the Ethiopian capital of Addis Ababa.[37] In response, Ethiopian forces intervened in Luuq to destroy al Ittihad's safe haven. After this defeat, al Ittihad declined in prominence and by 2004 was widely regarded as defunct.

However, the next Islamist group to control territory in Somalia proved to be more formidable. The Islamic Courts Union (ICU), whose core leadership included a number of holdovers from al Ittihad, was initially a loose confederation of judicial systems designed to provide stability in the face of the country's anarchy. Within a couple of years, however, the ICU became the strongest fighting force in the country.

The ICU came to international attention on June 5, 2006, when after months of fighting for Mogadishu, the warlords who had ruled Somalia's capital since Barre's collapse were decisively defeated. As the ICU seized Mogadishu, one warlord reportedly fled to a hospital while other warlords' forces were pushed from the city center to the outskirts. ICU chairman Sheikh Sharif Sheikh Ahmed told citizens in a radio broadcast, "We want to restore peace and stability to Mogadishu. We are ready to meet and talk to anybody and any group for the interest of the people."[38]

After taking Mogadishu, the ICU won a rapid series of strategic gains throughout the country. It took control of critical port cities such as Kismayo, meeting with little resistance as it advanced. Typical of this period was the ICU's capture of Beledweyne on August 9, 2006. The local governor fled to Ethiopia almost immediately after fighting broke out between his forces and ICU militiamen.

By late October 2006, the ICU controlled most of Somalia's key strategic points, was able to move supplies from the country's south to its north, and had effectively encircled the U.N.-recognized TFG in the south-central city of Baidoa. The ICU imposed a harsh version of sharia in the territory it controlled, with far-reaching restrictions. It conducted mass arrests of citizens watching movies, abolished live music at weddings, killed several people for watching soccer, and arrested a karate instructor and his female students because the lessons involved mixing of the sexes.

Strict implementation of sharia usually alienates local populations, so as the ICU gained power, it was determined to enhance its "soft power." Somalia's business community favored the ICU's emphasis on stability and the rule of law over the previous anarchic conditions and saw the ICU's rule as a means of reducing security costs. A 2006 report by the U.N. Monitoring Group on Somalia noted that checkpoints established by warlords before the ICU's rise cost businesses several million dollars a year, and the ICU's elimination of certain extortionate checkpoints reduced these expenses, often by up to 50 percent.[39] In addition to winning the business community's sympathies, the ICU provided some benefit to citizens who previously had to live under insecure conditions in which crime was pervasive.

But Western analysts saw the ICU's rise as a threat because of its hard-line Islamist beliefs and the connections of some of its leaders with al Qaeda. These analysts watched with trepidation as the ICU encircled Somalia's TFG in Baidoa, putting it under siege. All that prevented the government's destruction were Ethiopian soldiers manning roadblocks around the city.

In December 2006, the ICU had amassed, and it seemed to be preparing a final assault to wipe out the TFG. But as this attack on Baidoa began, Ethiopia responded with overwhelming force. Most accounts hold that Ethiopia launched an immediate invasion of Somalia with the intention of reversing the ICU's countrywide gains, but Andre LeSage, a senior research fellow for Africa at National Defense University in Washington, D.C., is skeptical.

"Frankly, I don't think anybody knows Ethiopia's plans when it went into Somalia in December 2006," he told me. "One of the assessments that I've heard is that when the Ethiopians wanted to push back against the ICU, they basically fell through the ICU forces and ended up on the outskirts of Mogadishu quickly. At that point, the elders in Mogadishu, who had basically kicked the ICU out, wanted the Ethiopians to come in."[40]

Regardless of its initial intent, Ethiopia ended up sweeping through Somalia and reversing the ICU's gains. The United States not only approved of Ethiopia's advance but even provided it with military support. The perceived U.S. and Ethiopian interests in pushing back the ICU were clear. The United States was concerned about the ICU's connections with al Qaeda, and Ethiopia's primary concern was the terrorist attacks that had been carried out in its territory when al Ittihad controlled Luuq. Ethiopia assumed that the ICU would present an even larger security problem.

As the Ethiopian forces rolled into Somalia, the ICU could not match Ethiopian airpower. Moreover, U.S. air and ground forces, including the elite Task Force 88, supported Ethiopia's intervention.[41] The Ethiopians entered Mogadishu on December 28, 2006, and quickly reversed virtually all of the ICU's strategic gains throughout the country.

The Ethiopian Invasion and Its Aftermath

The Ethiopian invasion did not turn out well. Before I turn to the mistakes and other problems related to the invasion, it is worth examining the security concerns that U.S. analysts had about the ICU's rise. This is particularly pertinent because a revisionist scholarship has arisen arguing that the ICU should not have been viewed as a threat by American planners, that it was in fact a "relatively moderate" movement.[42] This revisionist view is bolstered by the fact that the Ethiopian invasion has had dire consequences; many observers are thus eager to look back at the rationale for the invasion and discredit it entirely. But the fact that the invasion has been costly (not least for the Somali people) and poorly executed does not therefore mean that the initial perception of the ICU was exaggerated.

Well-known civilian military affairs analyst Bill Roggio, in a devastating response to one of pundit Matthew Yglesias's contributions to this debate, argued that the ICU was properly viewed as a threat at the time of Ethiopia's invasion.[43] First, he noted that senior ICU leaders had trained in al Qaeda camps and were affiliated with al Qaeda. These leaders included Hasan Dahir Aweys, who led the ICU's consultative council; his protégé, Aden Hashi Ayro, founded al Shabaab.

Second, Roggio highlighted the existence of numerous militant training camps in Somalia during the ICU's rise and the fact that the ICU's island fortress of Ras Kamboni served as "a major command, control, and communications hub for al Qaeda in East Africa." Third, Roggio pointed to the presence of foreign fighters in Somalia in 2005 and 2006, often a key indicator of growing salafi jihadi movements, and the fact that the ICU used Arabic-language propaganda tapes that al Qaeda's media outfit al Sahab helped to produce.

ICU spokesmen often denied the presence of foreign fighters during their rise. In a June 2006 press conference, for example, ICU leader Sheikh Yusuf Indohaadde said, "We want to say in a loud voice that we have no enemies; we have no enmity toward anyone. There are no foreign terrorists here."[44] Yet less than three weeks later, the Associated Press obtained a copy of an ICU recruitment video that showed Indohaadde himself north of Mogadishu alongside fighters from the Gulf Arab states.[45]

So there were legitimate reasons for analysts to be concerned about the advance of the ICU. But in addition to these dangers, the potential for an insurgency to break out was obvious at the time the Ethiopians rolled into Somalia. The month before the Ethiopian invasion, the U.N.'s Monitoring Group on Somalia warned that the ICU was "fully capable of turning Somalia into what is currently an Iraq-type scenario, replete with roadside and suicide bombers, assassinations, and other forms of terrorist and insurgent-type activities."[46]

Shortly after the invasion, ICU chairman Sheikh Sharif Sheikh Ahmed called for an insurgency, and soon one was born. It consisted not only of those living in Somalia at the time of Ethiopia's invasion; members of the diaspora and also some non-Somali foreigners bolstered the insurgents' ranks. By May 2009, it was estimated that as many as a thousand foreign fighters may have traveled to Somalia.[47]

During the course of the insurgency, al Shabaab emerged as a distinct force. Previously it had been known as the ICU's militant youth wing, but a definitive break between al Shabaab and other insurgent groups occurred after September 2007, when the ICU attended a conference of opposition factions in the Eritrean capital of Asmara. The ICU emerged from the Asmara conference known as the Alliance for the Reliberation of Somalia (ARS). Al Shabaab boycotted the conference, and its leaders launched vitriolic attacks on the ARS soon after.

The Rise of al Shabaab

One important document explaining al Shabaab's outlook was written by an American jihadi known as Abu Mansoor al Amriki (born Omar Hammami in Alabama).[48] He gained notoriety in the United States in April 2009 after appearing in a jihadi propaganda video that featured, among other things, a very amateurish rap song about jihad. As journalist J. M. Berger has observed, "Only someone truly committed to the jihad could bear to listen to his attempts to sing for very long."[49]

In January 2008, Amriki wrote a document titled "A Message to the Mujahedin in Particular and Muslims in General" that rapidly made its way around jihadi websites. In it, he explained that al Shabaab had boycotted the Asmara conference because the group refused to work with the non-Muslim Eritrean state. He wrote that cooperation with infidels would corrupt the jihad because Eritrea would cause them to turn to politics rather than armed resistance, thus leaving "members of the Courts [ICU] in the lands of the *Kuffaar* [infidels], underneath their control, sitting in the road of politics which leads to the loss and defeat they were running from." Amriki also attacked the ICU, now the ARS, for having goals limited to Africa's infidel-drawn borders, whereas al Shabaab's goal was—like al Qaeda's—to reestablish the caliphate. Indeed, Amriki's message framed al Qaeda's vision as central to al Shabaab. He wrote that al Shabaab's *manhaj*, or religious methodology, was the same as that of Osama bin Laden, Ayman al Zawahiri, and AQI leader Abu Musab al Zarqawi.

Since then, other al Shabaab leaders have similarly clarified the group's global outlook and allegiance with al Qaeda. Saleh Ali Saleh Nabhan, al Shabaab's now-deceased chief military strategist, formally reached out to al Qaeda's senior leadership in a twenty-four-minute video address titled "March Forth," which circulated on jihadi websites beginning on August 30, 2008. In it, Nabhan offered salutations to bin Laden and pledged allegiance to "the courageous commander and my honorable leader." Also in August 2008, al Shabaab spokesman Sheikh Mukhtar Robow acknowledged that al Shabaab was negotiating over becoming a part of al Qaeda, saying, "We will take our orders from Sheikh Osama bin Laden because we are his students."

In November 2009, Fazul Abdullah Mohammed, al Shabaab's late intelligence chief, was named al Qaeda's East African commander. Upon being appointed, he said, "After Somalia we will proceed to Djibouti, Kenya, and Ethiopia."[50] And in February 2010, al Shabaab issued a statement saying that it had agreed "to connect the Horn of Africa jihad to the one led by al Qaeda and its leader Sheikh Osama Bin Laden."[51]

Although al Shabaab's reaching out to al Qaeda is disturbing enough, of greater concern is the fact that al Qaeda leaders have been receptive to the group's overtures. Al Qaeda leaders have simply ignored some other self-proclaimed al Qaeda affiliates, such as those that have popped up in Gaza.[52] But in contrast to the way al Qaeda disregarded those groups, bin Laden originally gave several rhetorical nods to the ICU in 2006, after its capture of Mogadishu. Thereafter, when Ethiopia invaded in response to the ICU's advance on Baidoa, Zawahiri appeared in a Web-based video in January 2007 calling for Muslims to fight the Ethiopians. "I appeal to the lions of Islam in Yemen, the state of faith and wisdom," he said. "I appeal to my brothers, the lions of Islam in the Arabian Peninsula, the cradle of conquests. And I also appeal to my brothers, the lions of Islam in Egypt, Sudan, the Arab Maghreb, and everywhere in the Muslim world to rise up to aid their Muslim brethren in Somalia."

Al Qaeda leaders have also lauded al Shabaab specifically. On November 19, 2008, Zawahiri responded to Nabhan's video pledging allegiance to bin Laden and al Qaeda with one of his own, in which he called al Shabaab "my brothers, the lions of Islam in Somalia." He urged al Shabaab's leaders and fighters not to lay down their arms "before the mujahid state of Islam" has been established.

Bin Laden issued a video address devoted to al Shabaab in March 2009 titled "Fight On, Champions of Somalia," in which he addressed "my patient, persevering Muslim brothers in mujahid Somalia." He explicitly endorsed al Shabaab and denounced Sheikh Sharif Sheikh Ahmed, who had left the resistance to lead Somalia's TFG. Bin Laden compared Sheikh Sharif to men like Ahmad Shah Masud, the Northern Alliance leader whom al Qaeda assassins killed just two days before the 9/11 attacks, saying that both Sheikh Sharif and Masud had "turned back on their heels": that is, apostatized from Islam. He explained that Sheikh Sharif had left the faith when he "agreed to partner infidel positive law with sharia to set up a government of national unity."

Al Shabaab became a powerful fighting force within Somalia, the dominant insurgent group. It is certainly more militarily capable than the TFG. The situation now is similar to that faced by the TFG in Baidoa in 2006: all that prevents its destruction is a foreign fighting force—no longer the Ethiopians, but the African Union Mission to Somalia (AMISOM). In addition to its capabilities within Somalia, al Shabaab also has a definitive transnational reach.

On July 11, 2010, al Shabaab carried out an attack outside of Somalia's borders for the first time, as twin bomb blasts rocked the Ugandan capital of Kampala while citizens gathered to watch the World Cup. Seventy-four people died, but the carnage could have been worse: the authorities disrupted two planned follow-up attacks. One of the disrupted attacks was meant for a Kampala nightclub, where an explosives-laden vest was found in a bag in the middle of the club.[53] The bag came to the attention of witnesses when they heard a cell phone ringing inside it. After seeing the deadly contents, they called the police, who found that the vest was rigged to a cell phone detonator.

The second planned follow-up attack was uncovered after additional suspects were arrested in Kampala. During the course of the arrests, the police found explosives and a suicide belt.

The Uganda bombings represented a political calculation on al Shabaab's part. After the withdrawal of Ethiopian troops from Somalia in January 2009, Uganda was one of only two countries (the other being Burundi) to devote troops to AMISOM's U.N.-sanctioned peacekeeping mission to stabilize the transitional government. The bombings were designed to make Uganda pay a price for this support.

Al Shabaab's leaders made this calculation clear. Prior to the attacks, al Shabaab's emir, Sheikh Muqtar Abdelrahman Abu Zubeyr, warned that the people of Uganda and Burundi would be targeted because of their countries' role in AMISOM. "You should know that the massacres against the children, women and the elderly of Mogadishu will be revenged against you," he said.[54] And after the Uganda bombings, al Shabaab spokesman Ali Mohamoud Rage confirmed the political calculus. "We are sending a message to every country who is willing to send troops to Somalia that they will face attacks on their territory," he said. "We will continue to retaliate against Ugandan and Burundian forces if they continue to stay here."[55]

Many observers believed it was significant that al Shabaab had passed a threshold by carrying out a bombing outside Somalia, and they worried that it could be a harbinger of further attacks to come.

A Broader Fight

Looking back on 2006–2007, it is clear that significant strategic problems grew in Pakistan and Somalia while American resources and attention were devoted to the surge in Iraq. Nor was the growth in jihadi groups limited to these two countries; during the same period, al Qaeda's affiliates in Yemen and in the Maghreb (northwest Africa) also grew stronger.

Thus, even as al Qaeda experienced what must be regarded as a major setback in Iraq—a broad-based resistance to its bloody agenda that discredited the group's claims to speak for the Iraqi people—in other locations it was able to expand its capabilities and further its strategic objectives.

One of those objectives, economic warfare, was fulfilled because al Qaeda can undertake attacks on Western economic targets from these new safe havens (it has done just that from both Pakistan and Yemen) and because the new foothold that the jihadis have gained will force the United States to expend more resources trying to counter their influence.

The other strategic objective, broadening the battlefield, is also clearly satisfied. As al Qaeda gains a significant presence in more countries, the United States is spread thinner and thinner, trying to understand, and operate in, these unfamiliar environments.

9

The War on Oil

Man's ascent throughout the ages has always been cali-
brated as a coefficient of power. From the earliest pre-
civilized societies, man's ability to lift, move, propel, and
ignite endowed him with the decisive advantage over every
competitor, human or not. True, the use of tools separates
man from beast. But the ability to dynamically utilize those
tools separates one man from another. Hence, the concepts
of *better*, *faster*, and *farther* have always been the measure of
any society's capacity to flourish, manufacture, defend, and
conquer—and thereby succeed, however transiently until
outdone by another.

—*Edwin Black*, Internal Combustion

On March 24, 2010, Saudi Arabia announced the arrest of 113
alleged al Qaeda militants who it claimed were planning attacks
on oil facilities. Fifty-eight of those arrested came from Saudi Arabia,
and fifty-two came from Yemen; the others were from Bangladesh,
Eritrea, and Somalia. Saudi security officials said that the suspects

were divided into three separate cells, and during the raids the security forces discovered weapons, ammunition, and suicide belts.

"The twelve in the two cells were suicide bombers," Mansour al Turki, a spokesman for Saudi security services, told Reuters. "We have compelling evidence against all of those arrested, that they were plotting terrorist attacks inside the kingdom." Turki described the suspects as members of a "deviant group that has chosen Yemen as a base for the launch of its criminal operations."[1] This was a direct reference to al Qaeda in the Arabian Peninsula (AQAP), al Qaeda's affiliate in Saudi Arabia and Yemen.

Initial arrests in Arab states often constitute bloated sweeps, with the innocent quietly released after the arrests are announced. Despite this, the report that terrorists in Saudi Arabia had focused on oil targets was unsurprising. Between 2004 and the mass arrests in March 2010, al Qaeda and other jihadi groups had come to see attacks against oil facilities, particularly in Saudi Arabia, as a critical aspect of their economic warfare strategy. And justifiably so: the United States is the world's largest oil importer, consuming around twenty-one million barrels every day, more than 65 percent of which is imported from foreign countries. Without adequate access to oil, or if the price of oil dramatically increased as the result of a terrorist strike, the U.S. economy would flounder and perhaps collapse.

The situation the United States confronts today is largely the inverse of what the Soviet Union faced in the 1980s. During the Afghan-Soviet war, Russia's economy was undermined by Saudi Arabia's increase in oil production. By dropping the world price of oil, Saudi Arabia reduced the income that the Soviet Union could obtain from its oil exports, causing significant harm to its economy. In contrast, the price of oil has dramatically increased since the 9/11 attacks and the onset of the war on terrorism—a worrying turn for the United States, with its ravenous appetite for imported oil.

Unlike in the 1980s, the post-9/11 changes in oil price are not due to economic warfare engineered by oil-producing states. Rather, several factors have spurred the current price rise, including the fact that the global economy grew significantly in the first decade of the twenty-first century—in China and India, in particular—and the demand for oil outstripped the pace of new discoveries. Beyond supply-and-demand considerations, oil is not traded in a free market. Instead, a cartel, the Organization of the Petroleum Exporting Countries (OPEC), plays a significant role in determining the global price of oil.

OPEC's ability to manipulate prices does not mean that it is engaged in economic warfare against the United States, however. There are entirely understandable reasons that oil producers like to make as much money as possible from their resources. Moreover, the potential for instability in oil-producing states also pushes the price of oil upward in the form of a *risk premium*—a concern that has been dramatically underscored by the revolutionary fervor that took hold in the Arab world in early 2011.

Bin Laden frequently compared the United States to the Soviet Union, drawing parallels between the way the Afghan mujahedin bled the Soviet Union's economy in the 1980s and al Qaeda's current attempts to do the same to America. Many Westerners were quick to dismiss his proclamations—with some justification, since bin Laden was a propagandist and a polemicist. Nonetheless, the fact remains that significant parallels can be drawn between the Soviet Union in the 1980s and the United States today. The way in which the price of oil has worked to undermine both economies should be of concern.

Al Qaeda's Decision to Attack the Oil Supply

Osama bin Laden did not always see attacks on oil as part of his fight against America. When he first declared war against the United States in 1996, bin Laden specified that oil was not one of al Qaeda's targets because the resource was "a large economical power essential for the soon to be established Islamic state."[2] That is, bin Laden was looking toward al Qaeda's ultimate goal of reestablishing the caliphate. When the caliphate was declared, it would benefit economically and strategically from its control of a significant portion of the world's oil—and for that reason, al Qaeda wouldn't jeopardize that future wealth by targeting oil while fighting for the caliphate's creation.

But the events and reactions that the 9/11 attacks set in motion made clear that the U.S. strategy for fighting al Qaeda was very costly for America. This may have influenced a change in jihadi strategy pertaining to oil.

One indication that jihadi thinkers had come to see oil as a desirable target was a treatise titled "The Laws of Targeting Petroleum-Related Interests and a Review of the Laws Pertaining to the Economic Jihad," which was posted online in March 2004. Written by al Qaeda strategist Rashid al Anzi, this document argued for the legitimacy of attacks against oil facilities.[3]

Anzi's argument began by explaining the importance of oil to the jihadi movement's foes. "Oil is a vital resource for the modern industrial world," he wrote, "and a resource that is fundamental for the economies of the industrialized infidel countries." Indeed, he explained that the widespread availability of oil "enabled America to dominate the world."

Anzi wrote that attacks on the oil supply could harm the jihadis' foes. He first claimed that a rising oil price hurts industrialized countries more than others and that it is particularly devastating to the United States, "the number one consumer of oil in the world." Anzi argued that attacks on the oil supply could raise the price in multiple ways. In addition to causing actual supply disruption, these attacks could create fears of a supply shortage and thus raise the price because the markets factor in future expectations. Attacks could also force an increase in insurance costs and raise the cost of guarding petroleum facilities.

The result of terrorist strikes would thus be an increase in oil expenditures as a proportion of Western countries' gross national product, as well as damage to America's economic reputation. "Everyone knows that America is totally dependent on oil in order to keep its economy going," he wrote. He thus believed that the end result of the attacks he advocated would be "the conversion of assets into other foreign currencies and increased demand for gold, while at the same time investor capital flows out of America."

Because of how critical oil is to the "infidels," and the potential for damaging America, Anzi concluded that oil targets are "a legitimate means of economic jihad." He divided these targets into four categories: pipelines, oil facilities, individual leaders from the petroleum industry, and oil wells. Anzi saw the first three as legitimate targets of attack, albeit with some caveats. He noted that pipelines "are among the easiest targets to attack" and claimed that the benefits of attacking them outweigh the costs. Oil facilities were also legitimate targets, although Anzi warned that they "are not to be targeted if they are privately owned by a Muslim." Anzi believed that individual leaders in the petroleum industry were easy targets. "The benefits of such operations far outweigh the disadvantages," he wrote, "as long as [spilling] the blood of the person who is being targeted is permissible."

Anzi did not sanction the targeting of oil wells themselves, however, as long as there was a sufficient alternative to attacking them. Although Anzi's argument for allowing attacks on oil targets may initially appear to be a sharp departure from bin Laden's 1996 promise that oil would not be part of the jihad, his requirement that jihadis avoid wells actually shows a continuity in logic. After all, it is through wells that the earth's hydrocarbon resources can be exploited. By focusing attacks on the means by which oil is brought to market, Anzi's framework ensures that even as jihadis harm their enemies' economy by disrupting the global oil supply, they leave in place the means by which a caliphate would be able to dominate the petroleum industry in the future.

After the publication of Anzi's treatise, bin Laden came around to a similar understanding of the permissibility of attacking oil targets, in an audio address titled "Depose the Tyrants," which was released on December 16, 2004. In it, bin Laden asserted that "the biggest reason for our enemies' control over our lands is to steal our oil." Thus, he asked his followers to "give everything you can to stop the greatest theft of oil in history." Bin Laden explained that the price of oil was too low, and that even the trading of oil on the free market constituted theft by Western countries. For this reason, the jihadi movement should take the situation into its own hands by attacking oil targets. "Keep on struggling," bin Laden said, "do not make it easy for them, and focus your operations on [oil], especially in Iraq and the Gulf, for that will be the death of them."[4]

The call to attack oil targets was echoed throughout al Qaeda's ranks. In a December 2005 video, Ayman al Zawahiri called for al Qaeda fighters to "focus their attacks on the stolen oil of the Muslims." Referring to the purchase of oil at then-market prices as history's greatest theft, he continued, "The enemies of Islam are consuming this vital resource with unparalleled greed. We must stop this theft any way we

can, in order to save this resource for the sake of the Muslim nation."[5]
Sawt al Jihad, the now-defunct online magazine of AQAP, claimed in
February 2007 that cutting the U.S. oil supply through terrorist attacks
"would contribute to the ending of the American occupation of Iraq
and Afghanistan."[6]

In January 2008 AQAP's Arabic-language magazine *Sada al
Malahim* featured an interview with the wanted jihadi Abu Hummam
al Qahtani. Qahtani said, "If the enemy's interests in the Arabian
Peninsula were devastated, his access to our petroleum interrupted,
and the oil refineries put out of order, this would cause the enemy to
collapse—and they won't merely be forced to withdraw from Iraq and
Afghanistan, but moreover would face a total collapse."[7] There has
also been discussion on jihadi Web forums about the desirability of
attacking oil installations.[8]

Terrorist Plots

Jihadi discussions of attacks on the oil supply are not just rhetoric. Of
particular concern in this regard are Saudi Arabian facilities, which
are a point of vulnerability for the entire world economy. Saudi Arabia
is critical to world oil markets. It produces almost 10 million barrels
per day, and it is the only country able to maintain an excess production capacity of around 1.5 million barrels per day (a *swing reserve*) in
order to keep the world price stable. Saudi production is vulnerable
to attack, however, because it depends on a limited number of hubs.
Gal Luft and Anne Korin of the Institute for the Analysis of Global
Security outline this in a 2003 article:

> Over half of Saudi Arabia's oil reserves are contained in
> just eight fields, among them the world's largest onshore
> oil field—Ghawar, which alone accounts for about half of
> the country's total oil production capacity—and Safaniya, the
> world's largest offshore oilfield. About two-thirds of Saudi
> Arabia's crude oil is processed in a single enormous facility
> called Abqaiq, 25 miles inland from the Gulf of Bahrain.
> On the Persian Gulf, Saudi Arabia has just two primary oil

export terminals: Ras Tanura—the world's largest offshore oil loading facility, through which a tenth of global oil supply flows daily—and Ras al Ju'aymah. On the Red Sea, a terminal called Yanbu is connected to Abqaiq via the 750-mile East-West pipeline. A terrorist attack on each one of these hubs of the Saudi oil complex or a simultaneous attack on a few of them is not a fictional scenario.[9]

Several incidents in Saudi Arabia show how jihadi terrorists are attempting to exploit this vulnerability. The first major incident occurred in September 2005, when a forty-eight-hour shootout with Islamist militants at a villa in the Saudi seaport of al Dammam ended with Saudi police introducing light artillery. When the police entered the compound to conduct a search in the aftermath of the fight, they found not only what *Newsweek* described as "enough weapons for a couple of platoons of guerilla fighters" but also forged documents that would have given the terrorists access to the country's key oil and gas facilities.[10] Saudi interior minister Prince Nayef bin Abdul Aziz confirmed to the daily newspaper *Okaz* that the cell had planned to attack energy facilities, noting that "there isn't a place that they could reach that they didn't think about."[11]

The most significant security incident to date targeting Saudi facilities came a few months later, on February 24, 2006. Terrorists affiliated with AQAP attacked the Saudi Aramco–operated refinery at Abqaiq, which processes two-thirds of Saudi Arabia's crude oil. In addition to this processing function, Abqaiq is home to one of the world's largest oil fields, containing 17 billion barrels of proven reserves. Khalid al Rodan of the Center for Strategic and International Studies has noted, "The proven reserves in the Abqaiq field alone are larger than the reserves of some major oil exporting countries: Mexico's total oil reserves are 14.8 billion barrels and Canada's conventional oil reserves are only 16.8 billion barrels."[12]

Immediately after the incident, a statement from Saudi Arabia's interior ministry explained that two explosives-laden cars tried to enter the facility through a side gate and that a firefight broke out when security officers challenged them. The interior ministry claimed that the explosives in the vehicles detonated, destroying them. Local news sources played down the incident, with Nawaf Obaid, a Saudi security adviser, telling the *Arab News* that it was proof of "how tight and impenetrable the existing Saudi security system is."[13] Nonetheless, the price of oil immediately jumped by $2.37 a barrel.

But the incident may have been a nearer miss than the rhetoric of Saudi officials allowed. Written evidence submitted to Britain's House of Commons by Neil Partrick, a senior analyst in the Economist Group's Economist Intelligence Unit, claimed that the terrorists—who wore Saudi Aramco uniforms and drove Saudi Aramco vehicles—managed to enter the first of three perimeter fences surrounding the refinery. They were fired upon only as they approached the second perimeter fence. Partrick wrote that the terrorists "had inside assistance from members of the formal security operation of the state-owned energy company" in acquiring the vehicles and uniforms, or else "security was sufficiently [lax] that these items could be obtained and entry to the site obtained."[14] Needless to say, neither possibility is reassuring.

There have been several significant arrests since the February 2006 attempt on Abqaiq. In April 2007, Saudi Arabia's interior ministry announced that it had foiled another al Qaeda–linked plot to attack oil facilities.[15] In 2008, the interior ministry arrested more than seven hundred suspected militants, with officials alleging that those arrested had been plotting to attack oil installations.[16] And on March 24, 2010, as already described, Saudi Arabia announced the arrest of more than a hundred alleged al Qaeda militants who it claimed were planning attacks on oil facilities.

If there were a catastrophic attack on Saudi oil installations—taking advantage of the limited number of production hubs to knock a significant amount of oil off the world market through either simultaneous attacks or a single massive strike—the impact on the world economy would be tremendous. Luft and Korin write that if a terrorist cell hijacked a plane and crashed it into either the Abqaiq or Ras Tanura facilities in a 9/11-type attack, it could "take up to 50% of Saudi oil off the market for at least six months and with it most of the world's spare capacity, sending oil prices through the ceiling."[17]

Former CIA case officer Robert Baer agrees, writing, "A single jumbo jet with a suicide bomber at the controls, hijacked during takeoff from Dubai and crashed into the heart of Ras Tanura, would be enough to bring the world's oil-addicted economies to their knees, America's along with them."[18] If a catastrophic attack were successfully executed, the substantially reduced worldwide supply of oil would be joined by an inflated risk premium. Julian Lee, a senior energy analyst at the Centre for Global Energy Studies in London, noted in 2004 that after a significant loss of Saudi oil, "it would be difficult to put an upper limit on the kind of panic reaction you would see in the global oil markets."[19]

In addition to the potential for a catastrophic attack on one of the key Saudi facilities, terrorist groups can also engage in disruptive attacks. This happened in Iraq, where oil facilities and personnel were often targeted during the course of the insurgency. Between the start of Operation Iraqi Freedom and mid-2008, researchers were able to document more than 450 unique attacks on Iraq's pipelines, oil installations, and oil personnel.[20] Because of these disruptive attacks, it took until 2008—five years after Saddam Hussein's regime fell—for Iraq to be able to return to a production level of 2.5 million barrels per day. (It had produced an average of 2.3 million barrels of oil a day during the last five years of Saddam's rule.)

Attacks carried out by the Movement for the Emancipation of the Niger Delta (MEND)—which is not a jihadi group but rather a militant organization whose concerns are more localized—provides an indication of the impact that disruptive attacks can have. MEND has been waging a campaign of pipeline, refinery, and oil field attacks since its February 2006 declaration of "total war" on the oil companies operating in Nigeria. In the midst of record-high oil prices in 2008, Saudi Arabia pledged to produce an extra two hundred thousand barrels of oil per day, beginning in July 2008, to provide relief to consumers. However, MEND and its copycats were able to knock more than that offline in a single week. An attack on Shell's Bonga field coupled with two attacks on Chevron's Abiteve crude oil line cut Nigeria's output by about four hundred thousand barrels per day. Although the Nigerian facilities were repaired, this demonstrates how disruptive attacks can thwart the market's supply expectations.

Attacks against oil targets will remain an important part of the war on Western economies being waged by al Qaeda as well as by its affiliates and copycats. The former head of the CIA's Bin Laden Unit, Michael Scheuer, notes that such attacks have been religiously validated, and "al Qaeda and its allies are well-placed throughout the Persian Gulf to attack oil facilities and officials."[21]

Al Qaeda's continuing interest in striking oil targets was verified by information uncovered following the raid that killed bin Laden. Based on evidence unearthed in that raid, the Department of Homeland Security issued a new bulletin on May 20, 2011, outlining al Qaeda's interest in targeting oil and natural gas infrastructure. "In 2010, there was continuing interest by members of al Qaeda in targeting oil tankers and commercial infrastructure at sea," said a DHS spokesman in a statement referencing the bulletin. He added that there was no information suggesting an imminent threat, but the department "wanted to make our partners aware of the alleged interest."[22]

Oil as Strategy

Moving beyond the threat of terrorist attacks on the oil supply, America's *oil addiction*—a term that is widely used today across the political spectrum—makes for bad national strategy.[23] Oil enjoys an absolute monopoly over the U.S. transportation sector, for it provides about 96 percent of the fuel that powers the country's transportation. This is not an easy monopoly to break up. Just as the concept of path dependence would predict (see chapter 3), decades of investment have been made in an infrastructure—highways rather than rail, a vehicle fleet that can be powered only by oil—that only reinforces oil's dominance. The tremendous strategic problems caused by oil's monopoly over America's transportation sector have been obvious since at least the Arab oil embargo directed at the United States in 1973–1974.

Since one of the major arguments in this book is that al Qaeda is attempting to systematically undermine the U.S. economy, let's begin by examining the economic impact of our oil dependence. It goes without saying that primary energy is fundamental. With it economies can flourish, but without it they wither. The exclusive reliance on oil for our transportation needs has made it a strategic commodity, a good that if disrupted or made unaffordable will cause our economy to collapse.

This situation is exacerbated by the fact that the United States now holds only 3 percent of the conventional global oil reserves yet uses 25 percent of the world's daily oil production. We import more than 65 percent of the oil we use—more than twice the ratio of imports to daily consumption at the time of the 1973–1974 Arab oil embargo. This amounts to a daily purchase of twelve million barrels of imported oil.

Market volatility makes it difficult to say with precision how much American wealth is transferred overseas annually to pay for oil imports— after all, there can be massive fluctuations in the price of oil over a period of days or weeks—but as of the time of this writing, it amounts to about $500 billion being sent overseas annually. Even in 2005, the United States spent about $200,000 *per minute* on imports of foreign oil.[24]

Between January 2007 and the summer of 2008, the price of oil doubled in just eighteen months, hitting $145.31 a barrel on July 3, 2008. After the U.S. economy dramatically collapsed in September 2008, oil and gas prices also plummeted. For a short time, American drivers paid less than $2 a gallon for gasoline in some cities. But by the end of 2010, it was clear that this respite from high prices had most likely ended. "The price of oil is poised for another run at $100 a barrel after a global economic rebound sent it surging 34 percent since May," the *Huffington Post* reported on December 31, 2010. "That could push gasoline prices to $4 a gallon by summer in some parts of the country, experts say."[25]

Turmoil in the Arab world has contributed to high oil prices. Before the end of February, two long-serving Arab dictators—Tunisia's Zine El Abidine Ben Ali and Egypt's Hosni Mubarak—were toppled from power after their citizens revolted, and there was a further wave of unrest throughout the region. In just a month—between January 23 and February 23—the price of Brent crude oil traded in London surged from $96 a barrel to above $111. This price rise was not based on actual supply disruptions, but rather on future expectations. The *Economist* noted, "The big worry is that spreading unrest will culminate in another shock akin to the oil embargo of 1973, the Iranian revolution or Iraq's invasion of Kuwait."[26]

Although the price of oil could recede again if and when the situation stabilizes in the Arab world, most industry analysts believe that it will remain high for the foreseeable future. As the United States attempts to put its fragile economy back on its feet, the price of oil may undermine that. Daniel Indiviglio, an associate editor at the *Atlantic*, wrote in February 2011 that a rising oil price endangers the U.S. economic recovery in multiple ways: it weakens consumer spending, because consumers have "less money to spend on discretionary items"; it hampers the jobs recovery, because "higher energy costs could soak up some of the money that would have been used to bring on more employees"; it produces spending trade-offs that slow the housing market; it dampens tourism by increasing the cost of travel; and it forces a decline in exports because shipping costs are higher.[27]

As I have already mentioned, today the United States faces a strategic situation that is largely the inverse of what the Soviet Union faced in the 1980s regarding the price of oil. Low oil prices reduced Russia's export-driven revenue, while today's high oil prices make it difficult for America to absorb the costs that al Qaeda is dedicated to imposing on the United States.

Nor is the economic impact on the United States the only strategic concern related to its oil dependence. At the same time that a high oil price makes Western industrialized countries economic losers, it is also creating new winners—and the beneficiaries of these massive wealth transfers are often unfriendly to America. To understand this, one need look no further than Iranian president Mahmoud Ahmadinejad or Venezuela's Hugo Chavez, who famously boasted that "the American empire will be destroyed" at a 2006 OPEC conference. Dependence on foreign oil also has a distorting impact on the conduct of diplomacy. For example, oil politics have obviously impeded the use of multilateral sanctions in response to Iran's development of nuclear weapons.[28]

Consequently, there are multiple strategic costs to America's continued dependence on oil imports. And one of these costs, the impact on the U.S. economy, has a direct impact on al Qaeda's efforts to see the United States go the route of the Soviet Union.

10

The Thousand Cuts

[The United States] is a superpower that has a huge military force and a large economy, but all of this is established on a weak basis. Therefore, it is possible to target this weak basis and concentrate on the weakest points. If the United States is hit at ten percent of these points, it will fail and abandon the leadership of the world.

— *Abu al Fida al Tunsi,* Thunderbolts of Proof
on the People of Indolence and Deception

The dramatic collapse of the U.S. economy in September 2008 signaled a new and more perilous era for America. It also ushered in a new phase in al Qaeda's strategy for destroying the United States.

The collapse made the country seem mortal. When Osama bin Laden declared war on America in 1996, he explained that the U.S. economy was the driver of the country's military dominance—and after September 2008, it seemed that the U.S. economy *had actually been shattered*, thus dramatically weakening America's global position. Because of this, al Qaeda and its affiliates believed that their strategy could evolve.

Whereas once the United States wouldn't have been bothered unless it was struck by the most dramatic blows, the weakened economy now meant that even smaller attacks could have a large impact.

This shift in al Qaeda's strategy was aided by the inefficient homeland security bureaucracy that the United States had erected. Al Qaeda is a nimble organization that can adapt to defenses (such as aviation security checkpoints) relatively easily, at a low cost. Meanwhile, each successful adaptation that the terrorist group undertakes significantly drives up the costs for the United States. Essentially, the economic collapse has put al Qaeda in an advantageous strategic position that— even despite bin Laden's death—has it thinking about the endgame in this war.

The Collapse

America's economic collapse was composed of two massive stock free falls that occurred in a single week, triggered by a credit crisis. In the first free fall, Wall Street's markets opened on Monday, September 15, 2008, with traders furiously selling off stocks based on three pieces of news showing that economic storm clouds were no longer on the horizon but rather that the rains of crisis were pouring down.

The first piece of news came just after midnight on Monday morning: the venerable investment bank Lehman Brothers, which had been scrambling for a buyer to solve its financial straits, was unable to find one. Lehman Brothers announced that it would be filing for bankruptcy. The second piece of news hit the same day, when Merrill Lynch—which had announced a breathtaking $55.2 billion in losses related to subprime collateralized debt obligations—announced that it had been sold to Bank of America.[1] And the third piece of news involved the plan of American International Group (AIG) to sell some of its own troubled assets.[2] Rumors swirled that if AIG didn't raise enough capital, its stock would be downgraded.

The collapse of a bubble in subprime lending stood at the heart of this financial collapse. Subprime lending involves making loans to people deemed to be credit risks, those who may be unable to maintain a repayment schedule. Because of the possibility that the loans will not be repaid, subprime lending is inherently risky.

As the bursting subprime bubble battered Wall Street's investment banks, New York governor David Paterson's decision to bend lending rules to allow one of AIG's subsidiaries to loan it $20 billion wasn't enough to stave off a panic. The Dow Jones average lost more than five hundred points, for the worst day that Wall Street had seen in seven years. Before the day had ended, AIG's stock was in fact downgraded, and traders learned that more bad news was coming: Washington Mutual was also in deep trouble, looking for a "white knight."

The second free fall happened on Wednesday, September 17, when the Dow Jones average dropped by 450 points. CNN notes that "despite reporting better-than-expected results, Goldman Sachs shares dipped below $100 a share for the first time since 2005. Morgan Stanley took a tumble as well, as rumors circulated that it would merge with troubled bank Wachovia."[3] Jeffrey Friedman, a senior fellow at Boston University's Institute for Advance of the Social Sciences, writes, "The deflation of the subprime bubble in 2006–7 was the proximate cause of the collapse of the financial sector in 2008."[4]

There was no easy fix for these economic woes. Despite multiple government bailouts designed to address the problem, the U.S. economy—and the economies of other Western countries—remained on the brink, and consumer confidence shattered.

Jihadi Reactions

Jihadi spokesmen claimed responsibility for America's economic collapse. Ayman al Zawahiri said that the jihadi movement caused the U.S. crisis in an August 2009 interview released by al Qaeda's media company, Al Sahab Establishment for Media Production. He explained, "The economic recession today, caused by the battles and raids against America, was solved by the central bank through a huge decrease in interest, which increased fluidity and competition to lend, which pushed the public to borrow more than they can pay back. That caused incapability by the public to pay back, so the financial institution fell, and that was followed by a disastrous economic crisis." He did not, however, argue that terrorist strikes against the United States represented the sole cause of the crisis. Rather, he stated that "America held the burden of huge losses in Afghanistan, Iraq and Somalia," thus giving a nod to the manner in which the country's draining wars bled the economy.[5]

A propaganda video released by Al Sahab in September 2009 took a similar line. It claimed that "the blessed invasions against America, and its wars in Iraq and Afghanistan, are the main factors that expedited the emergence of the fall of the capitalistic economics that governs the rest of the economy of the world."[6] There have been similar claims of credit from other jihadi leaders.[7]

Bin Laden himself released an audiotape in September 2009 linking the U.S. war on al Qaeda and other jihadi groups to America's astronomically high debt. Referring to America's decision to invade Afghanistan, bin Laden again invoked the ghost of the Soviet Union. "Russian generals," he said, "who learned lessons from the battles in Afghanistan, had anticipated the result of the war before its start, but you do not like those who give you advice. This is a losing war, God willing, as it is funded by money that is borrowed based on exorbitant usury." Bin Laden continued, "The accumulated debts incurred as a result of this war have almost done away with the U.S. economy as a whole."[8]

These claims are, in part, representative of the hubris that jihadi spokesmen have long displayed. Bin Laden wasn't actually responsible for the Soviet Union's collapse, yet time and again he has referred to himself as its architect. Many jihadi claims about the role that they played in the financial sector's collapse are similarly exaggerated. Specifically, Zawahiri's claim that the jihadi movement caused the subprime bubble isn't sustainable. There are specific risks involved in subprime lending, and there had been another subprime bubble in the 1990s. The bestselling author Michael Lewis describes how the bubble looked during that period:

> All these subprime lending companies were growing so rapidly, and using such goofy accounting, that they could

mask the fact that they had no real earnings, just illusory, accounting-driven, ones. They had the essential feature of a Ponzi scheme: to maintain the fiction that they were profitable enterprises, they needed more and more capital to create more and more subprime loans.[9]

That subprime bubble collapsed, and by 2002, the United States had no more subprime lending companies. Yet despite this collapse and the fundamental dangers of subprime lending, the market for these loans returned. By 2005, U.S. lending institutions had doled out $652 billion worth of subprime mortgage loans.[10] Contrary to Zawahiri's claim that the fight against al Qaeda produced the subprime crisis, subprime lending grew even while interest rates *increased*. This is not how subprime lending is supposed to function.

"Even more shocking," Lewis writes, "was that the terms of the loans were changing, in ways that increased the likelihood they would go bad. Back in 1996, 65 percent of subprime loans had been fixed-rate, meaning that typical subprime borrowers might be getting screwed, but at least they knew for sure how much they owed each month until they paid off the loan. By 2005, 75 percent of subprime loans were some form of floating-rate, usually fixed for the first two years."[11]

This created a rather obvious bubble for those who could pierce the obscurantism of subprime lending (and the market was quite confusing by design) to understand what was really going on. Once the subprime loans moved from fixed rate to the more onerous floating rate, a large number of borrowers were going to default.

And that is precisely what happened: borrowers started defaulting en masse as previous fixed-rate loans moved to a floating rate. Zawahiri's claim that the fight against al Qaeda caused the subprime bubble represents a hubristic misunderstanding of the U.S. economy or else a propagandistic claim that is indifferent to the truth of the matter.

Nevertheless, the costs of protecting the country and engaging in wars overseas are substantial. Jihadi strategy recognizes this fact, and since the financial sector collapse, it has further adapted to exploit America's economic weakness.

Jihadi Adaptations

The perception that post–financial collapse America had now become mortal is shared by jihadi spokesmen as well as the movement's rank and file. "Due to this jihad, the U.S. economy is reeling today," radical Yemeni American cleric Anwar al Awlaki said in an interview that was posted on the Internet in May 2010. "America cannot withstand this Islamic nation. It is too weak. America's cunning is weaker than a spider web."[12]

Online jihadi commentators also refer frequently to the diminished U.S. economy and to America's mortality. In a March 2010 discussion thread in the global jihad–oriented Al Tahaddi Islamic Network website, a commenter asked, "Can the U.S. bear another strike similar to the events of 11 September?" Noting this trend, analyst Gabriel Weimann has observed that "recent jihadi chatter on the Internet suggests both exultation about the economic crisis gripping the West and a call for what can be labeled as 'Econo-Jihad,' targeting Western financial systems and economic infrastructure."[13]

Similarly, a February 2010 discussion thread on the Al Fallujah Islamic Forums focused on the "simple topic" of "how to quickly get rid of America, God willing."[14] The topic alone signals the jihadi movement's rising levels of confidence. Even after the 9/11 attacks, when al Qaeda showed that it was able to simultaneously destroy several of America's most vital and cherished buildings and kill thousands, defeating the United States seemed like a quixotic, unachievable goal. In bin Laden's October 2001 interview with Al Jazeera's Taysir Allouni (see chapter 3), Allouni expressed skepticism that al Qaeda had any chance of defeating a country as powerful as the United States.

Bin Laden himself did not talk of an imminent victory when he spoke to Allouni. Instead, he invoked the image of how powerful and indomitable the Soviet Union had appeared at the time it invaded Afghanistan. Contrary to everyone's expectations, the Soviet Union lost that war, and then it dissolved. The United States, bin Laden said, could meet with a similar fate. Thus, even after the 9/11 attacks were executed, speaking of quickly getting rid of America was inconceivable: bin Laden was trying to convince the world that doing so was even *possible*. The discussion on the Al Fallujah Islamic Forums about quickly getting rid of America thus shows the changing perceptions within the jihadi movement. Its supporters now believe not only that victory is achievable but also that it is imminent and can be ushered in quickly.

This perception of an imminent victory has produced adaptations in al Qaeda's strategy. The jihadi idea that defeating the United States is tied to undermining its economy is, of course, not new. But al Qaeda's strategy of economic warfare is entering a new phase based on the perception of America's mortality. This new phase has been described as "the strategy of a thousand cuts" in the November 2010 special issue of Al Qaeda in the Arabian Peninsula (AQAP)'s online magazine *Inspire* that commemorates the plot that employed bombs hidden in ink cartridges. Although that special issue of *Inspire* represents the best articulation of this new phase in al Qaeda's strategy, the basic contours were evident even before November 2010 in the statements of al Qaeda leaders as well as jihadi online discussions.

The cover of the November 2010 issue of *Inspire* features a photo of a UPS plane and the headline "$4,200." It is a pithy headline that provides deep insight into the direction that al Qaeda's strategy has taken, referring to the great disparity between the cost of executing terrorist attacks and the cost to Western countries of defending themselves from them. (See the chart on page 172 indicating these disparate costs for several major attacks.) In this case, $4,200 is what it cost AQAP to execute the cartridge-bomb plot, but it will cost Western countries far more than that as they attempt to prevent terrorists from successfully bringing planes down in the future through similar techniques.

In the special issue, Anwar al Awlaki (writing only under his title as AQAP's head of foreign operations) explains that AQAP settled on the idea of attacking cargo planes because of the principle that "if your opponent covers his right cheek, slap him on his left."[15] This is a very purposeful inversion of Jesus's biblical teaching that "if someone strikes you on the right cheek, turn to him the other also."[16] In this case, Western countries had been forced to spend billions of dollars on aviation security in response to such attacks as 9/11, Richard Reid's attempted shoe bombing, the 2006 liquid bombs plot, and Umar Farouk Abdulmutallab's underpants bomb.

These countries thus covered their right cheek, but the left cheek remained unguarded: cargo planes remained a point of vulnerability,

Cost Comparison for Terrorist Attacks:
Jihadi Groups' Costs versus Victims' Costs

Plot Name	Cost for Jihadi Groups	Cost for Victims
East African embassy bombings (1998)	Approx. $10,000	$21 billion
USS *Cole* bombing	Less than $10,000	$243 million
September 11, 2001	$500,000	$1 trillion
Madrid and London attacks ("3/11" and "7/7")	Approx. $20,000	$9.75 billion*
Mumbai Attacks	$893,000	Approx. $2.4 billion
Christmas Day bombing	Less than $7,000	$1.2 billion per year
Times Square plot	Approx. $2,000	$200 million
Operation Hemorrhage	$4,200	$17 million**

*Includes Spain's cost ($253 million), Britain's cost ($5 billion), and the cost of the Transit Security Grant Program that the United States implemented in response to the 2004 Madrid and 2005 London attacks, as well as five weeks of heightened terror alerts following the London bombing.

**Estimate includes amount spent on counterterrorism operations in Yemen and the Certified Cargo Screening Program.

for two reasons. First, as an article in *Inspire* by Ikrimah al Muhajir explains at length, some specific technical adaptations allowed AQAP to disguise the PETN bombs used in that plot from the security scanners. "With all the intelligence information the enemy had," he writes, "they could not detect the explosives even though the printers were inspected twice in the U.K. They only discovered the explosives when they had the exact tracking number of the package."[17]

The second reason cargo planes remained a point of vulnerability is that not all parcels shipped on them are screened in advance. In fact, Awlaki recognized, in his contribution to *Inspire*, that for this reason the jihadis' foes were faced with a dilemma once AQAP was able to successfully place bombs on cargo planes. "You either spend billions of dollars to inspect each and every package in the world," he wrote, "or you do nothing and we keep trying again."[18]

In chapter 1, I noted that *National Review*'s Jonah Goldberg described terrorists' repeated targeting of airplanes as a "schoolboy fixation." But the terrorists aren't unnecessarily fixated, childlike, on a single target. Rather, Goldberg is the ignorant one. Awlaki's calculation is in fact correct. Despite billions upon billions of dollars that have been thrown into aviation security, al Qaeda remains able to locate points of vulnerability that need to be fixed at great expense, lest the terrorists be able to continue attacking until they bring down more planes. And aviation is a point of vulnerability for the entire world economy; even if Goldberg doesn't understand this, the jihadis certainly do.

Awlaki explained in *Inspire*, "The air freight is a multi-billion dollar industry. FedEx alone flies a fleet of 600 aircraft and ships an average of four million packages per day. It is a huge worldwide industry. For the trade between North America and Europe, air cargo is indispensable and to be able to force the West to install stringent security measures sufficient enough to stop our explosive devices would add a heavy economic burden to an already faltering economy."[19]

Inspire lucidly explains that large strikes, such as those of 9/11, are no longer required to defeat the United States. "To bring down America we do not need to strike big," it claims. "In such an environment of security phobia that is sweeping America, it is more feasible to stage smaller attacks that involve less players and less time to launch and thus we may circumvent the security barriers America worked so hard to erect."[20] Al Qaeda's strategy is to launch smaller yet more frequent attacks to drive up its enemies' security costs.

These attacks do not even have to be carried out by individuals who are recognizable members of al Qaeda. There has long been a debate among counterterrorism analysts over whether al Qaeda should be understood, more than anything else, as an idea—this despite the acknowledgment in the 2007 National Intelligence Estimate (see chapter 8) that al Qaeda, as an organization, had regenerated its homeland attack capabilities. As a *Los Angeles Times* piece championing this position put it, al Qaeda should be seen as "more of an ideology than an organization."[21]

These calls to see al Qaeda as an ideology above all else will most likely be given new life in the wake of bin Laden's death. As I will show momentarily, understanding al Qaeda in this manner is misguided: al Qaeda the organization remains potent. But because small attacks are perceived as effective and do not even have to be tied to al Qaeda's central leadership, al Qaeda the organization is attempting, in this phase of its economic warfare strategy, to more effectively harness al Qaeda the idea by prompting those who share its ideology to lash out on their own. As an *Inspire* article by Ibrahim al Banna implores, "Dear Muslim, hasten to join the ranks of the mujahedin or to form cells to perform operations against the disbelievers in their own land."[22]

The organization al Qaeda can harness the idea of al Qaeda by encouraging its self-motivated supporters to focus on targets that will advance the organization's strategy of warfare. We can already see al Qaeda spokesmen doing just that. For example, in a March 2010 video message, Adam Gadahn praised Fort Hood shooter Nidal Hasan and encouraged other Muslims to follow his example.

"The mujahid brother Nidal Hasan, by the grace of Allah and with a single 30-minute battle, singlehandedly brought the morale of the American military and public to its lowest point in years," Gadahn said in "A Call to Arms," a video released in March 2010. "The mujahid brother Nidal Hasan, lightly armed but with a big heart, a strong will and a confident step, again brought into sharp focus the weaknesses and vulnerabilities of America, and again proved wrong those who claim America cannot be hit where it hurts."

Although Hasan's target was not economic in nature, Gadahn linked this emulation of Nidal Hasan by other would-be jihadis to the economy, saying that by copying the Fort Hood shooter his audience could "further undermine the West's already struggling economies with carefully timed and targeted attacks on symbols of capitalism which will again shake consumer confidence and stifle spending."

In this vein, al Qaeda released a one-hundred-minute video in June 2011 urging individual jihad. New al Qaeda emir Ayman al Zawahiri was featured in this video, as was Gadahn, who urged Muslims to buy guns and attack targets of opportunity in the United States.

Indeed, rank-and-file jihadis and their online supporters seem to have internalized the importance of striking economic targets. In two online discussions I have already mentioned—Al Tahaddi Islamic

Network, on whether the United States could bear another strike like 9/11, and Al Fallujah Islamic Forums, on how to be rid of America— the respondents overwhelmingly saw economic targets as critical. The targets they considered included banks, oil wells, auto producers in Detroit ("the backbone of their economy"), electrical plants, and stock exchanges. Even a discussion of assassinating President Obama was couched in economic terms, as one commentator explained, "If you blow up Obama, then their economy will crumble."[23]

In this new strategy of a thousand cuts, whether attacks succeed in killing "infidels" is largely beside the point. If an attack breaches the enemy's security measures, it will significantly drive up future security costs, even if it kills nobody and inflicts no structural damage. As Awlaki notes in *Inspire*, blowing up cargo planes in the ink-cartridge plot "would have made us very pleased but according to our plan and specified objectives it was only a plus."[24] The attack could be considered a success even without killing anybody.

Elsewhere in the issue, this is described as "leverage." Not only does an attack that cost AQAP $4,200 to execute force the enemy to expend many times that amount, but also "in terms of time and effort, three months of work for a team of less than six brothers would end up costing the West hundreds of thousands, if not millions, of hours of work in an attempt to protect itself from our packages of death."[25] That article continues:

> During the initial discussions of the team it was determined that the success of the operation was to be based on two factors. The first is that the packages pass through the latest security equipment. The second, the spread of fear that would cause the West to invest billions of dollars in new security procedures. We have succeeded in the former and we are now witnessing the inception of the latter. We will continue with similar operations and we do not mind at all in this stage if they are intercepted. It is such a good bargain for us to spread fear amongst the enemy and keep him on his toes in exchange for a few months of work and a few thousand bucks.

In a triumphalist tone, the passage concluded, "For our enemies to think that intercepting such a package is evidence of their success is truly ridiculous."

Indeed it is. Other jihadi statements reflect an awareness that even "failed" attacks can achieve their objectives. In March 2010, for example, Gadahn explained that even attacks that kill nobody can be considered successes because they "bring major cities to a halt, cost the enemy billions and send his corporations into bankruptcy."[26]

The notion that success can be attained solely through driving up security costs, without actually destroying the enemy's targets, has also been embraced by al Qaeda's online supporters. One message making this point at length was posted to the Al Fallujah Islamic Forums in December 2009. The author mockingly addresses the security services monitoring the Web forum, asking them to write the following in their reports:

> A Very Serious Threat
> Source: A Radical Islamist Forum
> Warn them that they must protect every federal build-ing and skyscraper, such as: Library Tower (California), Sears Tower (Chicago), Plaza Bank (Washington State), the Empire State Building (New York), suspension bridges in New York, and the financial district in New York.
> Nightclubs frequented by Americans and the British in Thailand, Philippines, Indonesia (especially our dear Bali Island), the oil company owned by the former Secretary of State Henry Kissinger in Sumatra (Indonesia), and U.S. ships and oil tankers in the Strait of Hormuz, Gibraltar, and the Port of Singapore.
> Let us not forget any airport, seaport, or stadium. Tell them to protect [these places] no matter the cost, day and night, around the clock throughout Christmas and the holi-day season.[27]

The point is clear: Security is expensive, and driving up costs can wear down Western economies. These economies can be harmed by failed attacks or even by phantom threats. Indeed, the message then encourages the United States "not to spare millions of dollars to protect these targets" by increasing the number of guards, closely searching all who enter and exit the enumerated locations, and even preventing flying objects from approaching the targets. "Tell them to stop anything that moves on land, flies in the air, and swims on or under the river," it says. "Tell them that the life of the American citizen is in danger, and that his life is more significant than billions of dollars. . . . Hand in hand, we will be with you until you are bankrupt and your economy collapses."

One can see how well al Qaeda has incorporated the small-actor lessons that Ivan Arreguín-Toft wrote of when analogizing the new wars that the United States might face to the Ali-Foreman boxing match (see chapter 2). Al Qaeda and its affiliates are well aware of how the costs of guaranteeing security from the threat of terrorism drive up America's expenses and the national debt. They are well aware that these expenses are contributing to a looming economic Armageddon.

Jihadi militants are replicating Muhammad Ali's strategy for defeating George Foreman by turning America's strength against it. In the jihadis' view, as the United States spends more and more to defend itself from terrorism, it makes itself weaker, easier to knock out.

11

A Formidable Adversary

We cannot mortgage the material assets of our grandchildren without risking the loss of their political and spiritual heritage. We want democracy to survive for all generations to come, not to become the insolvent phantom of tomorrow.

—*President Dwight D. Eisenhower, 1961 farewell address*

A l Qaeda the organization remains vibrant even after Osama bin Laden's death. I have traced al Qaeda's rebound after the U.S. invasion of Afghanistan, showing how it regrouped in Pakistan. Even as the capabilities of the organization's core leadership were growing, Western analysts were slow to recognize the group's regeneration. They assumed, falsely, that al Qaeda's central leadership had been marginalized, and this belief persisted even while the core organization was significantly involved in terrorist plots in the West, such as the July 2005 bombings in London.

This history is instructive because it may be about to repeat. From 2002 through 2005, many analysts believed that al Qaeda's core was marginalized, because the major militant operations they saw were unconnected to the jihadi group's central leadership. This reasoning was flawed from the outset, because it was entirely possible—and turned out to be the case—that affiliates and other jihadis were stepping to the forefront while al Qaeda's command recovered from the loss of its safe haven.

Similarly, we are entering another period in which we may see more attacks that are unconnected to al Qaeda's central leadership. This is true because the organizational command will be regrouping after bin Laden's death—although much of the authority had already devolved to Ayman al Zawahiri in an effort to ensure that al Qaeda could survive its leader's death.[1] It is also true because of the contours of the current phase of al Qaeda's strategy: the group wants to hit the United States with smaller and more frequent attacks, and there is no reason that these attacks require specific operational guidance or approval from top levels of the organization.

It is unclear, as of this writing (shortly after bin Laden's death), whether there will indeed be more attacks in the near future that are not connected to al Qaeda's core leaders. If I am correct that this phenomenon will occur, some commentators and analysts will again declare al Qaeda's core leadership dead or marginalized based on similarly flawed reasoning—based on the dubious idea that seeing plots unconnected to the group is proof of its demise. Such claims should be treated skeptically, just as they should have been received with more of a critical eye in 2002.

This chapter analyzes al Qaeda's current capabilities and the threat it will pose in the future. It examines the group's structure and the weaknesses that many analysts attribute to it (including the fact that it was not a real factor in the Arab spring) and looks also at the group's strengths. After more than a decade since the 9/11 attacks al Qaeda's leader has been killed; but despite that, the organization still has a significant presence in multiple geographic regions, sees many of its goals being satisfied, and believes that its own future is brighter than America's.

Al Qaeda's Structure

In an article published in *Foreign Affairs* in early 2011, Leah Farrall, a former senior counterterrorism intelligence analyst for the Australian federal police, provided a balanced conceptual analysis of al Qaeda.[2]

Farrall's framework stands up remarkably well in light of what is known about the documents recovered from bin Laden's compound in Abbottabad, which undercut some of the conventional wisdom in the counterterrorism field—including the idea that bin Laden was simply a figurehead or that we have entered a phase of "leaderless jihad."

Farrall argued that al Qaeda's strength cannot be evaluated in isolation from that of its subsidiaries. Subsequent revelations have underscored this point: information pulled from bin Laden's compound shows that al Qaeda's central leadership has been active in providing direction and planning for attacks by affiliates in Yemen and Somalia.[3] Farrall writes that al Qaeda in the Arabian Peninsula (AQAP) is best understood as a branch of al Qaeda rather than a franchise because of its unique history: it "was created by, and continues to operate under, the leadership of core al Qaeda members."[4] This branch, AQAP, and true franchises (such as al Qaeda in the Islamic Maghreb or al Qaeda in Iraq), over which the core leadership does not enjoy full command and control, constitute a dispersed organizational structure.

Farrall wrote, "Due to its dispersed structure, al Qaeda operates as a devolved network hierarchy, in which levels of command authority are not always clear; personal ties between militants carry weight and, at times, transcend the command structure between core, branch, and franchises. For their part, al Qaeda's core members focus on exercising strategic command and control to ensure the centralization of the organization's actions and message, rather than directly managing its branch and franchises."

Al Qaeda's core leadership exercises the greatest degree of command and control over external operations, attacks that fall outside the subsidiaries' assigned areas of operations. Farrall noted that there are set parameters for strikes that fall outside a subsidiary's traditional area of operations, such as encouraging the use of suicide bombers or "strikes on preapproved classes of targets, such as public transportation, government buildings, and vital infrastructure."

Although the subsidiaries are given great leeway in striking locations that the core leadership has authorized attacks on, Farrall noted that al Qaeda nonetheless emphasizes the necessity of consulting with the group's central leadership prior to engaging in "large-scale plots, plots directed against a new location or a new class of targets, and plots utilizing a tactic that has not been previously sanctioned, such as the use of chemical, biological, or radiological devices."

After examining both al Qaeda's core and its subsidiaries, Farrall assessed the group as stronger now than it was on September 11, 2001. After all, today it has a larger number of members, its geographic scope is greater, and it has achieved "a level of ideological sophistication and influence it lacked ten years ago."

Recent terrorist plots have confirmed that al Qaeda is a rejuvenated organization and that its core leadership has been an important part of that picture. For example, when news of a large-scale al Qaeda plot in Europe to execute multiple Mumbai-style "urban warfare" attacks surfaced in October 2010, it revealed how new leaders like Ilyas Kashmiri and Younis al Mauretani were able to assemble enough recruits (including British, French, and German nationals and perhaps one former Turkish air force officer) to perpetrate multiple large-scale attacks.[5] Intelligence officials said that bin Laden was personally involved, using couriers to provide strategic direction.[6] And a man who was killed in a series of drone strikes in Pakistan that had been prompted by news of the terror plots, Abdul Jabbar, was being groomed to serve as emir for a British branch of al Qaeda prior to his death.[7] These are indications of a group that is looking to expand rather than falling apart.

Al Qaeda's Weaknesses

Al Qaeda certainly has its share of weaknesses. I will describe three major ones here. The first is the fact that even though al Qaeda purports to stand up to the West on behalf of the *umma* (the Islamic community), its Muslim victims far outnumber the non-Muslims it has killed. A study published in December 2009 by the Combating Terrorism Center at West Point concludes that "the vast majority of al Qaeda's victims are Muslims: the analysis here shows that only 15% of the fatalities resulting from al Qaeda attacks between 2004 and 2008 were Westerners."[8]

This cynical indifference to killing fellow Muslims has caused some prominent defections from the jihadi group's ranks. Most notable is Sayyid Imam al Sharif, also known as Dr. Fadl, a prominent jihadi theorist who began to write against al Qaeda from an Egyptian prison. A key criticism was the manner in which al Qaeda had shed Muslim blood. "Every drop of blood that was shed or is being shed in Afghanistan and Iraq is the responsibility of bin Laden and Zawahiri and their followers," Sharif wrote.

Although al Qaeda spokesmen have been publicly dismissive of Sharif's defection, claiming that he was coerced by Egyptian authorities, the significant amount of effort they have devoted to refuting his attacks shows that they take him more seriously than they let on. Zawahiri published a two-hundred-page "letter" titled "The Exoneration" in response. As Diaa Rashwan of Egypt's Al Ahram Centre for Political and Strategic Studies told the *New Yorker*, "It's the first time in history that bin Laden and Zawahiri have responded in this way to internal dissent."[9]

In areas that al Qaeda has been able to control geographically (such as Iraq's Anbar province in 2006), the Muslim population that felt the most direct consequences has turned against it. Al Qaeda's wanton brutality has likewise turned public opinion against it on other critical battlegrounds. In Pakistan, for example, the killing of innocents by al Qaeda suicide bombers has caused the public to sour on the group (though, unfortunately, this doesn't mean forces of fundamentalism have been marginalized in the country).[10] Alia Brahimi, an academic at the London School of Economics, notes, "It is difficult to maintain that al Qaeda is the vanguard group acting in defense of the entire *umma* when the victims of Al Qaeda bombings are the people who comprise the *umma*."[11]

Al Qaeda's second weakness is the challenges that have been made to its theology; these are significant because a significant portion of al Qaeda's raison d'être is religious in nature. A major challenge has come from the Amman Message, a project spearheaded by the Royal Aal al Bayt Institute for Islamic Thought, a nominally nongovernmental institute in Jordan that receives significant backing from the monarchy.

The Amman Message produced a document dealing with *takfir* (the practice of declaring that "bad" Muslims have been cast out of Islam) that attracted the endorsements of an impressive array of Islamic scholars. The document holds that a broad array of Muslim sects fall under the banner of Islam and that it is impermissible "to declare as apostates any group of Muslims who believes in God . . . and His

Messenger . . . and does not deny any necessarily self-evident tenet of religion."[12] It was embraced by more than 550 scholars from numerous jurisprudential schools. These signatories represent a true cross-section of contemporary Islamic thought.

The Amman Message project also produced a seventy-nine-page report titled *Jihad and the Islamic Law of War*, which offers a refutation of al Qaeda's justifications for combat. It compares the atrocities al Qaeda justifies to bring about its utopian vision of the caliphate's reestablishment to Vladimir Lenin's statement "You cannot make an omelet without breaking eggs." The report insists that Islam does not countenance utopian ideology. "When one can justify any act in the name of a worldly utopia," it warns, "then one has passed into pure utilitarianism."[13]

There have been other similar condemnations. One cornerstone of al Qaeda's theology has been the famous fourteenth-century Mardin fatwa issued by Taqi al Din ibn Taymiyya that provides a justification for political violence. In March 2010, a conference of Muslim jurists at Turkey's Mardin Artuklu University revisited the fatwa and rejected the use that groups like al Qaeda made of it.[14] Other clerics and institutions have written or spoken at length against al Qaeda's justifications for warfare, including Egypt's Amr Khaled, Muhammad Sayyid Tantawi, and Yusuf al Qaradawi; Pakistan's Tahir ul Qadri; Morocco's Sheikh Abdelbari Zemzemi; and the Islamic Commission of Spain.

Although many of these condemnations do not go as far as Westerners would like, and in some cases their sincerity has been questioned, the condemnations do represent a weakness on al Qaeda's part. Since a large part of the group's legitimacy is rooted in its claims to piety and acting in service of Islam, having prominent religious scholars condemn it on these very grounds presents a significant challenge.

A third possible weakness on al Qaeda's part may come from the upheaval that has swept through the Arab world in 2011, the so-called Arab spring, as nonviolent protests toppled two dictators from power and further unrest threatens other changes in leadership. Peter Bergen told me that he considers these events devastating to al Qaeda's narrative. "Have you seen a single person carrying a placard with Osama bin Laden's face on it?" he asked. "Has anybody been mouthing al Qaeda's talking points? Have you seen a single American flag burning? It's an ideological catastrophe."[15]

Thus, after bin Laden's death, a number of analysts chimed in with the idea that al Qaeda had died even before bin Laden, that the Arab spring had killed it.[16] There are two primary rationales for this claim. First, those who think the Arab spring killed al Qaeda say that the nonviolent overthrow of Egypt's Hosni Mubarak and Tunisia's Zine El Abidine Ben Ali disproves al Qaeda's contention that violence is the only answer to the region's corrupt leadership. Second, they argue that al Qaeda's general irrelevance to the popular protests shows that the group's attraction is limited.

The Arab spring may indeed significantly weaken al Qaeda in the future. But the idea that the jihadi group is already dead because of the revolts is, quite simply, preposterous. Declaring it dead now is every bit as premature as proclaiming al Qaeda irrelevant after its leaders fled their former safe haven in Afghanistan in 2001. There are five reasons that this claim should be understood as a massive exaggeration.

The first reason is that some analysts have an unrealistically static conception of al Qaeda as an organization. That is, they seem to think that once they have identified a weakness of the jihadi group, there is nothing that al Qaeda can do to adapt. The weakness they have identified will inevitably destroy al Qaeda, they believe. But this conception is obviously wrong; al Qaeda is in fact a learning organization, and it has sought to address its perceived weaknesses, including its absence from the Arab spring.

Indeed, al Qaeda has released several propaganda messages addressing the Arab spring. Zawahiri released a five-part statement titled "To Our People in Egypt," which provided a historical analysis of the country's bad governance and a plea for the revolutionaries to turn toward fundamentalist Islam. A large part of his typically long-winded argument was condemning the country's secularism. "The Egyptian regime is a secular, tyrannical, and nationalistic regime," he said. Continuing in this vein, Zawahiri asked, "If a government claims to be Islamic, such as in Saudi Arabia, or that it is not fighting Islam, like in Egypt, but that government is loyal and submissive to the will of the foreign invader, could we say that it is an independent and legitimate government? Or should we say that it is a government allied with the foreign infidel invader, and is therefore illegitimate?"[17]

Senior al Qaeda leader Abu Yahya al Libi, who hails from Libya, released a thirty-one-minute video in March 2011 concerning that country's uprising. "The toppling of these collaborating and corrupt regimes is not the end of the true path of change, for which we should strive," he said. "It is merely a step, to be followed by other steps, and an effort, to be followed by other efforts, in order for all of us to reach the goal for which all true Muslims strive: making the word of Allah supreme."[18]

The second reason not to pronounce al Qaeda dead is that, as jihadi spokesmen have pointed out, proponents of this view almost certainly place too much emphasis on the claim that al Qaeda thinks violence is the *only* way to create change. Indeed, in a special issue of AQAP's *Inspire* devoted to the Arab revolts (the issue's cover is headlined "The Tsunami of Change"), Yahya Ibrahim writes, "Al Qaeda is not against regime changes through protests but it is against the idea that the change should be only through peaceful means to the exclusion of the use of force. In fact Shaykh Ayman al Zawahiri spoke in support of the protests that swept Egypt back in 2007 and he alluded to the fact that even if the protests were peaceful the people need to prepare themselves militarily. The accuracy of this view is proven by the turn of events in Libya."[19] In other words, al Qaeda is happy to see nonviolent change; it views the overthrow of these longtime U.S. allies as a harbinger of American decline. But al Qaeda also believes, according to this formulation, that violent rather than nonviolent change may also be necessary.

The third reason to reject the notion that the Arab spring killed al Qaeda is the way the jihadi group might take advantage of the chaos to make operational gains. A number of jihadis have either escaped or been released from prison in the region. The escape of thousands of prisoners from Egyptian jails in January 2011, including militants, has been widely reported. Subsequent to Mubarak's fall, Hani al Saba'i, an Islamist figure who runs the London-based Al Maqrizi Center for Historical Studies, posted the names of a number of violent Islamists who had been freed from Egypt's prisons.[20] A senior U.S. military intelligence analyst who has closely followed regional developments told me, "A significant talent pool that was previously incarcerated is now back on the streets."[21] There have been isolated reports of Islamists being released in Tunisia, and there is definite potential for similar developments in Yemen, a country that has seen al Qaeda detainees escape en masse in the past.

Al Qaeda has also made some territorial gains during the confusion and has sought to further leverage the situation, including by seizing arms. I will discuss al Qaeda's territorial advances in Yemen momentarily; it has also sought to capitalize on the situation in Libya. Some of the rebel forces opposing Muammar Qaddafi fought as insurgents against American forces in Iraq and Afghanistan, and former CIA officer Bruce Riedel has pointed out that there is a real lack of information in the U.S. intelligence community about the percentage of jihadis among the rebels. "The question we can't answer is, are they 2 percent of the opposition? Are they 20 percent? Or are they 80 percent?" he told the *New York Times*.[22]

Moreover, al Qaeda's North African affiliate, al Qaeda in the Islamic Maghreb (AQIM), has been able to obtain new weaponry during the Libyan chaos. Chad's president claimed that AQIM had stolen surface-to-air missiles from a Libyan arsenal, and an Algerian official told the press that he had monitored AQIM's shipments of seized arms from Libya to strongholds the group enjoys in the Sahara.[23] The bottom line is that the Arab revolts created a chaotic situation, and al Qaeda has a demonstrated ability to take advantage of chaos. The U.S. intelligence analyst with whom I discussed regional developments told me, "This is a recipe for chaos, and al Qaeda believes [it] can ride the wave."

The fourth reason to reject the idea that the Arab revolts have killed al Qaeda is that this view fundamentally misunderstands the nature of al Qaeda. It has always been a vanguard movement—that is, comprising a small percentage of the overall Muslim community—rather than one that possessed massive popular support. Even if al Qaeda would like large numbers of people to be on the streets chanting jihadi slogans, it doesn't *require* such levels of participation. All al Qaeda needs to do is maintain the dangerous militant organization it has had for the past two decades. Thus far, there is no indication that it will be unable to do so.

Finally, there's a very obvious reason that the Arab spring may prove to be *beneficial* to al Qaeda rather than fatal to the jihadi group: expectations in the Arab world are sky high and unlikely to be met. The revolts that comprise the Arab spring were not just about democracy. They were also about material needs, unemployment and food price inflation, poverty and empty stomachs. Will more jobs suddenly appear, or will the price of food suddenly decline?

Both Egypt and Tunisia have tourism-based economies, and tourism has been hurt by the instability that has accompanied regime change in both countries. In fact, Egypt's unemployment has risen rather than declined since Mubarak fell from power.[24] It's possible that quite apart from these material needs, even the hopes of democracy will be crushed. When expectations are so high, disappointment might also be enormous, even if things go relatively well. And when a society's lofty expectations are dashed, extremist ideologies have historically been able to flourish. Thus, we absolutely and unequivocally cannot say that al Qaeda died even before bin Laden did.

Other War Zones

Al Qaeda remains a formidable adversary in various regions of the world in which the United States has been engaged in the past decade. This section reviews these war zones and shows that al Qaeda has succeeded in its quest to broaden its conflict with America. The purpose is not to provide a comprehensive account of what is happening in these areas, but rather to shed insight on how al Qaeda views them strategically.

Afghanistan

America's post-9/11 war against Islamist militancy began in Afghanistan. Although the United States quickly toppled the Taliban, the Afghanistan War soon became an economy-of-force mission when resources were moved to fight the Iraq War.

There is a saying attributed to the Taliban: "They may have the watches, but we have the time." That is, the Americans and coalition forces enjoy technological superiority, which gives them the advantage for the moment, but the United States will not be in the country forever. The Taliban will remain after the Americans leave, and thus the

Afghans should choose their side carefully. Indeed, America is now looking to leave Afghanistan. It is clear that the United States will not remain in Afghanistan for another decade. In 2011, various actors with a stake in Afghanistan's future have begun to aggressively assert their interests in anticipation of the American drawdown.[25]

With the United States looking to transition out, a recent strategic analysis noted that one vital U.S. interest in the country is to prevent al Qaeda and its affiliates "from returning to safe havens in Afghanistan akin to those they enjoyed prior to the terrorist attacks of September 11, 2001."[26] One prong of U.S. strategy has been the attempt to create a process of political reconciliation for Afghanistan.

As this process moves forward, the late Pakistani journalist Syed Saleem Shahzad—who was well-connected within the jihadi movement before his untimely death—noted that contrary to U.S. hopes, "al Qaeda was gradually returning to the eastern Afghan provinces of Nuristan and Kunar, setting up bases for the first time in years in the wake of the withdrawal of U.S. troops from the area to more populated centers."

Shahzad spoke with one of al Qaeda's strategists about this and was told that with the United States occupied by the uprisings in the Arab world, al Qaeda was looking for a breakthrough in Afghanistan. "I don't think that the situation in the Arab world will evaporate into the air in the next several months," the strategist said. "Therefore any breakthrough in Afghanistan will pave the way for al Qaeda to reorganize its cadre and march to its ultimate war theater—the Middle East."[27]

Al Qaeda therefore remains a force in Afghanistan and hopes to capitalize on America's drawdown.

Pakistan

Afghanistan's neighbor Pakistan has been viewed as critical to operations in Afghanistan since the war began. Before the U.S. invasion, Deputy Secretary of State Richard Armitage gave Pakistan the ultimatum that (in Musharraf's words) "we had to decide whether we were with America or with the terrorists, but that if we chose the terrorists, then we should be prepared to be bombed back to the Stone Age."[28]

Despite these threats, Pakistan is, of course, the country to which al Qaeda's leaders fled in order to regroup after their sanctuary in Afghanistan was lost. Pakistan's Inter-Services Intelligence agency (ISI) has deep-rooted connections to Islamist militancy, and it has continued to play a role in supporting the Taliban insurgency in Afghanistan. But even though Pakistan has been a thorn in America's side in Afghanistan—and most certainly has the blood of U.S. soldiers on its hands—the country could be far worse, from a security perspective. After all, it is a nation with nuclear weapons, simmering unrest, and a strong fundamentalist movement. The concern among observers is that if the unrest is brought to a boil, then unlike in the Arab states, fundamentalist movements will be at the fore.

There are multiple reasons that unrest in Pakistan could grow. The political system is notoriously corrupt; it may be democratic in form, but it is oligarchic in practice. The *New York Times* has noted, "Parliament today remains dominated by the families of a favored few, who use their perch to maintain a corrupt patronage system and protect their own interests as Pakistan's landed and industrial class."[29] In the past three years the country has experienced a food-price inflation of 64 percent while the purchasing power of the average wage earner has declined by 20 percent. Pakistan's unemployment rate stands at 34 percent, and the government's bungled response to the flooding that devastated the country in 2010 further eroded public confidence. Thus, the *New York Times* found great pessimism about Pakistan's future among informed observers:

> The big question on many minds is how, and when, a critical mass of despair among this nation's 180 million people and the unifying Islamist ideology might be converted into collective action. Some diplomats and analysts compare the combustible mix of religious ideology and economic frustration, overlaid with the distaste for America, to Iran in 1979. Only one thing is missing: a leader. "What's lacking is a person or [an] institution to link the economic aspirations of the lower class with the psychological frustration of the committed Islamists," a Western diplomat said this week. "Our assessment is this: This is like Tehran, 1979."[30]

In January 2011, the governor of Punjab province, Salman Taseer, was assassinated by a bodyguard because Taseer opposed the country's blasphemy laws. These laws, implemented under military dictator Muhammad Zia ul-Haq, provide that any utterance deemed derogatory to the Prophet Muhammad can be punished by death.[31] An obvious problem with blasphemy laws is their potential to be abused as a tool for oppressing religious minorities, which has in fact occurred in Pakistan.

The *Times* article noted that the treatment Taseer's assassin received further underscores concerns about widespread fundamentalist sentiments in Pakistan. "The security guard, Malik Mumtaz Hussain Qadri, has catapulted to the front row of contemporary Pakistan and was hailed by lawyers, mainstream politicians and religious leaders," it reported. Frequent public rallies have even been held in support of him.

Predictions that unrest in Pakistan could lead to something like the Islamic revolution in Iran have been made before, so it is quite possible that these nightmare scenarios won't come to pass. But the trend lines in the country are moving in the wrong direction. Resource scarcity has been a big part of the country's unrest, including the aforementioned escalating food prices as well as acute energy shortages. Resource problems in Pakistan are only deepening.[32] Thus extreme political volatility, and powerful fundamentalist movements, could be a permanent part of Pakistan's landscape for the foreseeable future.

Even if Pakistan doesn't experience a fundamentalist takeover, al Qaeda still enjoys an advantageous situation there. Although the organization is targeted by U.S. drone strikes that have killed several of its leaders, those attacks have not destroyed the group.

Indeed, interrogations of Westerners who have traveled to the border region of Afghanistan and Pakistan to liaise with al Qaeda reveal that the organization has taken protective measures to adapt to drone strikes.[33] Furthermore, there are concerns that these strikes may play a contributing role in Pakistan's instability. "However effective the CIA may believe its program to be," noted the BBC, "it has damaged America's reputation in Pakistan still further, fuelling anti-American propaganda and bringing yet more recruits to the militants' cause."[34]

Iraq

Although al Qaeda in Iraq (AQI) was defeated and discredited in 2007–2008, it is seeking to capitalize on America's drawdown. Indeed, anyone with an interest in Iraq's future is taking a keen interest in the imminent U.S. departure. As Iranian president Mahmoud Ahmadinejad reportedly told Iraq's foreign minister, "Americans planted a tree in Iraq. They watered that tree, pruned it, and cared for it. Ask your American friends why they're leaving now before the tree bears fruit."[35]

If Iraq backslides into chaos, AQI could well end up the beneficiary. Basil al Shuwayli, the director of Baghdad's intelligence directorate, has described al Qaeda as "the most serious challenge" to Iraq's security.[36]

In particular, AQI has sought to take advantage of the frustrations caused by the Iraqi government's inability to incorporate the participants in the Sons of Iraq (SoI) program, which at its height had more than 103,000 Sunnis in it. Only 9,000 SoI participants have been hired for the country's security forces. The *New York Times* noted that even those who have been offered positions with the government are often given either temporary or menial positions.[37] So on the one hand, SoI members are frustrated with Iraq's government, while on the other, AQI has engaged in retaliatory attacks on SoI.

Natham al Jubouri, a former Awakening movement leader in Salahuddin province, has said, "At this point, Awakening members have two options: Stay with the government, which would be a threat to their lives, or help al Qaeda by being a double agent. The Awakening is like a database for al Qaeda that can be used to target places that had been out of reach before."[38] Al Qaeda's carrot-and-stick approach to the Awakening—threatening the participants with retaliatory attacks on the one hand and offering to buy them off on the other—has been corroborated by others involved in SoI.[39]

A complaint leveled by a SoI member called Sheikh Hussam in mid 2010 shows the depths of frustration in some corners of that once vibrant movement. "The Americans did not betray us," he said. "They sentenced us and our families to death. They supported us in fighting al Qaeda, but then suddenly they left us caught between two enemies—al Qaeda and Iran. That is America's legacy here."[40]

In addition to targeting SoI members, AQI has been trying to expand its power in other ways. It has engaged in kidnappings to raise money for its activities. It has also been using "sticky bombs" as a tactical advance; these are magnetic explosives that can be fastened to parked cars and later detonated remotely. This advance allows AQI to engage in targeted bombings without losing as many suicide attackers in the process.[41]

The development of sticky bombs has also given birth to a rather shocking Iraqi variant of *Punk'd* called *Put Him in Bucca*. (Camp Bucca was a high-security prison near the Kuwaiti border that the Americans ran until September 2009.) In the show, fake sticky bombs are planted in celebrities' cars, after which the producers are intent on "having an Iraqi army checkpoint find them and terrifying the celebrities into thinking that they are headed for maximum security prison."[42] Sometimes pop culture can really illuminate the troubles with which a country continues to struggle.

Yemen

Even before the Arab revolts broke out, Yemen had long been viewed as a tinderbox. Yemen expert Gregory Johnsen noted in *Foreign Policy* that the country is beset by multiple looming crises and a marked increase in the number of centers of power.[43] In addition to confronting the challenge posed by AQAP, Yemen also faces a rebellion from its Houthi inhabitants and the threat of secession in the south. (Yemen was once two countries before unification on May 22, 1990; the communist regime in South Yemen was one of bin Laden's first major areas of concern after he founded al Qaeda.)

But internal military threats are not the only, and not necessarily the greatest, challenge that Yemen faces. It is also beset by environmental and resource catastrophes. "The country's water table is nearly depleted from years of agricultural malpractice," Johnsen writes, "and its oil reserves are rapidly dwindling. This comes just when unemployment is soaring and an explosive birthrate promises only more young, jobless citizens in the coming years."

AQAP's growth has occurred against this backdrop. In March 2011, Christopher Boucek of the Carnegie Endowment for International Peace testified to Congress that "AQAP has emerged as the organization most likely to kill American nationals and to attack U.S. interests."[44] Reinforcing the idea that al Qaeda is a learning organization and not one that blindly repeats mistakes, Boucek noted that AQAP has learned from the missteps of other al Qaeda affiliates. Specifically, it does not target Yemeni civilians, and it possesses a sophisticated media operation, as exemplified by its publication of *Inspire*.

Moreover, Boucek said that when initial AQAP operations have proved unsuccessful, the group "has re-attacked the same target, such as the U.S. Embassy in Sana'a (attacked twice in 2009), Saudi Prince Muhammad bin Nayef (who has survived four reported assassination attempts by AQAP), and British diplomatic targets in Sana'a (attacked twice in 2010)."

Although the United States has targeted AQAP's leadership with missile strikes, AQAP, like al Qaeda in Pakistan, has developed defensive measures to deal with this targeting. After going underground in response to a late 2009 missile attack that came close to decapitating the group's key leaders, AQAP emerged with greater discipline. The measures it has implemented include adopting walkie-talkies rather than cell phones, passing messages through intermediaries, and heavily encrypting its electronic communications.[45]

The Arab spring protests rocking Yemen have been particularly fierce, with crowds demanding the resignation of President Ali Abdullah Saleh. There are credible reports that during the chaos, al Qaeda has been able to hold territory. On April 6, 2011, China's Xinhua news agency reported that AQAP had "seized control over swaths of hundreds of kilometers from Lodar city of Yemen's southern Abyan province to southeast Shabwa province's city of Rodhom." Tribal chieftains told Xinhua that AQAP had established checkpoints as well as military camps in that area.[46]

This is not meant to suggest that al Qaeda will hold this territory for a significant length of time. But the fact that the group was able to make any kind of territorial gains is indicative of its capabilities and provides a very dark hint of what may come as Yemen's looming environmental problems further weaken the central government's power.

There are allegations that Yemen's government has been encouraging al Qaeda's advances to cause Western governments to fear that regime change could empower the militants.[47] It is difficult to sort out such claims during the chaotic rush of events, but three points are worth making. First, regardless of whether AQAP has been encouraged by Yemen's government, it would not be able to capture territory if it lacked significant military capabilities. In other words, even if the government has a motive to exaggerate AQAP as a threat, that doesn't mean the threat is illusory. Second, al Qaeda has consistently shown the ability to take advantage of chaos. That it is doing so in Yemen shouldn't come as a surprise. Third, given the various factors Gregory Johnsen outlined that constitute a general unraveling in Yemen, we should expect the risks of significant instability to grow over time—and hence for AQAP to grow rather than diminish as a problem.

The Sahel and Algeria

AQIM, which is based in Africa's Sahel region (extending from Mauritania to Chad) and Algeria, has also grown in the past few years. An outgrowth of the Algerian organization Salafist Group for Preaching and Combat (GSPC), the jihadi group adopted AQIM as its moniker in 2007. When this occurred, a statement the group issued over the Internet said that it had waited to adopt the name because "we wanted the permission of Sheikh Osama, may God protect him."[48]

Tactically, AQIM has been known in particular for its use of suicide attacks. Although Algeria was wracked by bloody civil war in the 1990s, suicide attacks did not factor into this dark period in the country's history. And contrary to GSPC, whose area of operations was essentially limited to Algeria, AQIM has been able to carry out attacks in multiple countries. For example, AQIM struck Mauritania several times in 2008, including a shooting aimed at Israel's embassy and an ambush directed at a military patrol.[49]

To raise funds, AQIM has engaged in kidnappings, often of Westerners, along with its more traditional activities of smuggling (cigarettes and weapons) and drug trafficking. The kidnappings serve a dual strategic purpose: they raise money for the jihadi group, and the intimidation tactics depress tourism to the countries on which AQIM is waging war. Analysts Dario Cristiani and Riccardo Fabiani have noted that since 2008, AQIM "has created a kidnapping industry" that "usually involves local criminal groups kidnapping European tourists (whose governments are more likely to pay ransoms to obtain the release of hostages) and then selling them on to AQIM groups in the Sahel." [50]

The proceeds from the kidnappings are promptly reinvested in the organization. Although this "industry" has taken off since 2008, it is unlikely to supplant AQIM's other means of revenue generation. As Mathieu Guidere, a professor at France's University of Toulouse and the author of *Al Qaida à la Conquête du Maghreb*, has explained, the group's traditional sources of revenue provide income that can be expected at regular intervals. In contrast, he says, "Kidnapping is only an occasional and isolated source of revenue." [51]

AQIM may be based in Africa, but its reach into Western countries is viewed as a concern. Analysts believe that several dozen AQIM cells exist in such countries as Britain, France, Germany, Italy, and Spain. [52] Although the European cells are primarily tasked with raising money for the organization, there is always a concern that they could have a dual use: they could go operational at some point and strike targets of opportunity.

This concern is particularly acute because AQIM has threatened European countries. For example, it warned that it would strike France after that country implemented dress restrictions aimed at Muslim women. French commentators voiced concern about AQIM after the release of a bin Laden propaganda tape in October 2010 that focused specifically on their country. "Osama bin Laden's message is a clear encouragement to the leaders of the AQIM to step up their operations in France," complained a French observer. [53]

Overall, AQIM enjoys a relatively secure space in Africa's Sahel. It has a safe haven in the desert, and the vast desert also helps it to move through the borders of various countries in the region. [54]

America's Diminished Capabilities

All of the above regions where al Qaeda enjoys a significant presence are in addition to its successes in Somalia, where al Shabaab (see chapter 8) has been able to control significant territory. In short, al Qaeda can be considered a major challenge in an impressive number of geographic regions, including Afghanistan, Pakistan, Iraq, Yemen, the Sahel, and the Horn of Africa. The jihadi group is also capable of sponsoring major terrorist attacks against Western countries. There can thus be little question that al Qaeda has succeeded in its goal of making its conflict with the United States far broader than it was ten years ago.

Unfortunately, al Qaeda's other major goal has also been satisfied: America's economy is far weaker now than it was ten years ago. In 1999, not only was the U.S. economy strong, President Bill Clinton thought the United States would be rid of its national debt by 2015. "If we maintain our fiscal discipline, using the surplus to pay down the debt and using the savings to strengthen Social Security, America will entirely pay off the national debt by 2015," he said to reporters on the White House lawn in June 1999.[55] Today the economy is in a shambles, and the national debt has reached astronomical figures, standing at more than $14 trillion.

Of course, al Qaeda cannot claim the sole credit for this, or even the primary credit. Woeful financial mismanagement on the federal government's part, allowing spending to reach unprecedented levels while taxes were slashed, drove up the national debt. Meanwhile, an unregulated market for subprime lending by major financial institutions produced an enormous bubble that burst to the detriment of the entire economy. But our massive spending on intelligence, homeland security, and other counterterrorism needs has certainly been a contributing factor. "I don't think it's sustainable over time," former DHS inspector general Clark Kent Ervin said to me about current national security expenditures. "We really do have serious economic problems."[56]

National debt is not an inherent evil. Similar to a business borrowing money through the sale of stock, a government's borrowing can be seen as an investment in the economy's future. As economists Robert

Heilbroner and Lester Thurow note, "The government sector, like the business sector, also can justify its rising debt in terms of an increasing stock of real assets—dams and roads, skills and knowledge, and the like."[57] But the country's current staggering level of debt is far larger than one could see as a reasonable investment in America's economic future. Moreover, our national security expenditures are *defensive* in nature: Rather than building up infrastructure and the kinds of assets that are suggestive of prudent investment, they are designed only to prevent hostile forces from taking American lives and destroying American property.

The national debt threatens the U.S. fight against terrorism—indeed, threatens the nation's future—in multiple ways. Chairman of the Joint Chiefs of Staff Michael Mullen has rightly called our national debt the number one national security threat that America faces.[58] Osama bin Laden believed that American military might could not be sustained without a sound economy.

Harvard University historian Niall Ferguson agrees. He wrote in *Newsweek* in 2009 that America's "ability to manage its finances is closely tied to its ability to remain the predominant global military power." Not mincing words, Ferguson added, "This is how empires decline. It begins with a debt explosion. It ends with an inexorable reduction in the resources available for the Army, Navy, and Air Force." This is why, Ferguson says, voters are correct to worry about the U.S. debt crisis. "If the United States doesn't come up soon with a credible plan to restore the federal budget to balance over the next five to 10 years, the danger is very real that a debt crisis could lead to a major weakening of American power."[59]

Other observers agree that the U.S. defense budget is due for cuts that will hamper the country's ability to continue to project military power. "In the federal budget, built of great lumpy, immoveable blocks of medical care and pensions, something has to give," the *Times* of London has noted, "and it's going to be defense."[60]

A June 2010 report from the Center for Strategic and Budgetary Assessments states, "Given the bleak U.S. fiscal outlook, and the need for major fiscal belt tightening, how likely is it that the American people will sustain a level of spending on national defense sufficient to maintain the military at its current size and enable it to modernize sufficiently to be able to address threats beyond our two current wars? The simple answer is: not likely at all."[61] Defense officials also believe that military spending will be cut.[62]

By 2019, the annual interest on the national debt will be more than $700 billion, which is more than the current size of the Defense Department's entire budget. The *New York Times* anticipates that significant domestic political fights will result. "The competing demands could deepen political battles over the size and role of the government, the trade-offs between taxes and spending, the choices between helping older generations versus younger ones, and the bottom-line questions about who should ultimately shoulder the burden," it notes.[63]

But clearly these hard choices will not be confined to the domestic policy arena. We confront significant challenges from al Qaeda and its affiliates in Afghanistan, Pakistan, Iraq, Yemen, the Sahel, and the Horn of Africa. How long can the United States remain engaged in these disparate regions? Who will pick up the slack?

Pretending that the country does not confront hard choices is simply not a realistic option. As William H. Gross, the managing director of the bond-management firm Pimco Group, told the *New York Times*, "What a good country or a good squirrel should be doing is stashing away nuts for the winter. The United States is not only not saving nuts, it's eating the ones left over from the last winter."[64]

Indeed, this is where the Soviet example is so haunting. In Yegor Gaidar's analysis (see chapter 2), the Soviet Union's collapse was brought about by spiraling public debt caused by the collapse of world oil prices (which depressed Soviet revenues) as well as a grain crisis. Rather than making hard choices—giving up its hold over Eastern Europe, rationing food, or cutting its military-industrial complex—the Soviet Union decided to ignore the problem and borrow money from overseas, until its credit rating collapsed.

There are some differences in the situation that the United States confronts (it has been battered by high rather than low oil prices, for example), but overall, these parallels should trouble America. "If the deficit isn't reined in, investors eventually could refuse to continue lending Uncle Sam the money required to run the government—everything from the wars in Iraq and Afghanistan to unemployment insurance, Social Security and Medicare," *USA Today* noted in August 2010. "Once ignited, worries about U.S. creditworthiness could quickly snowball. The nightmare scenario: Investors shun U.S. government securities, forcing an abrupt resolution of the deficit via draconian spending cuts and tax increases like nothing in U.S. history."[65]

There are already signs that investors are beginning to question America's economic future. On April 18, 2011, Standard & Poor's Ratings Services announced that it was lowering the outlook on U.S. debt from "stable" to "negative." This change was the result of pessimism about whether Congress would address the country's debt woes. As the congressional newspaper *The Hill* reported, although S&P will continue to give U.S. bonds a rating of AAA or A-1+, this downgraded debt rating "means there is a one-in-three chance it will lower the rating for the bonds—and force Treasury to raise interest rates on U.S. debt—within two years."[66]

When we look at the differences between September 2001 and September 2011 from al Qaeda's perspective, it is clear how much the jihadi group has gained. Even though it has lost Osama bin Laden and its safe haven in Afghanistan, its fight against the United States is broader, and al Qaeda and its affiliates are key players in more regions than they were engaged in a decade ago. Indeed, jihadi groups threaten to control territory in several of them.

Meanwhile, the U.S. economy is shattered, it faces an almost unthinkable debt burden, and its policy makers have largely been consigned to arguing with each other on the sidelines as the country's traditional allies—Egypt's Mubarak, Tunisia's Ben Ali, Yemen's Saleh, and others—are overthrown or see their power erode. Although some observers think that these waves of change discredit al Qaeda and will undermine it, the jihadi group thinks that they instead demonstrate America's decline. When al Qaeda looks at the global landscape, it believes with reason that it is the United States, not al Qaeda, that will have the most trouble adapting to the changes that are already upon us.

That is why al Qaeda believes, with justification, that it is winning.

12

How to Survive al Qaeda

Throughout our history, Americans have displayed an extraordinary degree of resolve, nimbleness, and self-sacrifice in times of war. Today we are breaking with that tradition. Our nation faces grave peril, but we seem unwilling to mobilize at home to confront the threat before us.

— *Stephen Flynn, 2005*

The saddest aspect of al Qaeda's success in the past decade is that the deepest wounds the United States suffered weren't caused by the jihadi group. Rather, they were self-inflicted. The problems began with America's failure to understand al Qaeda's overarching strategy immediately after the 9/11 attacks and continued with the striking fact that no official strategic assessment was undertaken thereafter. Although officials were busy trying to prevent another major attack on the country, it is unthinkable that we went to war with this foe— and the war on terrorism has indeed been a war—without performing any real strategic assessment.

Our failure to understand al Qaeda's strategy has had recognizable costs. If you were to structure a plan for fighting a small adversary like al Qaeda, with its particular strategies, it would largely be the *opposite* of the system that the United States put in place in the post-9/11 world. To fight an adaptive foe that seeks to undermine your economy, you need a nimble, flexible, and relatively inexpensive system of homeland defense. Instead, the system we adopted was bureaucratic, rigid, and incredibly costly. To fight a small foe who wants to broaden the conflict and make your every blow wear you down (as happened to boxer George Foreman in his fight with Muhammad Ali), you need to keep the battlefield as small and focused as possible. Instead, the United States allowed al Qaeda to turn Iraq and other countries into frontline states in this war.

The good news is that even though many of the problems that the United States is now confronting are of its own creation, it is capable of crafting solutions. This final chapter outlines what America needs to do to fight terrorism more effectively.

Understand Al Qaeda's Strategy

It is fundamental that to understand an enemy, we must comprehend its ends (desired goals), as well as the ways and means through which it intends to reach those goals.

America's failure to understand al Qaeda's strategy has proven costly. We cannot, of course, undo past mistakes, but we can make sure that we do not repeat the same errors. U.S. officials can start by understanding the evolution of al Qaeda's strategy and where it stands as of 2011. One thing the history of the jihadi group makes clear, however, is that al Qaeda is an adaptive organization. Its strategic approach has evolved based on its enemies' reactions; it has always sought to exploit the weaknesses, vulnerabilities, and opportunities unwittingly presented to it.

Adaptations will certainly occur in the wake of bin Laden's death. American planners should understand the group's strategic history but also carefully watch the ways that this strategic outlook will continue to evolve over time. (Also, given advances in technology that can give groups collective power once reserved exclusively for nation-states, al Qaeda will not be the last nonstate challenger that America encounters as a strategic threat. In the future, the United States shouldn't undertake another large-scale venture designed to counter a nonstate threat without first embarking on a detailed strategic assessment of its adversary.)

With this strategic knowledge of al Qaeda, the United States must structure its defenses and its offensive posture against the jihadi network in a manner that is designed to thwart the network's designs. Al Qaeda currently has a strong asymmetric warfare strategy, and it believes that the United States will be unable to adapt to it. Al Qaeda's operatives have been able to find vulnerabilities even in aviation security, which has been hardened far more than any other set of targets.

Al Qaeda believes that its relatively small and inexpensive adaptations will continue to thwart its enemies' defenses and that each time it slips an operative past the security measures designed to detect him—even if that operative doesn't succeed in killing a single "infidel"—it will force costly and intrusive adaptations upon its adversary. This can be seen from the last few plots targeting aviation. Al Qaeda's strategy is, essentially, to make the United States collapse under the weight of its own defenses.

So how can the United States more effectively counter this strategy? That is the question I now explore.

Address the Politicization of Terrorism

As U.S. planners gain a thorough understanding of al Qaeda's strategy and reevaluate their own defenses in this light, it is critical to tackle the structural impediments to effectively combating terrorism. One of the biggest impediments over the past decade has been the politicization of terrorism and national security. As I have shown (see chapter 4), every political party that has used terrorism and national security to win elections from 2002 onward has had serious paradigmatic flaws in its approach to these issues. In some cases the election results have hastened major national mistakes, such as when the 2002 midterm election was seen as a mandate for the United States to invade Iraq.

Two dangers are posed as long as terrorism and national security is a major area of political contention. First, both parties will seek partisan advantage on the issue. Rather than resulting in healthy competition that produces better policy, this runs the risk of bad policy being adopted as the parties play to their respective bases. Second, the politicization of national security inherently runs up costs to the nation, because spending large sums of money can be used as a proxy for toughness. When politicians have to make decisions about resource allocation in light of a possible terrorist risk, they will almost always overallocate resources. After all, having taken action when a threat proves to be false might be wasteful, but not having taken action when a threat proves to be true could be politically fatal.

Some might argue that I am exaggerating the harm of this situation because it is better to err on the side of caution when we're dealing with terrorism. Indeed, that might be our choice as a society: But such a choice should be the product of consideration, not forced by a fear of voter backlash coupled with the knowledge that overspending carries little political consequence. Fear of unfair political attack is a terrible driver of policy. Moreover, given our understanding of where al Qaeda's strategy currently stands—its "strategy of a thousand cuts" involving smaller, more frequent attacks designed to drive up security expenses—it would be irrational to select maximally expensive defenses without giving due consideration to the enemy's strategy. After all, maximally expensive defenses are precisely what al Qaeda is counting on.

Obviously, complaining about the politicization of terrorism is not enough. It is easy to say that this issue should be dealt with more maturely, but it is more difficult to actually create more productive discourse. Now is an opportune time to do so, however, because of the continuity from the last two years of the Bush administration through the first three years of the Obama administration on terrorism and national security, and also because bin Laden's death and the tenth anniversary of the 9/11 attacks may create space to reevaluate the issue and thus reduce its politicization.

This is not to say that the continuity from one administration through the next means that the Bush-Obama approach has it right, nor does it mean that voices advocating different approaches should be marginalized. Indeed, one purpose of this book is to advocate a different paradigm for pursuing the fight against terrorism. Rather, two key problems are worth addressing on the politicization of terrorism and national security. The first is the fact that many political attacks have been irrational grandstanding, intended solely for partisan gain. The second is the downside of the democratization of communication technology.

There are, of course, many clear advantages to advances in communication technology. Important voices that would have been marginalized or ignored two decades ago have been able to play a role in public debates. At its best, access to numerous competing sources of information can produce instantaneous fact-checking and expose one to a diversity of perspectives, thus producing more accurate and nuanced analysis. But there is also a clear dark side to these advances. They not only empower deserving voices that illuminate otherwise neglected aspects of an issue, they can also empower the voices of those who don't really deserve a podium: the bigots, the demagogues, and the charlatans.

Even one individual can hold America's foreign policy hostage to some degree. This was the case with Terry Jones, an obscure Florida pastor who became a major international news story in September 2010 when he threatened to burn a Qur'an. Even General David Petraeus weighed in on Jones's threats, arguing that burning Islam's holy book would endanger U.S. forces. Although Jones didn't follow through on his threat in 2010, in March 2011 he organized a mock trial of the Qur'an in which he served as the judge. (This "trial" also featured attorneys for the prosecution and defense, as well as witnesses.) At the end, Jones declared the Qur'an guilty, and it was set aflame.

Less than two weeks later, an angry crowd in Mazar-e Sharif, Afghanistan, attacked a U.N. compound and killed at least eight people. Although there were multiple responsible parties for this outbreak of violence—not least the crowd itself, as well as President Hamid Karzai—this illustrates how one lone extremist can cause deaths halfway around the world and threaten critical U.S. foreign-policy objectives.[1] One aid worker in Afghanistan commented at the time, "This is not the beginning of the end for the international community in Afghanistan. This is the end. Terry Jones and others will continue to pull anti-Islam stunts and opportunistic extremists here will use those actions to incite attacks against foreigners. Unless we, the internationals, want our guards to fire on unarmed protesters from now on, the day has come for us to leave Afghanistan."[2]

It will be virtually impossible to stop rogue individuals like Jones from igniting similar controversies. Their impact can be mitigated, but one reality of life in the early twenty-first century is that lone nuts can influence geopolitics in ways they couldn't have twenty years ago. In 1991, Jones would most likely have been consigned to the letters-to-the-editor section of the local newspaper, his Qur'an-burning antics earning no more than local exposure. What can be addressed, though, is the tendency of fringe voices to hijack serious discussions about national security and counterterrorism, and in that way produce bad policy and a woeful misallocation of resources.

What's needed is the strengthening of a moderate center on terrorism and national security, a collection of experts and professionals— from the right, the left, and those without partisan affiliation—who can gather periodically, discuss pressing issues, and hear both official thinking on the matter and the views of their colleagues. I will explain the mechanisms through which a moderate center can be strengthened momentarily, but first I want to explain the reasons for doing so.

The purpose of strengthening a moderate center isn't to squelch anybody's right to speak on these issues or to ensure absolute agreement on America's counterterrorism and national security policies. Indeed, the issues are complex, and answers are often shaded in gray rather than being black and white, so it is healthy to have disagreement and debate. The first reason to have a strong moderate center is to have a mechanism to rebut wrongheaded or sensationalistic issues that occasionally come to dominate national security discussions when one party seeks to leverage them for political gain.

An example of this occurred in February 2006, when it was announced that the Bush administration had approved a deal in which Dubai Ports of the United Arab Emirates (DP World) would take over the operation of twenty-one U.S. seaports. Immediately politicians from both parties, but primarily Democrats, skewered the administration for approving the deal, arguing that it would significantly increase the risk of terrorism. The political debate was incredibly poor, albeit with the interesting twist that the Democrats were now perceived as tougher on security than the Republicans were. Both sides seemed to immediately leap to the rhetorical excesses that sometimes typified the other, with the Democrats hyperbolizing the threats posed by the deal and the administration just as casually accusing its foes of racial and religious prejudice. (In a clear demonstration that politics sometimes makes for strange bedfellows, the left-wing *Nation* sided with the administration, similarly accusing the deal's opponents of "anti-Arab bigotry.")[3] Matthew Duss, a policy analyst at the left-leaning think tank Center for American Progress, told me, "I think this was seen by Democrats as an opportunity to establish their nationalist and anti-terrorist credibility. They'd been beaten up by Bush so long on these issues that they saw this as an opportunity to reverse the roles."[4]

The bottom line, though, is that the security concerns were massively overblown. Port management responsibilities would have gone to DP World under the deal, but the Coast Guard would have remained responsible for port security regardless of who managed the ports, and U.S. Customs and Border Protection would have maintained responsibility for container and cargo security. In other words, the security procedures wouldn't have changed even if DP World had taken over port operations.

In addition, it was highly unlikely that the nationalities of the port employees would change substantially after a purchase by DP World: the ports had previously been run by the British company P&O Steamship Navigation, and P&O's purchase of the ports didn't produce a sudden infusion of British workers. Critics of the sale also overlooked the fact that DP World had every incentive to ensure the ports' security. Rather than being a fly-by-night operation that came out of nowhere to buy up P&O, DP World is a multibillion-dollar operation that bought the British company for $6.8 billion. If a terrorist attack came through one of its ports, DP World's business could be shattered.

There are numerous other examples of false issues dominating national security discourse for distinct periods. One is the hysteria that has surrounded the idea that a nuclear weapon could be shipped into the United States through one of its ports. Given our porous borders to the north and the south, plus the fact that radiation monitoring occurs at American ports, putting a nuclear device in a package and shipping it to a U.S. address is among the *least* likely means of introducing it to the country—particularly when you factor in the chance that such a package could be lost in the mail.

Another false issue was the controversy that surrounded Rashad Hussain, the U.S. special envoy to the Organization of the Islamic Conference (and someone I have known for more than a dozen years), after his appointment. When reports surfaced that Hussain had criticized some terrorism prosecutions while a student at Yale Law School—doing so from a rather typical civil libertarian perspective— the public discourse took an ugly turn. He was lambasted in the *Washington Examiner*, for example, as "a voice of radical Islam."[5] The White House stood behind Hussain's appointment, and the storm passed, but not before the story spiraled somewhat out of control and he was subjected to ugly attacks.[6]

A strong moderate center could help to counter off-base or irrational political issues that come to dominate political discussion by allowing knowledgeable, serious professionals to more effectively bring sanity and a sense of perspective to these discussions.

The second reason to have a strong moderate center is that it could be used to create space for serious discussion about how much spending on homeland security and counterterrorism is justified, given that our terrorist foes are now counting on our security spending to make us easier to break. "It's hard for anybody to have an attack occur on their watch," Ben Sheppard of the Institute for Alternative Futures told me. "Regardless of which party is in power, the other will say it occurred because there weren't sufficient counterterrorism policies in place. There's an expectation that all terrorist attacks are preventable."[7]

Even though politicians and other officials have said publicly that we cannot prevent all terrorist attacks, the country seems to operate as though we actually have a zero-risk paradigm for terrorism. This leads to exorbitant spending on homeland security.

Sheppard continued, "What's probably a better approach is for politicians to communicate with the public and say we have limited resources. Even with the best intelligence and resources devoted to the task, one or two attacks may get through. The politicians need to set the right expectations." Sheppard noted that the difference between the United States and Britain is that terrorism is rarely a significant political issue in the latter. (There are some exceptions to this, but they are issue-specific, such as controversy over whether the government should extend the length of time terrorism suspects can be detained without charge.)

Forty-year CIA veteran Charlie Allen concurred. "I would look at a lot of the programs," he told me, "a lot of the expenditures for homeland security, and make sure they're based on a realistic threat assessment, make sure that they're defensible. My view is that we probably should trim some."[8] This is a far easier discussion to have in a less hotly contested partisan atmosphere.

The third reason for a moderate center is that experts have an impact on the public understanding of national security. William McCants, a well-regarded research analyst at the Center for Naval Analyses and a former senior adviser for Countering Violent Extremism at the U.S. Department of State, has noted that "the media relies on experts."[9] If experts from competing political perspectives were more vigilant about cutting down ominous-sounding nonstories, that could alter the way the media treats these issues. Instead, under the current system, baseless national security controversies frequently arise—such as the three examples mentioned earlier. Sometimes experts chime in on these controversies to provide a more rational perspective in the media; sometimes they don't. But this takes place in a rather ad hoc manner.

How can a moderate center be strengthened? This is an area where cooperation between the private sector and the government can play a significant role. One way to bolster a moderate center is by the creation of a forum for frank, open, fast communication among recognizable thinkers, experts, and government officials involved in the policy process.

A private organization—a think tank or a foundation interested in crafting a more reasonable national security discussion—could convene a regular, moderated forum in which officials and national security theorists, who represent a range of perspectives but who all have genuine expertise and are pragmatic, could interact to discuss pressing issues. Meeting periodically in person would help to develop contacts that might not otherwise exist, build up trust among competing perspectives, and explore how peers who are grappling with these issues view current approaches to tackling jihadi militancy. Such face-to-face meetings would of course be supplemented by the kind of instantaneous communication that is typical of twenty-first-century life, such as an e-mail listserv that can continue these discussions.

Such a forum, which would allow discussion between the government and private stakeholders who are capable of driving the public discussion, could counter the tendency for nonissues to become politically important. It would provide the potential for rapid reaction by genuine experts who could quickly consider and weigh in on developing controversies. Of course, such a forum wouldn't work if an administration attempted to use it to advance a partisan agenda. But assembling a range of thinkers who are knowledgeable and honest rather than obsequious could serve as a check against such abuses. It is desperately important to make terrorism a less political issue, and there is no better time than now—before there's another major attack.

Reduce the Expense of National Security

At the beginning of this book, I asked a simple yet vital question: do our security outlays make us more rather than less vulnerable? We are currently faced with two related problems. First, at the current level, in the way that our system of homeland defense is structured, our security outlays do indeed make us more vulnerable. Al Qaeda's strategy is premised on this, recognizing that it is easy to drive up U.S. security expenditures. Second, many commentators who recognize these outrageous expenditures—as several articles and cable news shows pointed out in the wake of bin Laden's death—have no real framework for *how* security expenses should be reduced. If one simply slashed spending while maintaining our current security framework, it would, in fact, almost certainly make us less safe. This will be true unless we're able to modify the system so that we can get more security while expending *fewer* resources.

The fundamental problem with our system of homeland security is that it has been structured in an extremely expensive manner from top to bottom. This includes the measures used to defend against terrorism, because the country's hesitance to embrace a system of terrorist profiling has led to an unnecessarily costly system and also one that is less effective; without a terrorist profile, security personnel are left trying to guard against a greater number of potential threats. It is a system in which it is difficult to even assess whether our security has been improved by the massive post-9/11 expansion of the intelligence community, and it is a system in which expensive contractors still play a dominant role among the personnel who are charged with protecting the country.

Terrorist Profiling

Many debates about our national security policies are frustrating, dominated by red herrings and straw men. Nowhere is this truer than in debates over terrorist profiling. Many of the arguments that have been offered against profiling are in fact completely irrelevant; foremost among these is the argument, made by countless talking heads on cable channels, that many al Qaeda terrorists are not Arab, as though this were some sort of revelation that proves profiling ineffective. The opponents of profiling frequently argue against the crudest, most inefficient system of profiling imaginable, and then they conclude that because they have proved this system ineffective, they have discredited all possible systems of terrorist profiling.

The system of behavioral profiling that TSA has begun to implement should be sustained and expanded. TSA began to test the Screening of Passengers by Observation Techniques (SPOT) program in October 2003. Stephen M. Lord, the director of homeland security and justice issues at the Government Accountability Office, explained, "The SPOT program utilizes behavior observation and analysis techniques to identify potentially high-risk passengers. TSA designed SPOT to provide behavior detection officers (BDO) with a means of identifying persons who may pose a potential security risk at TSA-regulated airports by focusing on behaviors and appearances that deviate from an established baseline and that may be indicative of stress, fear, or deception."[10]

When further investigation is justified by the various indicators that SPOT employs, a passenger is directed to referral screening in the checkpoint area, which involves additional questioning as well as a physical search by BDOs and other officers. If a closer look is merited thereafter, the passenger is then referred to a law enforcement officer who can determine whether there are grounds for such further actions as detention or arrest. According to Lord, as of April 2011, BDOs had been deployed to 161 of the nation's 462 TSA-regulated airports.

Other countries have succeeded in utilizing profiling in aviation security and other contexts without trampling on civil liberties. Israel comes up frequently in discussions about passenger profiling. As former TSA head nominee Erroll Southers has written, lessons from Israel's aviation security can be applicable to the United States. "Despite the differences in size and scope," Southers wrote, "the State of Israel does one thing better than most; it prioritizes 'the human element' on both sides of the counter-terrorism equation." Southers argued that though profiling is controversial in the United States, the behavior-based profiling at Israel's Ben Gurion International Airport "does not put security and civil liberties at odds, nor should it in the United States."[11]

Emphasizing this need for "the human element," many Israeli security professionals are dismissive of the expensive machinery that Western governments are investing in instead. Rafi Sela, an Israeli aviation security expert, told Canada's parliament in April 2010, "I don't know why everybody is running to buy these expensive and useless machines. I can overcome the body scanners with enough explosives to bring down a Boeing 747. That's why we haven't put them in our airport."[12]

Meanwhile, countries that have not embraced profiling have come to realize that their security suffers as a result. In late 2010, BAA, a leading British-based airport company, called for a review of British airport security because of its predictability. BAA's director of security, Ian Hutcheson, said that the rules employed at British airports, as opposed to behavioral detection and other profiling tools, create a system that "is too prescriptive, which gives this consistency of security which plays into terrorists' hands."[13]

Sheldon Jacobson, a University of Illinois at Urbana-Champaign computer science professor who has studied aviation security since

1996, has argued that our spending is actually making us less secure. "Spending billions of dollars on screening the wrong people uses up finite resources," he wrote. "If we keep focusing on stopping terrorist tactics rather than stopping the terrorists themselves, the aviation security system will never reach an acceptable level of security. More screening can actually result in less security by directing security attention and resources (which by definition, are finite) onto people who are not a threat, which in turn moves such attention and resources away from people who are a threat."[14]

I see the case for profiling as a rather obvious issue. The major impediment to its acceptance is that it seems the public hasn't yet fully comprehended the finite nature of our resources: many still embrace the notion that clunky, inefficient defenses against terrorism are in fact noble. As the reality of our constrained resources is fully understood, our public debate will change. The sooner this happens, the better off we will be.

Analytic Reform

Are we better off with the massive expansion of the intelligence community that occurred after 9/11? Is our raw intelligence better? Has our analysis improved? Is it having a significant operational impact? These are difficult questions to answer, but they must be asked—and explored with diligence and humility.

Any exploration of trimming and reforming the intelligence community requires a detailed knowledge not only of the explosive growth of the intelligence apparatus but also the value that is being derived from the various agencies. Astute observers within the intelligence community believe that cuts can and should be made. "How many of these 800,000 people within the intelligence community are actively advancing U.S. interests?" one analyst said to me. "If they aren't doing so, there's a legitimate question to be asked: Why are you here?"[15]

Any effort to trim our intelligence apparatus should involve intelligence veterans and other informed professionals who are free of commercial conflicts of interest and can provide apolitical recommendations on structural reforms. The reason for objective, knowledgeable observers to play a key role in any review is obvious. Cuts that prove to be too deep could not only endanger our country's security but also necessitate a future *expansion* of the intelligence apparatus after the overbreadth of the cuts became obvious. And when more personnel were added later, many of them might be expensive contractors rather than governmental employees, which is precisely what happened in the wake of the 9/11 attacks. We do not want to risk a tragic cycle of making the wrong cuts, being hit by another terrorist strike, and then inefficiently building back up our intelligence infrastructure in response.

Other aspects of the culture of the intelligence community that might limit its effectiveness should be explored. There is a distinct lack of specialists, and the tendency to produce generalists can result in "Google-deep" conclusions that analysts with a bit more background and context would immediately recognize as flawed. At present, no professional incentives exist for analysts to develop into specialists. This drives up costs. The intelligence community often has to hire contractors as specialists, and because those doing the hiring have difficulty telling the difference between a good and a bad specialist, more are hired than are needed. Thus there is dead weight.

"You have a massive amount of very general, duplicative work that could be streamlined just through proper coordination," the aforementioned analyst told me. In addition to the inefficiencies associated with this situation, analytical shortcomings are also produced. In this culture of nonspecialists, analysts are dissuaded from drawing controversial conclusions. Platitudes are often used in lieu of actual analysis because the analysts lack the confidence and experience to take positions that some might regard as controversial. This can lead to analytic errors.

It goes without saying that not all analysts fall into this trap. I have known many astute intelligence analysts whose perspectives I deeply respect. But to not admit that this is part of the current culture of intelligence analysis would represent an extreme denial.

The intelligence community should establish long-term professional incentives for analysts to develop significant expertise in their areas of focus. It is necessary to maintain specialists in every key area. The fact that the United States knew so little about Libya when we were *preparing to go to war* with Qaddafi's regime is a damning indict-ment of the intelligence community's current structure.

In addition, we should strive for more of a *qualitative* element in evaluating our analysts. "Analysts should be able to show their work," one analyst told me, "which would be required at any private organiza-tion." Performance-based pay could be one solution. "I'm very much in favor of pay for performance," Charlie Allen told me. "In my view the only way we should work is pay for performance. I found DHS, with its analysis occurring under civil service rules, not as agile, not as quick." Of course, if analysts are to be paid for their performance, there must be personnel in place who are capable of evaluating that performance. When such evaluations are undertaken by human resource depart-ments that lack subject-matter expertise or the requisite tools to assess analytic tradecraft, performance measurements may be used that are actually irrelevant. If "evaluation" becomes an exercise in meaningless box-checking, it might as well not be tried at all.

Reform of the intelligence community should not be undertaken lightly, and doing so without the requisite detailed knowledge of the intelligence apparatus could be costly. Nonetheless, the principles for reform are actually simple: a more skilled corps of analysts with deeper knowledge of the areas they're studying won't just improve our intel-ligence but will also allow us to adapt better to al Qaeda and other foes engaged in asymmetric warfare. This will save us money in the long run.

Civil Service Reform

The elephant in the room, in so many of our discussions about the overuse of private contractors, is civil service reform. Right now, it is extremely difficult to both hire and fire federal employees, who enjoy a broad array of civil service protections. Indeed, these protections make it almost impossible to fire underperforming federal employees. They will often be shuffled to other departments—or in some grotesque cases, even promoted—in response to their lack of performance.

Charlie Allen, speaking to me about the difficulties he experi-enced with underperforming employees, said that he was often forced to move them out of key positions. "But if I could have fired people more easily, I would have done that," he said. This illuminates one obvious reason for the government's preference for contractors over federal employees: at least an underperforming contractor can be fired, or the contract not renewed. In contrast, an underperforming federal employee will remain a permanent drag on the federal budget.

Past civil service reform efforts have been less than successful. For example, although the Civil Service Reform Act of 1978 (CSRA) was sweeping, designed to make the government more businesslike, it is widely thought to have been poorly implemented. One recent academic study noted that "today, civil service reformers are again seeking management flexibility, somewhat ironically, by escaping from the rules-bound processes and institutions that evolved under CSRA."[16]

Civil service reform is an area in which far more aggressive change than we have been accustomed to would be good for our country. Easing the restrictions on the firing of underperforming federal employees would improve our corps of analysts and other national security professionals and reduce our reliance on expensive contractors. The caveat is that such professionals would need to be protected from political retribution: analysts should not have to worry about being fired because their conclusions don't conform to a party line.

But the problem of preventing political retribution is not the obstacle to meaningful civil service reform. Rather, there are a lot of people invested in the present system. (Remember path dependency?) This includes, of course, personnel within the federal bureaucracy who don't want to see their employment protections erode. This is a significant constituency: the Bureau of Labor Statistics notes that with about two million civilian employees, the federal government is the largest employer in the United States.[17]

Other key players, including federal contractors, have also made significant investments in the present system, assuming that robust civil service protection will not change. Because there is a built-in constituency opposed to civil service reform, many observers see it as a political nonstarter. "Civil service reform won't happen," Daniel Byman, a professor in Georgetown University's Security Studies program, told me, "but if I could wave a magic wand and pass it, that would be a huge gain."[18]

Other observers are more optimistic. Clark Kent Ervin, the former DHS inspector general, told me, "It's absolutely time to have civil service reform. I'm convinced of it." Prior to his time at DHS, Ervin was the State Department's inspector general. He moved to State after serving in state government in Texas—and while in Texas government, he summarily fired several people.

"I arrived at the State Department in 2001," he said, "had a bumbling executive assistant, and could not get rid of her." His point in comparing the federal government to Texas is that even in government it should be possible to have a system that allows for an optimized workforce. Ervin believes that there should be an appeals process to prevent firing for mercurial or arbitrary reasons, but that government employment should be more similar to civilian at-will employment, in which letting go of an underperforming employee is relatively easy.[19]

Ervin believes that civil service reform is possible now, in this climate of economic chaos, and that "there are huge bipartisan majorities for it." He may or may not be correct. But regardless of whether civil service reform is a *feasible* idea, it may well be a *necessary* one.

Build Resilience

Despite our best efforts, another terrorist attack may succeed. We should be building up our societal resilience. As DHS has defined it, resilience is "the ability of systems, infrastructures, government, business, and citizenry to resist, absorb, and recover from or adapt to an adverse occurrence that may cause harm, destruction, or loss of national significance."[20] Ben Sheppard of the Institute for Alternative Futures has focused on societal resilience in his research. He told me that when one looks at resilience, it is important to look not just at infrastructural resilience but also at the psychological aspect.[21]

Indeed, in debates on whether the current levels of spending on counterterrorism and national security are justified, the assertion is frequently made that the American people simply "couldn't handle" another major attack. In other words, the American people are perceived as lacking psychological resilience, and some of the resource misallocation in this area is justified by this lack of resilience. Of course, it is absurd to purposefully misallocate governmental resources out of a fear of public reaction; this hardly amounts to responsible policy making. An important aspect of preparing ourselves for the future is bolstering our resilience, both infrastructural and psychological, against the threat of terrorism and other dangers.

Sheppard told me that from an infrastructural perspective, it is important to "identify what vulnerabilities we'll have in five, ten, fifteen years so we can work on them now. Fifteen years ago the cell phone and Internet would not be seen as critical infrastructure the way they are now. You should ask the question of what new technologies could be adopted and what can be done to increase resilience in those various areas. We need to stop being reactive and be more proactive."

In terms of psychological resilience, the public of various nations has proven to be more resilient to terrorist attacks than policy makers often assume. Lawrence Freedman, a professor of war studies at King's College in London, notes that "public opinion is considered so fragile that even occasional atrocities, perhaps with chemical or radiological weapons, are assumed to have psychological effects well beyond the original change to life and property." However, Freedman writes, in reality the public is quite resilient, and the available evidence doesn't support the idea of a panic-prone public.[22]

One of the most important contributions to our understanding of public reaction in the wake of terrorist attacks is Sheppard's 2009 book *The Psychology of Strategic Terrorism*, which comprehensively examines a number of different case studies, including the reaction in Israel when Saddam Hussein launched Scud missiles against it during the 1991 Persian Gulf War, the sarin attack that the Aum Shinrikyo cult launched in the Tokyo subways in 1995, the 9/11 attacks, the anthrax attacks in the United States just after 9/11, and the Israeli reaction to the Palestinians' second intifada in 2000. After using multiple analytic methods to understand the public reaction to all of these events, Sheppard concludes that "the public is largely resilient to attacks and responds in a calm and reasonable way."[23] One of the key aspects of averting a public panic when a crisis does arise is credible risk communication.

This does not mean that we should be confident in and complacent about current levels of psychological resilience, but it does suggest that politicians may initially exaggerate the degree of public overreaction that even a major attack would produce. Indeed, although the public of various countries has often proved to be more resilient than was assumed, many observers believe that the United States is not doing well in fostering psychological resilience. "My impression is that we're doing rather poorly," Byman told me. "We've ratcheted up a zero-tolerance approach to terrorism."

Similarly, Bert Tussing, the director of the Homeland Defense and Security Issues Group at the U.S. Army War College, told me, "One thing we're not doing enough of is trying to reinstill a sense of community in our people. For a long time, when we looked at emergencies we thought of communities—faith-based organizations, families— taking care of one another. I think that unwittingly and without malice aforethought, working as a government to take care of people, we've instilled something between an entitlement and a victim mentality. People don't have ownership of their own fate, and when that happens, you slip into a victim mentality, waiting for the government to come to your rescue."[24]

One example of how to empower citizens is a program called the Community Emergency Response Team (CERT). The CERT concept was developed by the Los Angeles Fire Department in 1985, was later adopted by FEMA, and is now managed by the Citizen Corps within the Department of Homeland Security. The program teaches citizens how to prepare for a disaster and how to serve as auxiliary responders when one occurs.

The CERT program of Phoenix, Arizona's fire department is highly developed. As Deputy Fire Chief John Maldonado told my co-author for a project I worked on several years ago, the Phoenix department would be overwhelmed by a major catastrophe because the city is so sprawling, with only fifty-two stations in 550 square miles.[25] Consequently, the department has focused on teaching community members how to assist it and themselves in disaster situations.

The City of Phoenix's official website notes that if a major emergency strikes the Phoenix area, CERT members are expected to "give critical support to first responders, provide immediate assistance to victims, and organize spontaneous volunteers at a disaster site." CERT members can take a train-the-trainer course (conducted by FEMA or the state's training office for emergency management) and then conduct training sessions of more than twenty hours for other volunteers, who upon completion become CERT members themselves. The training includes "disaster preparedness, disaster fire suppression, basic disaster medical operations, light search and rescue operations, and terrorism awareness."[26]

The value of CERT volunteers can be seen in the response to Hurricane Katrina, when the state of Arizona deployed a CERT team to set up Phoenix's Veterans Memorial Coliseum as a shelter to receive victims from Louisiana. In what was dubbed Operation Good Neighbor, volunteers helped to transport and register evacuees and deliver meals to them. The Phoenix Citizen Corps Committee credits the mission's relative success to CERT members' familiarity with its command structure. "Although many church and volunteer groups helped with activities," the Committee noted, "it was clear that CERT members had an understanding of *how* an incident is structured and assigned."[27]

Tussing suggests that principles of disaster response can be incorporated into primary and secondary education to foster a more psychologically prepared and resilient nation. He referenced how his own children have returned from school enthusiastic about recycling or aware of the dangers posed by smoking. "I think getting to the schools, instilling this in our children when they're young, and tailoring the message over time is one very good way of doing it," he told me. Byman agreed, telling me that it makes sense to have "a sustained effort to educate people from the junior high level on up as to the true dangers, and how to respond, so people feel empowered."

Preparing citizens to play a role in responding to terrorist attacks and other major crises can serve a dual purpose. On the one hand, it can build more psychological resilience in the populace—before, during, and after crises. On the other hand, it can improve crisis response.

Avoid Campaigns Like the Libyan No-Fly Zone

I have just discussed how to keep our costs down in the fight against terrorism. Not all U.S. foreign policy has to be conducted through the lens of our fight against al Qaeda and other jihadi groups, but America's various foreign policy decisions should at least be undertaken with an *awareness* of the fight against jihadi militancy. Al Qaeda and its affiliates are a major force in multiple geographic regions—including Afghanistan, Pakistan, Iraq, Yemen, the Sahel, and the Horn of Africa—thus ensuring that the United States has a real national interest in all of these places. Precisely because America's resources are limited, it is critical that there be a legitimate national interest at stake in future military operations and that there be a solid justification if these operations are likely to result in the world becoming an even broader battlefield.

Against this paradigmatic backdrop, the nonsensical nature of the no-fly zone that the United States decided to establish in Libya in March 2011 becomes apparent. There was both public and international pressure for America to do something as the Arab revolts spread to Libya and it seemed that President Muammar Qaddafi was going to ruthlessly suppress an uprising in Benghazi. Both Anne-Marie Slaughter, the former head of the State Department's policy planning, and Secretary of State Hillary Clinton raised the specter of the slaughters in Rwanda in the 1990s as justification for why the United States should now act in Libya. *New York Times* columnist Nicholas Kristof, explaining why the U.S. establishment of a no-fly zone was the right response, wrote, "The tide in Libya seems to have shifted, with the Qaddafi forces reimposing control over Tripoli and much of western Libya. Now Qaddafi is systematically using his air power to gain ground even in the east."[28]

There were two problems with the public debate over intervening militarily in Libya. One was the question of why the United States would choose to intervene militarily in that particular uprising. Around the time that Qaddafi was preparing to quash the rebellion in Benghazi, the world also witnessed violent crackdowns on protesters in Bahrain, Syria, and Yemen. In Ivory Coast, Laurent Gbagbo had refused to relinquish power even after losing an election, and his regime was also engaged in a bloody crackdown. "Since 1998, more than 5 million people have died in the Congo's civil war, and both sides have used the . . . rape of women as an instrument of war," wrote Joshua Foust, a fellow at the American Security Project. "Yet that appalling atrocity—orders of magnitude worse than what Qaddafi has put his people through, worse than the Rwandan Genocide, worse than almost anything since the great communist purges of [the] last century—barely merited a peep from the international community, much less calls for full-fledged military intervention."[29] Why establish a no-fly zone in Libya when there were so many other grave humanitarian atrocities?

A more troubling question is what national interest was at stake to justify intervening militarily. In the hundreds of op-ed pieces penned in defense of U.S. intervention, little was said about this. Instead, the humanitarian aspect of the mission was emphasized. "Inspired by events in Tunisia and Egypt, the Libyan people rose up spontaneously against four decades of repression by Col. Muammar Qaddafi," Senator John Kerry wrote in a March 10 op-ed that compared the Libyan uprising to the failed Shiite' revolts against Saddam Hussein in 1991. Kerry claimed that just like those 1991 uprisings that ended in bloodshed, Libya's struggle involved "ordinary people facing off against an autocrat's airpower and well-armed soldiers, counting on the free world to protect them against massacre after we've applauded and bolstered their bravery with our words."[30]

This is an astoundingly irrational justification for military action. The situation in Libya in fact had precious little in common with the 1991 uprisings, in which overthrowing Saddam Hussein had been encouraged by the highest office in the United States—by the president himself—after America had just won a war against Saddam. In 1991, there really was a legitimate expectation, one that was tragically dashed, that America would try to protect those who rose up against Saddam Hussein. In contrast, under Kerry's paradigm, any American *praise* for revolutionaries standing up for their freedom in any part of the world suddenly confers a *responsibility* on the United States to protect them if the regime they're opposing cracks down. Such a conception of when America has a duty to intervene is a recipe for countless costly and unnecessary wars.

Similarly, when former president Bill Clinton endorsed a no-fly zone over Libya at the *Newsweek* and *Daily Beast* second annual Women in the World summit, he emphasized the fact that anti-Qaddafi rebels had asked for U.S. assistance, that America possessed "the planes to make an appropriate contribution," and that because Qaddafi was drawing in mercenaries to fight the revolutionaries, "it's not a fair fight."[31] Clinton's remarks demonstrate why U.S. intervention makes sense from the rebels' perspective; they do not show why undertaking military action in Libya makes sense for the United States. There are plenty of unfair fights in the world that do not merit U.S. intervention.

The lack of attention to whether there were real national interests at stake in Libya was a bipartisan failure. Senator John McCain, President Barack Obama's opponent in the 2008 election, called for a no-fly zone while criticizing the administration for not acting quickly enough. "Every place we go they are looking to America for leadership," he said, referring to his travels through the Middle East, "for assistance, for moral support and ratification of the sacrifices they have made in defense of democracy. America should lead."[32] This is another example of a politician dictating what U.S. policy should be based on other countries' requests or expectations. Actual U.S. interests did not factor into Senator McCain's equation.

When one considers the U.S. establishment of a no-fly zone in Libya in light of al Qaeda's strategic goals, the jihadi group's two overarching goals are advanced by American intervention. First, going to war with Libya broadens the battlefield in which the United States is engaged. Although there was seemingly no strategic interest in going to war with Libya before the no-fly zone was established, the United States turned Qaddafi into a mortal foe the minute it started bombing him. This was highly problematic, because the American planners had no endgame, no exit plan in mind when the bombing of Libya commenced.

Qaddafi's forces made predictable adaptations to the Western jets' onslaught. As the Associated Press noted, Qaddafi's forces "rapidly reorganized" after the no-fly zone was established, "shedding their heavy armor and relying on light forces to harry and repeatedly ambush the lightly armed rebels."[33] These adaptations were predictable, since Serbian leader Slobodan Milosevic did the same when the United

States was bombing him during Operation Allied Force in 1999, and he was able to continue controlling territory by doing so.[34]

Yet the United States lacked any considered response to these adaptations and to the fact that Qaddafi's regime did not immediately fall as a result of the no-fly-zone's establishment. Thus policy makers bandied about various ideas that would escalate the war, such as introducing ground troops or arming or training the rebels. The United States inexorably moved toward ever deeper involvement in a conflict in which it had very little at stake to begin with—and thus we ended up with a broader battlefield, one more war in which America was deeply involved.

As for al Qaeda's second major strategic goal, the Libyan no-fly zone also imposed significant costs upon the United States. Although many Americans see a no-fly zone as a cheap alternative to a ground invasion, it is anything but. The no-fly zone that the United States established in Iraq after the end of the Persian Gulf War cost about $1 billion a year, at a time when fuel was far less expensive.[35] The most comprehensive study on the cost of a no-fly zone over Libya, published by the Center for Strategic and Budgetary Assessments, found that the cost would depend on the kind of no-fly zone the United States implemented but that it would range from $390 million to $8.8 billion for six months of operations.[36] It is already clear that the low-end costs envisioned in that report are too low: after the United States established the no-fly zone, it cost more than $400 million in the first week of operations and more than $600 million in the first month.[37]

In addition to the financial cost of the mission, the costs imposed on military personnel must be considered. The 1st Battalion of the 2nd Marines (1-2), which deployed as part of the operations in Libya, had returned from Musa Qala—one of the toughest operational areas in Afghanistan—in late 2010 and had to deploy to Libya about six months after its return to the continental United States.

I spoke to a company-grade Marine Corps officer who had recently returned from Afghanistan, and he told me that one of his friends, a logistics officer in 1-2, received only forty-eight hours' notice that he would deploy for the Libya operation. Supporting an operation like a no-fly zone requires not just pilots but a whole host of service personnel: mechanics, refuelers, ordnance technicians, and all the personnel who are required to staff an aircraft carrier. "You're basically wearing people thin because of the requirements to deploy, the constant cycle of going back and not being able to take time for yourself and your family," the officer told me. "What you'll find is that a lot of those talented NCOs [noncommissioned officers] with experience will just leave. In fact, you're seeing that right now."[38]

There is a principled argument to be made for liberal internationalism as a foreign-policy doctrine, but such a doctrine must be tempered by the resources available to pursue an interventionist foreign policy when only humanitarian interests—and not national security interests—are at stake. At a time when America's debt rating is being downgraded, committing to a military intervention that may cost billions of dollars is irresponsible. The former assistant secretary of state for public affairs, P. J. Crowley, commented via Twitter, "To those worried about the cost of military operations in Libya, it hardly rivals the $750 billion spent in Iraq, plus the human toll."[39] This argument is nonsense on stilts—particularly coming from someone like Crowley, who correctly recognizes the Iraq War as a major blunder. The fact that the intervention in Libya is less costly than the Iraq War, which imposed an incredible burden on America's economy and constrained its response to the 2008 credit crisis, does not therefore mean that the United States can afford this war or that the war is in our country's interests.

Not only does America's intervention in Libya serve to advance both of al Qaeda's strategic goals—by involving the United States in an ever broader battlefield against a rogue's gallery of foes and by imposing considerable costs upon America—but it hampers the fight against al Qaeda in another way. The *Atlantic*'s Jeffrey Goldberg observed, "One of the things you notice in Washington is that even our government's most talented servants, like most of their fellow humans, have little ability to focus on more than one or two pressing issues at any given moment. Yes, they can speak on eight or ten issues at once, but granting sustained, deep attention to a hard problem is different than juggling questions at a press conference."[40]

Goldberg classified Libya as a seventh-tier national security problem at best. Among the six issues from the "back-of-the-envelope list" that he considered more pressing than Libya, three—Afghanistan and

Pakistan, Iraq, and AQAP in Yemen—involved areas where al Qaeda was involved in some capacity. One can add the growth of al Qaeda in the Sahel and Horn of Africa as other issues that are more important than Libya, from a national security perspective. Being involved in a new war, one in which U.S. responsibilities could potentially continue to expand, does not leave the country with the focus or resources to deal effectively with the areas where al Qaeda poses a real and legitimate threat.

Address Our Oil Addiction

Even if terrorists weren't attempting to disrupt the global supply of oil, our sole reliance on oil to power our transportation sector would still be an enormous strategic problem.

At the outset, it's important to note that oil dependence is a liquid-fuel problem. Both parties have been complicit in confusing this point, with Democrats suggesting that solar and wind power can reduce our oil dependence and the Republicans pointing to nuclear power as an oil alternative. Both sets of claims are grossly inaccurate: solar, wind, and nuclear power could be used to provide the country with *electricity*, but oil dependence is unrelated to the electrical grid. As Ken Silverstein, the editor of *EnergyBiz Insider*, has noted: "Oil, in this country, now comprises 2 percent of total electric generation. But it still provides 96 percent of the fuel in the transportation sector."[41] Most electricity generation comes from a combination of coal, natural gas, nuclear, and renewable sources—not from oil. Bruce Dale, a professor of chemical engineering at Michigan State University, bluntly summarized the current political discourse to me. "Politicians don't know what the hell they're talking about," he said. "They don't know you can't put the energy of a windmill into a car."[42]

Whenever I have made this point in my public speeches, an audience member will inevitably think he's caught me overlooking something. "But if we build electric cars, we can run them from solar or wind power," he will piously proclaim. This is one of those observations that might seem compelling for about five seconds, until you think it through. The fatal flaw in this logic is that the growth of electric vehicles is not at all hampered by a lack of electricity to power them. Rather, they haven't achieved significant market penetration because they're considerably more expensive than other cars.

Building up solar and wind power in the hope that they will one day be used to power electric vehicles that not enough people are buying is akin to addressing Detroit's crime problems by building more farms in the hope that the food they grow can one day be used to feed the city's police, if the police force ever grows. In both cases, there is obviously a more direct solution: subsidize electric vehicles or build up the police force rather than investing in unneeded electricity or food that could *perhaps* one day support them.

The first two years of the Obama administration saw some policy advances on oil dependence issues that will have a rather limited (albeit positive) immediate effect. First, Congress passed policies designed to promote auto efficiency. Ambitious new corporate average fuel economy (CAFE) standards, which mandate fuel economy increases of 33 percent by 2016 and 40 percent by 2020, are the centerpiece of these efforts.[43]

Second, a set of policies was designed to begin the electrification of the transportation sector through such means as plug-in hybrid electric vehicles, which can be plugged into the power grid and run off electricity for miles before burning a drop of petroleum. The administration's stimulus bill included $400 million for electrifying transportation, and the White House separately announced $2.4 billion in grants toward the manufacturing and deployment of next-generation batteries and electric vehicles.[44]

However, some analysts warn that electrification of the transportation sector will be slow, and thus the impact on oil dependence limited, especially in the near future. "Everybody imagines that in five years you'll see electric vehicles driving all over the place," David Victor, a professor at the University of California at San Diego's School of International Relations and Pacific Studies, told me. "The fact is that it will take longer than they think."[45]

Kateri Callahan, the president of the Alliance to Save Energy, shared his skepticism. "The battery is expensive," she told me, "and it doesn't deliver what you'd get from liquid fuels in terms of range. In order for an expensive item to displace an existing product, it has to offer more for the consumer."[46] Although the administration is right to promote electric vehicles as a form of fuel substitution, it is not clear that electric vehicles do provide the kind of benefit to the consumer that Callahan refers to—one that will help the vehicles to attain significant market penetration in the near future.

Thus, one of the crucial immediate actions the government should pursue—and one of the most significant missed opportunities during the first two years of the Obama administration—is the promotion of drop-in alternatives to oil, such as biofuels. It is true that biofuels have gotten somewhat of a bad public reputation in recent years, largely because of an intense PR campaign against them funded by the oil industry. But they hold far more promise than critics admit, in large part because criticisms attack the current generation of biofuels without considering the potential for technological improvements.

One such improvement would be the development of cellulosic ethanol. Contrary to current biofuels, which are derived from grains or oilseeds, cellulosic ethanol can be derived from such sources as switchgrass. For this reason, cellulosic ethanol offers a solution to one of the most troubling aspects of current generation biofuels: the trade-off between food and fuel. For cellulosic ethanol to work, scientists must address the technical issue of converting cellulose into a starch or sugar so it can be fermented into ethanol. "In principle this should be possible," writes engineer Robert Zubrin, "because grazing animals such as horses, deer, and cattle perform exactly this trick in their stomachs all the time—this is why they can eat leaves."[47]

If this technical barrier is overcome, biofuels can actually *reduce* food costs: the same process that converts this material into a starch or sugar could also address the problem of limited digestibility of straws and grasses as animal feeds.[48] It is a mistake to assume that biofuels for some reason cannot experience the kind of breakthroughs that we see in all other technologies in our lives.

But when it comes to displacing fossil fuels, biofuels have been held back by a chicken-and-egg dilemma. That is, the market for biofuels is too small because so few people have flex-fuel cars that can be powered by them. This means that filling stations have little incentive to carry biofuels—less than 1 percent of the 170,000 gas stations in the United States has an ethanol pump—which in turn discourages people from buying flex-fuel cars.[49]

In 2008, a potential solution to this problem won widespread support from politicians in both parties: the Open Fuel Standard Act.[50] The bill (S3303 and HR6559) would have required that at least 50 percent of each light-duty automobile manufacturer's annual inventory be "fuel-choice enabling" (that is, either flex-fuel vehicles or cars capable of operating on biodiesel) by 2012 and that at least 80 percent of these inventories be fuel-choice enabling by 2015. In other words, it would have forced automakers to give new car owners the ability to fill their tanks with alternative fuels if they chose. This would have broken the chicken-and-egg impasse that has been holding up alternative fuels, and it might have helped next-generation biofuel projects look more attractive to investors.

Many analysts correctly view the Open Fuel Standard Act as an important step because it challenges the monopoly that oil enjoys over the transportation sector by paving the way for biofuels to compete at the pump. Gal Luft of the Institute for the Analysis of Global Security told me, "The most important thing is to stop this horrible folly of putting out cars that can run on nothing but oil. Everybody talks about the oil problem, but meanwhile you're committing yourself to it by ensuring that the transportation sector can run on nothing else."[51]

Fighting Terrorism in an Age of Constrained Resources

The first time I was accused of secretly supporting al Qaeda's radical Somali affiliate al Shabaab on national television occurred in July 2010. A few days earlier, al Shabaab had struck outside Somalia's borders for the first time, carrying out deadly suicide attacks in Kampala, Uganda, that killed citizens guilty of no crime but watching the World Cup. Because I have written extensively about al Shabaab, Fox Business Channel booked me to discuss these developments.

When I went on the air, however, I realized that something was very wrong with the segment. As it was introduced, the host, David Asman, said, "Homeland Security briefs believe that as many as *hundreds* of members of that same al Qaeda faction are slipping across our southern border, which the administration has insisted is actually secure." He asked whether the administration was turning "a blind eye to the greatest threat of all." Asman and the other guest—Michelle Dallacroce of a group called Veteran Mothers against Illegal Amnesty—spoke of the severe danger posed by these hundreds of members of al Shabaab allegedly streaming into the country, and they concluded that the United States should immediately mobilize the National Guard to seal off the border with Mexico.

When it was my turn to speak, I tried to take a step back to assess the data points on which they drew this conclusion. There were three relevant points, none of which came close to establishing that we faced such a level of threat. The first was a DHS warning to Texas authorities to "be on the lookout for a suspected member of the Somalia-based al Shabaab terrorist group who might be attempting to travel to the United States through Mexico." The second data point was a court case in Texas that involved a human smuggling ring that had brought East Africans into the country. Press reports suggested that some of the people smuggled into the United States may have been Somalis affiliated with al Shabaab. The third data point was a court case in Virginia, in which a smuggler allegedly brought two hundred Somalis across the border—but there was no allegation that all of these men, or even a high percentage, were affiliated with al Shabaab.

I genuinely found these data points alarming, but they were a far cry from a scenario in which hundreds of members of al Shabaab were entering the country *right at that moment*—which, if true, might actually justify an expensive mobilization of the National Guard.

But Asman would hear none of it. "Daveed, hold on a second," he said. "I understand what you're saying, and you are very precise, as well you should be. But 9/11 was all about *not connecting the dots*. Had there been enough security people who had connected the dots, we might have been able to avoid what happened on 9/11. We are not connecting the dots now."

He argued that we needed to err on the side of caution. When I invoked our limited resources as a reason that we shouldn't be so casual about mobilizing the National Guard to seal the border with Mexico, he and Dallacroce went wild. "The point is," he said, "9/11 was all about not connecting the dots. I see some dots there, and I'm worried enough so I think we should take the cautionary step of putting the troops on the border."

Dallacroce, given the final word, said, "I think this gentleman is totally missing the point here. We're not saying that we want the border secured just because of al Shabaab." Then, accusatorily, she added, "And I don't know if you're protecting those people."

Being accused of secretly supporting al Shabaab on national television was more comedy than tragedy. Nobody in his or her right mind could take Dallacroce's accusation seriously; the idea that I was actually a commander of al Shabaab became a running joke with a group of my friends. But the interview raised a serious issue, because it reflected the grotesquely wasteful approach that we've had to homeland security.

What would we have gained from mobilizing the National Guard? That solution might have seemed obvious to the viewers, but only because the facts had been manipulated. The claim that hundreds of members of al Shabaab are entering the country *right now* conveys a greater sense of urgency than the truth, which was that two rings that had smuggled Somalis into the United States were broken up, and some of those Somalis may have been part of al Shabaab. The latter statement still provides reason for concern, but it is a far cry from the former. Indeed, under the latter formulation, mobilizing the National Guard seems like a dubious proposition.

The fact is, we're now in a world of severely constrained resources. Security decisions are not as simple as, Should we take this seriously, yes or no? Rather, all decisions are made in the context of limited budgets and numerous potential threats. That makes it important to respond vigilantly but not to overreact. Overreaction to any given threat can in fact make us *less safe* by causing the misallocation of resources, as well as such unmeasured costs as *crisis fatigue*. This is particularly true when we're talking about a massive undertaking like mobilizing the National Guard.

The sad reality of the twenty-first century is that we cannot respond with full vigor to every perceived threat, or we won't have the resources left over to address those that are most pressing. The sad reality is that lives will be lost in other parts of the world, like Libya, and we won't be able to do anything about it. This should give us no comfort, but we must be realistic. When we are facing a crushing national debt, the interest payments for which are projected to eclipse our current defense budget by 2019, we cannot afford to overreact to every terrorist threat and to intervene in every conflict.

The course to maintaining American power in the twenty-first century begins with *conserving* our resources. And this must be as true of our counterterrorism and military efforts as it is of any other segment of the federal budget.

Acknowledgments

At the inception of this project, I did not intend it to be a book. I initially had the more modest goal of publishing an academic article about al Qaeda's economic strategy; I had in fact submitted a piece on just that topic to a specialized journal. I had been waiting to hear back from that publication for several months and was beginning to lose patience by November 2010, when al Qaeda in the Arabian Peninsula (AQAP) released a special issue of its English-language online magazine, *Inspire*, that was dedicated to its recent ink-cartridge bomb plot. That issue, focused as it was on the disparity between what the plot cost AQAP and what it cost Western countries to defend themselves, strongly verified my conclusions about the direction that al Qaeda's strategy was taking.

Rather than continuing to wait on the academic journal that was sitting on my article, I decided to adapt my basic argument about al Qaeda's economic strategy for publication in *Foreign Policy*. The first person I would like to thank is Blake Hounshell, my editor at *Foreign Policy* and an incisive analyst, who decided to publish that piece.

It immediately generated a great deal of public discussion; among other things, it caught the attention of my editor at John Wiley & Sons, Stephen Power. Stephen reached out to my agent, Gary Morris, to see if I might be interested in adapting the *Foreign Policy* article into a book, and it didn't take me long to say yes. If Stephen hadn't approached me, this book project would never have begun. I thus owe an enormous debt of gratitude to Stephen and Gary, both of whom have shown great dedication to this project throughout.

This book was by no means a solo effort. Tara Vassefi has worked as my researcher since January 2010. Her competence, loyalty, and raw enthusiasm for this project has made working with her an enormous joy. These qualities also made her an outstanding manager of the team of interns who assembled some of the raw research materials that I relied on in preparing the manuscript. It is no exaggeration to say that this book couldn't have been completed in such a timely manner without Tara's remarkable efforts and that the book would have been worse without her contributions.

Lauren Mellinger also worked on this book as a full-time researcher, and she did outstanding work.

Unfortunately, as is the case for many think tanks in Washington, D.C., our interns have been unpaid. This is a reflection of the U.S. economy rather than of the interns' actual value. The members of our intern class who worked on the bulk of this book—Leah Barkoukis, Swarup Das, and Nathaniel Thomas—have my gratitude for their contributions. I would also like to acknowledge the class of interns who followed them—Clava Brodsky, Marielle Costanza, and John Patten— who helped to answer my research queries during the final round of substantive revisions to the manuscript. One of the best researchers I've had the pleasure of knowing, Seungwon Chung (one of my former interns), worked on the chart illustrating the disparity between the economic costs of carrying out terrorist attacks and those imposed on the attacks' victims.

Many people provided invaluable assistance as I undertook the research for this book. Although there are too many to name, I am appreciative of all who allowed me to interview them.

A number of people provided incisive comments as I worked on the manuscript. Three young colleagues in the field—Dan Darling, Brett Wallace, and Aaron Zelin—read the entire book and offered their comments and suggestions. Their feedback was extremely helpful in fine-tuning my argument and in finding particular angles and sources of information that I might otherwise have overlooked. It is a particular honor to have had these three read over the manuscript, because they're all brilliant thinkers. You will hear more about all of them in the future.

I also gave various chapters to colleagues with particular expertise in the subjects I was addressing. I would like to thank everyone who took the time to offer feedback in this manner, including Andrew Exum, Lieutenant Colonel Derek Jones, Jeremy Scahill, Adam White, and several people within government whom I cannot name but whose comments are appreciated nonetheless.

In addition to these readers, I found a number of friends and colleagues who were willing to read various chapters as I wrote them, checking for clarity, strength of argument, and the like. My sincere thanks to Caitlin Fitz Gerald, Andrew Lebovich, and Lauren Morgan for doing me this favor. I'm certain that I've neglected to name at least one person who read parts of the book for me. If you're the one I forgot, please accept my apologies—and let me know, so I can give you proper thanks in the paperback edition.

I was blessed to receive blurbs from a number of colleagues from diverse backgrounds, including those with serious experience in law enforcement, intelligence, diplomacy, academia, and journalism. I have the utmost respect for these colleagues who were kind enough to provide endorsements for this book, and I am honored that their names are also associated with this project.

I wrote this book while working at the Foundation for Defense of Democracies. Even a casual reading of this volume will reveal my heterodoxy as a thinker. I know that the organization hasn't always agreed with my public positions, but I would like to thank its leadership—in particular, Clifford D. May, Mark Dubowitz, and Jonathan Schanzer—for their leniency and good humor and for allowing me the intellectual freedom that is necessary to produce scholarship of genuine value.

Finally, I would like to thank my beautiful and brilliant wife, Amy Powell. She was supportive throughout the period in which I worked on the book, as she always has been with my professional work. This volume was an all-consuming effort, leaving me with too little time for Amy and often putting me in a rather agitated mood. Amy: I owe you another vacation, to make up for the one that this book (and I) managed to disrupt.

The academic journal to which I submitted the article that comprises the core of my argument about al Qaeda's economic strategy still hasn't responded to my submission. I assume that with the publication of this volume, it has become a moot point.

Notes

1. Bin Laden Is Dead; His Strategy Lives

The chapter epigraph is from Fareed Zakaria, "Al Qaeda Is Over," CNN, May 2, 2011.

1. From the full text of President Obama's speech on bin Laden's death, CBS News, May 2, 2011.
2. Jeff Martin, "Revelers Celebrate Osama bin Laden's Death outside White House," *DCist*, May 2, 2011.
3. Mohammed al Shafey, "Asharq Al Awsat Talks to CNN's Peter Bergen," *Asharq Al Awsat* (London), Aug. 13, 2010. In the interview, Peter Bergen remarks, "Bin Laden is a very effective leader. When people talk about him they say they love him. They say they love bin Laden; they don't say that they love Ayman al Zawahiri."
4. Lolita C. Baldor et al., "Source: Bin Laden Directing al Qaeda Figures," Associated Press, May 6, 2011.
5. Yahya Ibrahim, "$4,200," *Inspire*, Nov. 2010, p. 15.
6. Adam Goldman and Adam Schreck, "Bomb Plot Just Narrowly Averted, Officials Say," Associated Press, Oct. 31, 2010.
7. Quoted in George E. Condon Jr., "Hunt Is On for Bomb Maker," *National Journal*, Oct. 31, 2010.
8. Duncan Gardham, "Parcel Bomb Set to Go Off over the U.S., Police Say," *Telegraph* (London), Nov. 10, 2010.
9. Goldman and Schreck, "Bomb Plot Just Narrowly Averted."
10. "Details of Terror Plot Emerge," ABC News, Aug. 10, 2006.

11. Quoted in "Plot Would Have Killed Thousands," ABC News, Aug. 6, 2007.

12. "About Us," Bloggingheads.tv.

13. David Ignatius, "How the CIA Can Improve Its Operations in Afghanistan," *Washington Post*, Jan. 10, 2010.

14. Robert Baer, "The Khost CIA Bombing: Assessing the Damage in Afghanistan," *Time*, Jan. 8, 2010.

15. Jarret M. Brachman, *Global Jihadism: Theory and Practice* (London: Routledge, 2009), p. 5. For more on the concept of jihad, see David Cook, *Understanding Jihad* (Berkeley: University of California Press, 2005).

16. "Bin Laden Addresses American People on Causes, Outcome of 11 Sep Attacks," trans. Open Source Center, Al Jazeera, Oct. 29, 2004.

17. Anwar al Awlaki, "A Call to Jihad," video, posted to the Al Qimmah forum website, Mar. 22, 2010.

18. Abu al Fituh al Maghribi, "If I Were bin Laden I Would Have Declared It: The Success of the Strategy," trans. Open Source Center, *Vanguards of Khurasan*, Feb. 11, 2010.

19. Juan Miguel del Cid Gomez, "A Financial Profile of the Terrorism of al Qaeda and Its Affiliates," *Perspectives on Terrorism* (2010); Greg Bruno, "Al Qaeda's Financial Pressures," Council on Foreign Relations, Feb. 1, 2010; Nathan Vardi, "Is al Qaeda Bankrupt?" *Forbes*, Mar. 1, 2010.

20. Johanna Neuman, "It's Just Hip When a Congressman Is Asked to Strip," *Los Angeles Times*, Jan. 11, 2002.

21. "Bush Notes Progress in War on Terrorism," *Los Angeles Times*, Nov. 17, 2002.

22. *9/11 Commission Report: Final Report of the National Commission on Terrorist Attacks upon the United States* (New York: W. W. Norton, 2004), pp. 365–66.

23. Amy Belasco, *The Cost of Iraq, Afghanistan, and Other Global War on Terror Operations Since 9/11* (Washington, DC: Congressional Research Service, 2011).

24. Joseph E. Stiglitz and Linda J. Bilmes, *The Three Trillion Dollar War: The True Cost of the Iraq Conflict* (New York: W. W. Norton, 2008); Joseph E. Stiglitz and Linda J. Bilmes, "The True Cost of the Iraq War: $3 Trillion and Beyond," *Washington Post*, Sept. 5, 2010. Their argument is discussed further in chapter 6.

2. How to Beat a Superpower

The chapter epigraph is from Sun Tzu, *The Art of War*, trans. Thomas Cleary (Boston: Shambhala, 1988).

1. Peter Bergen, *The Osama bin Laden I Know: An Oral History of al Qaeda's Leader* (New York: Free Press, 2006), p. 14.

2. For an excellent discussion of what is known about Soviet thinking on the invasion, see Gregory Feifer, *The Great Gamble: The Soviet War in Afghanistan* (New York: Harper Perennial, 2009), pp. 9–54.

3. Seth G. Jones, *In the Graveyard of Empires: America's War in Afghanistan* (New York: W. W. Norton, 2010), p. 18.

4. Bruce Riedel, *The Search for al Qaeda: Its Leadership, Ideology, and Future* (Washington, DC: Brookings Institution Press, 2008), p. 42.

5. Peter L. Bergen, *The Longest War: The Enduring Conflict between America and al Qaeda* (New York: Free Press, 2011), p. 13.

6. Ibid., p. 14.

7. Steve Coll, *Ghost Wars: The Secret History of the CIA, Afghanistan, and bin Laden, from the Soviet Invasion to September 10, 2001* (New York: Penguin Books, 2004), p. 163.

8. "Bin Laden Addresses American People on Causes, Outcome of 11 Sep Attacks," trans. Open Source Center, Al Jazeera, Oct. 29, 2004.

9. Yegor Gaidar, "The Soviet Collapse: Grain and Oil," American Enterprise Institute, Apr. 19, 2007, www.aei.org/issue/25991.

10. Douglas B. Reynolds and Marek Kolodzeij, "Former Soviet Union Oil Production and GDP Decline: Granger Causality and the Multi-Cycle Hubbert Curve," in *Victory: The Reagan Administration's Secret Strategy That Hastened the Collapse of the Soviet Union*, ed. Peter Schweizer (New York: Atlantic Monthly Press, 1994).

11. Gaidar, "The Soviet Collapse."

12. Ibid.

13. Rafael Reuveny and Aseem Prakash, "The Afghanistan War and the Breakdown of the Soviet Union," *Review of International Studies*, 1999, pp. 693–708.

14. "Bin Ladin Addresses American People."

15. Osama bin Laden, "The Solution," trans. Nine Eleven Finding Answers (NEFA) Foundation, video, Sept. 7, 2007, www.nefafoundation.org/file/FeaturedDocs/2007_09_08_UBL.pdf.

16. "Egyptian Prime Minister on Middle East and Afghanistan," BBC Summary of World Broadcasts, Jan. 5, 1980.

17. James Dorsey, "Islamic Nations Fire Broadsides at Soviet Military Interventions," *Christian Science Monitor*, Jan. 30, 1980.

18. Mohammed M. Hafez, "Jihad after Iraq: Lessons from the Arab Afghans Phenomenon," *CTC Sentinel* (Combating Terrorism Center at West Point), Mar. 2008.

19. *9/11 Commission Report: Final Report of the National Commission on Terrorist Attacks upon the United States* (New York: W. W. Norton, 2004), p. 55.

20. Ayman al Zawahiri to Abu Musab al Zarqawi, July 2005, full text reprinted in "English Translation of Ayman al Zawahiri's Letter to Abu Musab al Zarqawi," *Weekly Standard*, Oct. 12, 2005.

21. Indictment, *United States v. Arnaout*, 02 CR 892 (N.D. Ill., 2002), p. 2.

22. *9/11 Commission Report*, p. 56.

23. Tareekh Osama memorandum, 1988, introduced by prosecution at Benevolence International Foundation trial, Northern District of Illinois, 2002–2003.

24. *9/11 Commission Report*, p. 56.

25. "Interior Organization," Combating Terrorism Center at West Point, Harmony Database, released Feb. 16, 2006.

26. "Employment Contract," Combating Terrorism Center at West Point, Harmony Database, released Feb. 16, 2006.

27. "Camp Acceptance Requirements," Combating Terrorism Center at West Point, Harmony Database, released Mar. 17, 2006.

28. Vahid Brown, "Al Qaeda Central and Local Affiliates," in *Self-Inflicted Wounds: Debates and Divisions within al Qaeda and Its Periphery*, ed. Assaf Moghadam and Brian Fishman (West Point, NY: Combating Terrorism Center, 2010), p. 80; Lawrence Wright, *The Looming Tower: Al Qaeda and the Road to 9/11* (New York: Vintage Books, 2007), pp. 173–75.

29. Bergen, *The Osama bin Laden I Know*, pp. 112–113; Wright, *The Looming Tower*, pp. 176–181.

30. Malik's Muttawa, Book 45, hadith number 45.5.17.

31. On al Qaeda's role in the downing of the American helicopter in Mogadishu, see Evan F. Kohlmann, *Shabaab al-Mujahideen: Migration and Jihad in the Horn of Africa* (New York: NEFA Foundation, 2009), p. 4. The incident itself is famously chronicled in Mark Bowden, *Black Hawk Down: A Story of Modern War* (New York: Grove Press, 2010).

32. Riedel, *The Search for al Qaeda*, p. 56.

33. Quoted in Abdel Bari Atwan, *The Secret History of al Qaeda* (Berkeley: University of California Press, 2006), p. 54.

34. Osama bin Laden, "Declaration of Jihad against the Americans Occupying the Land of the Two Holy Mosques," trans. Open Source Center, Aug. 23, 1996.

35. Michael Scheuer, *Imperial Hubris: Why the West Is Losing the War on Terror* (Washington, DC: Potomac Books, 2004), p. xviii.

36. Rosalind W. Gwynne, "Osama bin Laden, the Qur'an and Jihad," *Religion*, 2006, pp. 61–90. Religious refutations of al Qaeda's theological outlook that have been offered by Muslim scholars are discussed in chapter 11.

37. Bernard Lewis, *The Crisis of Islam: Holy War and Unholy Terror* (New York: Modern Library, 2003), pp. 31–32.

38. For explications of this salafi jihadi narrative, see Brynjar Lia, "Al Qaeda's Appeal: Understanding Its Unique Selling Points," *Perspectives on Terrorism*, 2008; Olivier Roy, *Al Qaeda in the West as a Youth Movement: The Power of a Narrative* (Brighton, UK: MICROCON, 2008).

39. Fawaz A. Gerges, *The Far Enemy: Why Jihad Went Global* (Cambridge: Cambridge University Press, 2009).

40. Thomas Hegghammer, "Jihadi-Salafis or Revolutionaries?" in *Global Salafism: Islam's New Religious Movement*, ed. Roel Meijer (London: Hurst, 2009), p. 256.

41. Historical Studies and Strategic Recommendations Division, "Strategic Study on Global Conflict and the Status of the Jihadist Trend," trans. Open Source Center, July 4, 2009.

42. "Bin Laden: Expel Jews, Christians from Holy Places," trans. Open Source Center, *Jang* (Rawalpindi), Nov. 18, 1998.

43. Abu Shiraz, "May 1998 Interview with Bin Laden Reported," trans. Open Source Center, *Pakistan* (Islamabad), Feb. 20, 1999; "Islamist Site Publishes Bin Laden's 'Letter to the American People,'" trans. Open Source Center, Oct. 26, 2002; "Al Qaeda Commander Calls for Overthrow of Qaddafi and Introduction of Sharia Law," Kavkaz Center (jihadi news agency), Mar. 14, 2011. See also the following Open Source Center translations: "Sirajuddin Haqqani Interview on Jihad in Afghanistan, Palestinian Cause," Apr. 27, 2010; "Islamic Army in Iraq Calls upon Mujahedin to Unite, Abide by Sharia Rules," Apr. 9, 2010; "Jihadist Leader al Qar'awi Interviewed on Jihad in Arabian Peninsula, Levant," Apr. 4, 2010.

44. Mary Habeck, *Knowing the Enemy: Jihadist Ideology and the War on Terror* (New Haven, CT: Yale University Press, 2006), pp. 60–65. For an extended salafi treatise on this point, see Abu Ameenah Bilal Philips, *The Fundamentals of Tawheed (Islamic Monotheism)* (Riyadh, Saudi Arabia: Tawheed, 1990).

45. Peter L. Bergen, *Holy War, Inc: Inside the Secret World of Osama Bin Laden* (New York: Free Press, 2001), p. 13.

46. Physicians for Human Rights, *The Taliban's War on Women: A Health and Human Rights Crisis in Afghanistan* (Boston: Physicians for Human Rights, 1998).

47. Ahmed Rashid, *Taliban* (New Haven: Yale Nota Bene, 2001), pp. 107, 115.

48. Asim Umayra, "The Destruction of the Khilafah: The Mother of All Crimes," talk given at Najah University, Nablus, West Bank, Apr. 15, 2000, quoted in Habeck, *Knowing the Enemy*, p. 8.

49. Bin Laden, "Declaration of Jihad Against the Americans." For other bin Laden references to the need to reestablish the caliphate, see the following

Open Source Center translations: "Pakistan Interviews Osama bin Laden," Mar. 18, 1997; "Daily Prints Osama bin Laden 'Letter' Calling for 'Global Islamic State,'" *Nawa-i-Waqt* (Rawalpindi), Jan. 7, 2001; "Full Text of Interview with al Qaeda Leader Osama bin Laden," Jihad Online News Network, Oct. 21, 2001.

50. Al Qaeda's training manual, exhibit introduced at East African embassy bombings trial, Southern District of New York, Jan.–May 2001, p. 11.

51. Zawahiri to Abu Musab al Zarqawi.

52. Lawrence Wright, "The Master Plan," *New Yorker*, Sept. 11, 2006.

53. Fouad Hussein, *Al Zarqawi: The Second Generation of al Qaeda*, part 15, serialized in *Al Quds Al Arabi* (London), May 30, 2005, trans. Open Source Center.

54. Scheuer, *Imperial Hubris*, p. xi. Scheuer's claim that Saudi ideology "can be met only by annihilating all non-Muslims" is inaccurate, for it ignores the option for non-Muslims who are considered People of the Book (namely, Christians and Jews) to become *dhimmis* (second-class citizens in an Islamic state living under a pact of protection). As *dhimmis*, they would be relatively free to practice their religion but would face a number of limitations, including being forced to pay the *jizya*, a tax that allows them to continue practicing their own faiths. For more on the treatment of the *dhimmis*, see A. S. Tritton, *The Caliphs and Their Non-Muslim Subjects* (Oxford: Oxford University Press, 1930). In the same way, even though bin Laden sees himself locked in an existential conflict with the non-Muslim world, this does not mean that victory for him entails killing all non-Muslims. Some of them could become subjugated *dhimmis* under his new regime.

55. For a sound discussion of Wahhabism, see Hamid Algar, *Wahhabism: A Critical Essay* (Oneonta, NY: Islamic Publications International, 2002).

56. Scheuer, *Imperial Hubris*, p. 7.

57. Sayyid Abul A'la Maududi, *Jihad fi Sabilillah* [Jihad in the cause of Allah] (1939; repr. Birmingham, UK: Islamic Mission Dawah Centre, n.d.), pp. 18–19.

58. *9/11 Commission Report*, p. 259.

59. Bob Woodward, *Bush at War* (New York: Simon and Schuster, 2002), p. 25.

60. Richard Clarke, *Against All Enemies: Inside America's War on Terror* (New York: Free Press, 2004), p. xiii.

61. "Bin Laden Determined to Strike in U.S.," Presidential Daily Brief, Aug. 6, 2001.

62. Robin Wright, "Top Focus before 9/11 Wasn't on Terrorism," *Washington Post*, Apr. 1, 2004.

63. Ivan Arreguín-Toft, "How the Weak Win Wars," *International Security*, Summer 2001, p. 93.

64. Ibid.

3. September 11, 2001

The chapter epigraph is from E. B. White, *Here Is New York* (New York: Little Bookroom, 1949), p. 54.

1. Richard Clarke, *Against All Enemies: Inside America's War on Terror* (New York: Free Press, 2004), p. 17.
2. Ibid., p. 18.
3. The FBI's investigation concluded that U.S. Army biodefense researcher Bruce Ivins—who committed suicide three weeks before the August 18, 2008, announcement—had mailed the anthrax letters. For subsequent work questioning Ivins's culpability, see Noah Shachtman, "Anthrax Redux: Did the Feds Nab the Wrong Guy?" *Wired*, Mar. 24, 2011.
4. U.S. Department of State, "Report of the Accountability Review Boards: Bombings of the U.S. Embassies in Nairobi, Kenya and Dar es Salaam, Tanzania on August 7, 1998," Jan. 1999.
5. U.S. Government Accountability Office, "Embassy Construction: State Has Made Progress Constructing New Embassies, but Better Planning Is Needed for Operations and Maintenance Requirements," June 2006, p. 1.
6. For a contemporaneous report on Abdel Rahman's conviction, see Joseph P. Fried, "Sheikh and Nine Followers Guilty of a Conspiracy of Terrorism," *New York Times*, Oct. 2, 1995.
7. Quoted in Peter L. Bergen, *The Osama bin Laden I Know: An Oral History of al Qaeda's Leader* (New York: Free Press, 2006), pp. 204–205.
8. Ibid., p. 208.
9. Alan Cullison, "Inside al Qaeda's Hard Drive," *Atlantic*, Sept. 2004.
10. Audiencia Nacional, Sala de lo Penal, Sección Tercera, "Sentencia Num. 36/2005," Madrid, Sept. 26, 2005. For discussion of the controversy surrounding this conviction, see Brynjar Lia, *Architect of Global Jihad: The Life of al Qaeda Strategist Abu Musab al Suri* (New York: Columbia University Press, 2008), pp. 193–99.
11. Quoted in Taysir Allouni, "A Discussion on the New Crusader Wars," trans. Open Source Center, Al Jazeera, Oct. 21, 2001.
12. Bruce Riedel, *The Search for al Qaeda: Its Leadership, Ideology and Future* (Washington, DC: Brookings Institution Press, 2008), p. 1.
13. "Bin Laden Addresses American People on Causes, Outcome of 11 Sep Attacks," trans. Open Source Center, Al Jazeera, Oct. 29, 2004.
14. Sun Tzu, *The Art of War*, trans. Thomas Cleary (Boston: Shambhala, 1988), p. 82.
15. Gen. Richard B. Myers, "National Military Strategic Plan for the War on Terrorism," Joint Chiefs of Staff, Feb. 1, 2006, p. 9.
16. Ibid., p. 13.
17. Ibid., p. 4.

18. *The U.S. Army/Marine Corps Counterinsurgency Field Manual* (Chicago: University of Chicago Press, 2007), p. 382.

19. "National Strategy for Combating Terrorism," National Security Council, Sept. 2006, p. 5.

20. *9/11 Commission Report: Final Report of the National Commission on Terrorist Attacks upon the United States* (New York: W. W. Norton, 2004), p. 50.

21. David Kaplan, "Mission Impossible: The Inside Story of How a Band of Reformers Tried—and Failed—to Change America's Spy Agencies," *U.S. News & World Report*, July 25, 2004.

22. Charlie Allen, interview with author, Washington, DC, Apr. 12, 2011.

23. Brian Michael Jenkins, interview with author by phone, Apr. 29, 2011.

24. *Bush v. Gore*, 531 U.S. 1046 (2000). A number of books have analyzed the legal dimensions of that Supreme Court decision. A particularly good contribution is Abner Greene, *Understanding the 2000 Election: A Guide to the Legal Battles That Decided the Presidency* (New York: New York University Press, 2001).

25. Steven Thomma and Ron Hutcheson, "As Going Gets Tough, Bush Is Able to Rise to Challenge," *Miami Herald*, Aug. 5, 2001.

26. ABC News/*Washington Post* Poll, "Backing for War on Terrorism," Sept. 20, 2001.

27. Michael S. James, "Terror, Iraq Could Jolt Bush-Kerry Race," ABC News, Mar. 5, 2004.

28. Tom Infield, "Attack Reverberates around the Nation," *Philadelphia Inquirer*, Sept. 12, 2001.

29. Alison Mitchell and Richard L. Berke, "Differences Are Put Aside as Lawmakers Reconvene," *New York Times*, Sept. 13, 2001.

30. Quoted in R. W. Apple Jr., "No Middle Ground," *New York Times*, Sept. 14, 2001.

31. Paul Pierson, *Politics in Time: History, Institutions, and Social Analysis* (Princeton, NJ: Princeton University Press, 2004), p. 10.

32. W. Brian Arthur, *Increasing Returns and Path Dependence in the Economy* (Ann Arbor: University of Michigan Press, 1994).

4. Our Politicized Fight against Terrorism

The chapter epigraph is quoted in Marc Santora, "Giuliani Broadens His Message on Terrorism," *New York Times*, Apr. 26, 2007.

1. *9/11 Commission Report: Final Report of the National Commission on Terrorist Attacks upon the United States* (New York: W. W. Norton, 2004), p. 38.

2. Tim Padgett, "The Interrupted Reading: The Kids with George W. Bush on 9/11," *Time*, May 3, 2011.

3. *9/11 Commission Report*, p. 38.
4. David Kohn, "The President's Story," *60 Minutes*, CBS, Sept. 10, 2003.
5. Ibid.
6. George W. Bush, Address to the Nation, Sept. 11, 2001.
7. Daniel Johnson, "War to the Death between America and Islamic Terrorists," *Daily Telegraph* (London), Sept. 12, 2001.
8. Elisabeth Bumiller and Frank Bruni, "In This Crisis, Bush Is Writing His Own Script," *New York Times*, Sept. 19, 2001.
9. Eric Pooley, "Mayor of the World," *Time*, Dec. 31, 2001.
10. Ibid.
11. Fred Siegel, *The Prince of the City: Giuliani, New York and the Genius of American Life* (New York: Encounter Books, 2007), p. x.
12. Michael R. Blood, "Rudy Shines under Pressure," *New York Daily News*, Sept. 14, 2001.
13. Joyce Purnick, "In a Crisis, the Giuliani We Wanted," *New York Times*, Sept. 13, 2001.
14. Chris Cillizza, "*Post*-ABC Poll: Clinton, Giuliani Lead Primary Fields," *Washington Post*, Jan. 20, 2007.
15. Frank Newport and Jeffrey M. Jones, "Giuliani, McCain Have Competing Strengths in Republicans' Eyes," Gallup, Feb. 1, 2007.
16. "From America's Mayor to America's President?," *Economist* (London), May 3, 2007.
17. Frank Newport, "The Best and Worst Aspects of a Possible Giuliani Presidency," Gallup, Aug. 3, 2007.
18. Michael Crowley, "The Indecider," *New York*, Oct. 25, 2009.
19. Donald Lambro, "A Sluggish Economy and Next Year's Vote," *Washington Times*, July 16, 2001.
20. Richard L. Berke, "After Shift in Senate, Some in G.O.P. Are Fearing Wider Impact in 2002," *New York Times*, June 8, 2001.
21. Jeffrey M. Jones, "Issues in the 2002 Election: Terrorism," Gallup, Aug. 13, 2002.
22. James Carney, "General Karl Rove, Reporting for Duty," *Time*, Sept. 29, 2002.
23. Ibid.
24. Major Garrett, "Daschle Blasts Bush for Politicizing National Security," Fox News, Sept. 26, 2002.
25. Howard Fineman, "How Bush Did It," *Newsweek*, Nov. 18, 2002.
26. R. W. Apple Jr., "Victory, and Challenges," *New York Times*, Nov. 7, 2002.
27. Quoted in "Bush Wins Big," *Independent* (London), Nov, 7, 2002.
28. Fineman, "How Bush Did It."

29. Charles Krauthammer, "Election 2002: It's the Terrorism, Stupid," *Time*, Nov. 18, 2002.

30. Quoted in Sean Loughlin, "Bush Presidency Defined by Terrorist Attacks," CNN, Aug. 30, 2004.

31. "Remarks by Former Mayor Rudolph Giuliani," transcript, *New York Times*, Aug. 30, 2004.

32. "Full Text: Arnold Schwarzenegger's Speech," transcript, BBC, Sept. 1, 2004.

33. At the 1988 Republican National Convention, Schwarzenegger told the crowd, "When it comes to the American future, [Democratic nominee] Michael Dukakis will be the real Terminator!" And on the set of the 1994 film *True Lies*, Schwarzenegger told his co-star Tom Arnold, "Listen, buddy, I only played the Terminator, but you married one." This was a reference to Arnold's ex-wife Roseanne Barr.

34. David M. Halbfinger and David E. Sanger, "Bush and Kerry Clash Over Iraq and a Timetable," *New York Times*, Sept. 7, 2004.

35. "Text of Bush-Kerry Debate," transcript, CBS, Sept. 30, 2004.

36. Joseph Curl, "Bush Derides Kerry Stance on Defense," *Washington Times*, Oct. 3, 2004.

37. "Transcript: First Presidential Debate," *Washington Post*, Sept. 30, 2004.

38. "Transcript: Vice Presidential Debate," *Washington Post*, Oct. 5, 2004.

39. Michael Moore, "Heads Up . . . from Michael Moore," *MichaelMoore .com*, Apr. 14, 2004, http://www.michaelmoore.com/words/mikes-letter/ heads-up-from-michael-moore.

40. Quoted in Elisabeth Bumiller and David M. Halbfinger, "Bush and Kerry Follow Debate with Sharp Jabs," *New York Times*, Oct. 2, 2004.

41. "Bin Laden Addresses American People on Causes, Outcome of 11 Sep Attacks," trans. Open Source Center, Al Jazeera, Oct. 29, 2004.

42. For a competent debunking of the idea that bin Laden was on dialysis, written several years before the al Qaeda leader's death, see Richard Miniter, *Disinformation: 22 Media Myths That Undermine the War on Terror* (Washington, DC: Regnery Publishing, 2005), pp. 33–38.

43. Ellen Knickmeyer and K. I. Ibrahim, "Bombing Shatters Mosque in Iraq," *Washington Post*, Feb. 23, 2006.

44. Thomas E. Ricks, *The Gamble: General David Petraeus and the American Military Adventure in Iraq, 2006–2008* (New York: Penguin Press, 2009), p. 33.

45. Quoted in Vali Nasr, *The Shia Revival: How Conflicts within Islam Will Shape the Future* (New York: W. W. Norton, 2007), p. 205.

46. Ricks, *The Gamble*, p. 36.

47. Colonel Peter Devlin, "State of the Insurgency in al Anbar," intelligence assessment, Aug 17, 2006, p. 2.

48. Mike Glover, "Bayh Urges Democrats to Focus on Terrorism," Associated Press, Feb. 12, 2006.

49. "Democrats Will Use Anniversaries of 9/11, Katrina, to Hammer GOP," *White House Bulletin*, Aug. 18, 2006.

50. Jennifer Medina, "Democrats Counter G.O.P. and Lieberman on Iraq," *New York Times*, Aug. 17, 2006.

51. Greg Smith et al., "Religious Groups React to the 2006 Election," Pew Research Center, Nov. 27, 2006.

52. Gary Langer, "Midterm Election: Referendum on War," ABC News, Oct. 23, 2006.

53. "The House Debate: A Sampling," *New York Times*, Feb. 16, 2007.

54. "Post-Presidential Address Commentary for Jan. 10," *Hardball with Chris Mathews*, MSNBC, transcript text updated Jan. 24, 2007. Despite the fact that Senator Obama argued that increasing U.S. troop levels would increase violence, he later falsely denied having said this. In the January 2008 debate of Democratic presidential candidates in New Hampshire, he said, "Now, I had no doubt—and I said at the time, when I opposed the surge—that given how wonderfully our troops perform, if we place 30,000 more troops in there, then we would see an improvement in the security situation and we would see a reduction in the violence." "The Democratic Debate in New Hampshire," transcript, *New York Times*, Jan. 5, 2008. He clearly and unequivocally said the opposite after the surge announcement. By mid-2008, Obama's campaign would delete his criticisms of the surge from its website. James Gordon Meek, "Barack Obama Purges Web Site Critique of Surge in Iraq," *New York Daily News*, July 14, 2008.

55. "Obama Talks War on Terror, Iran and Pakistan in First-Ever Interview with Bill O'Reilly," transcript, Fox News, Sept. 5, 2008.

56. Sheryl Gay Stolberg, "Bush's Strategy for Iraq Risks Confrontations," *New York Times*, Jan. 11, 2007.

57. Ari Shapiro, "Obama Tries to Shift Perceptions of Terrorism Policy," *Morning Edition*, National Public Radio, Jan. 7, 2010.

58. The most comprehensive treatment in this regard is Marc Lynch, *Rhetoric and Reality: Countering Terrorism in the Age of Obama* (Washington, DC: Center for a New American Security, June 2010).

59. Alex Leary, "Voters' No. 1 Issue? Not War," *St. Petersburg Times*, July 5, 2010.

60. Gary Langer, "Exit Polls: Economy, Voter Anger Drive Republican Victory," ABC News, Nov. 2, 2010.

5. Our Inefficient Fight against Terrorism

The chapter epigraph is from Clark Kent Ervin, *Open Target: Where America Is Vulnerable to Attack* (New York: Palgrave Macmillan, 2006), p. xi.

1. Fouad Hussein, *Al Zarqawi: The Second Generation of al Qaeda*, part 15 (serialized in *Al Quds Al Arabi*, published May 30, 2005), trans. Open Source Center.

2. Jarret M. Brachman and William F. McCants, *Stealing al Qaeda's Playbook* (West Point, NY: Combating Terrorism Center, 2006), p. 6.

3. Abu Bakr Naji, *The Management of Savagery: The Most Critical Stage through Which the Umma Will Pass*, trans. William McCants (West Point, NY: Combating Terrorism Center, , 2006), p. 19.

4. See the following Open Source Center translations: "Jihadist Forum Participant Describes 'Benefits of Targeting Embassies,'" Apr. 5, 2010; "Jihadist Leader al-Qar'awi Interviewed on Jihad in Arabian Peninsula, Levant," Apr. 4, 2010; "Jihadist Shaykh Writes Book Urging Muslims to Follow Jihad Path, Argues United States Weak," Mar. 26, 2010.

5. Brian Knowlton, "President Pledges 'Unprecedented' Spending on U.S. Security," *International Herald Tribune*, July 21, 2005.

6. James Gordon Meek and Greg Gittrich, "Al Qaeda Plot Targets Us," *New York Daily News*, Aug. 2, 2004.

7. Quoted in Peter L. Bergen, *The Longest War: The Enduring Conflict between America and al Qaeda* (New York: Free Press, 2011), p. 129.

8. Jamie Wilson and Richard Norton-Taylor, "New York on High Alert as Foiled Plots Revealed," *Guardian* (Manchester), Oct. 8, 2005.

9. Shannon Troetel, "NYPD Scaling Back Subway Security," CNN, Oct. 10, 2005.

10. Shawn McCarthy, "Subway Security Beefed Up after Mayor Issues Warning," *Globe and Mail* (Toronto), Oct. 7, 2005.

11. "Baltimore Tunnel Reopens after Threat," CNN, Oct. 19, 2005.

12. Ervin, *Open Target*, p. 35.

13. Michael Scherer, "Not Mild-Mannered Enough," *Mother Jones*, Mar./Apr. 2005.

14. Ervin, *Open Target*, p. 39.

15. Ibid., p. 191.

16. Brian Friel, "Security Sweep," *Government Executive*, Mar. 15, 2003.

17. Ervin, *Open Target*, p. 197.

18. Scott Higham and Robert O'Harrow Jr., "The High Cost of a Rush to Security," *Washington Post*, June 30, 2005.

19. U.S. Department of Homeland Security, Office of Inspector General, "Evaluation of TSA's Contract for the Installation and Maintenance of Explosive Detection Equipment at United States Airports," OIG-04–44,

Sept. 2004; Scott Higham and Robert O'Harrow Jr., "Contractor Accused of Overbilling U.S.," *Washington Post*, Oct. 23, 2005.

20. Martin Edwin Andersen and Jeremy Torobin, "Cash-Strapped TSA Spent $200K on Awards Ceremony," *Congressional Quarterly*, Feb. 11, 2004.

21. Senator Susan Collins, "Senator Collins Voices Concern about New Report Faulting TSA for Lax Oversight of Supporting Contracts," press release, Apr. 16, 2010.

22. U.S. Department of Homeland Security, Office of Inspector General, "Semiannual Report to the Congress: October 1, 2003–March 31, 2004," Apr. 30, 2004, p. 43.

23. U.S. Department of Homeland Security, Office of Inspector General, "Semiannual Report to the Congress: October 1, 2004–March 31, 2005," May 1, 2005, p. 21.

24. Ervin, *Open Target*, p. 206.

25. Dana Priest and William M. Arkin, "A Hidden World, Growing beyond Control," *Washington Post*, July 19, 2010.

26. Ibid.

27. Senior U.S. intelligence analyst, interview with author, Washington, DC, Feb. 10, 2011.

28. Quoted in Priest and Arkin, "A Hidden World."

29. Ibid.

30. Ibid.

31. Dan Eggen et al., "Plane Suspect Was Listed in Terror Database after Father Alerted U.S. Officials," *Washington Post*, Dec. 27, 2009.

32. Priest and Arkin, "A Hidden World."

33. Charlie Allen, interview with author, Washington, DC, Apr. 12, 2011.

34. Ronald Sanders, "Results of the Fiscal Year 2007 U.S. Intelligence Community Inventory of Core Contractor Personnel," transcript of Bush administration conference call, Aug. 27, 2008.

35. Dana Priest and William M. Arkin, "National Security Inc.," *Washington Post*, July 20, 2010.

36. Senators Joseph Lieberman and Susan Collins, "Senators Lieberman, Collins Astounded DHS Contract Workers Exceed Number of Civilian Employees," press release, Feb. 24, 2010; Jeanne Merserve, "Contractors Outnumber Full-Time Workers at DHS; Lawmakers 'Astounded,'" CNN, Feb. 24, 2010.

37. Priest and Arkin, "National Security Inc."

38. U.S. Senate Select Committee on Intelligence, "Intelligence Authorization Act for Fiscal Year 2008," Report 110–75, May 31, 2007.

39. Priest and Arkin, "National Security Inc."

40. Ibid.

41. Amanda Ripley, "The 'New' Homeland Security Math," *Time*, Sept. 24, 2007.

42. Representatives Anthony D. Weiner and Jeff Flake, "Security or Pork?: A Review of National Homeland Security Funding Boondoggles," Mar. 1, 2007.

43. Editorial, "Security? Or Boondoggle?" *Charleston Gazette* (WV), July 22, 2005.

44. Bob Kelley, "Osama Could Turn Up Anywhere," *Charleston Gazette* (WV), Oct. 15, 2005.

45. Charles Savage, "South Florida Unprepared to Seek Homeland Security Funds," *Miami Herald*, July 12, 2003.

46. Shawn Reese, "Distribution of Homeland Security Grants in FY2007 and P.L. 110–53, Implementing Recommendations of the 9/11 Commission Act," Congressional Research Service Report for Congress, Jan. 28, 2008.

47. Mike German, "Racial Profiling No Tool in Thwarting Terrorism," *San Francisco Chronicle*, Oct. 7, 2005.

48. Erroll Southers, interview with author, Los Angeles, Jan. 28, 2011.

49. Catherine Saillant, "Traveler Who Resisted TSA Pat-Down Is Glad His Moment of Fame Is Nearly Over," *Los Angeles Times*, Nov. 19, 2010.

50. Sharyn Alfonsi and Jennifer Metz, "National Opt-Out Day a Bust," ABC News, Nov. 24, 2010.

51. Quoted in Ray Henry, "TSA Chief Warns against Boycott of Airport Scans," Associated Press, Nov. 22, 2010.

52. Alfonsi and Metz, "National Opt-Out Day a Bust."

53. Southers, interview.

54. U.S. Travel Association, "A Better Way: Building a World-Class System for Aviation Security," Mar. 2011.

55. Malcolm Gladwell, "Safety in the Skies," *New Yorker*, Oct. 1, 2001.

56. Michael Totten, "Forget the 'Porn Machines,'" *New York Post*, Nov. 18, 2010.

57. Emily Berman, *Domestic Intelligence: New Powers, New Risks* (New York: Brennan Center for Justice, 2011), p. 45.

58. Ibid., p. 34.

59. Ibid., p. 32.

6. The Consequences of the Invasion of Iraq

The chapter epigraph is from T. E. Lawrence, "A Report on Mesopotamia," *Sunday Times* (London), Aug. 2, 1920.

1. Quoted in Thomas E. Ricks, *Fiasco: The American Military Adventure in Iraq* (New York: Penguin Books, 2006), p. 25.

2. Elaine Sciolino, "Bush's Foreign Policy Tutor: An Academic in the Public Eye," *New York Times*, June 16, 2000.

3. Michael R. Gordon, "Bush Would Stop U.S. Peacekeeping in Balkan Fight," *New York Times*, Oct. 21, 2000.

4. "George W. Bush Holds Campaign Rally in Grand Rapids, Michigan," transcript, CNN, Nov. 3, 2000, http://transcripts.cnn.com/TRANSCRIPTS/0011/03/se.04.html.

5. Colin L. Powell, testimony to the Committee on Foreign Relations, U.S. Senate, Feb. 5, 2002.

6. Quoted in Eric Schmitt and Steven Lee Myers, "Bush Administration Warns Iraq on Weapons Programs," *New York Times*, Jan. 23, 2001.

7. Jane Perlez, "Capitol Hawks Seek Tougher Line on Iraq," *New York Times*, Mar. 7, 2001.

8. Alan Sipress, "Powell Defends Stand on Iraq," *Washington Post*, Mar. 8, 2001.

9. Jim Hoagland, "While Bush Debates, Saddam Threatens," *Washington Post*, May 3, 2001.

10. Quoted in Ricks, *Fiasco*, p. 28.

11. The evidence of this early focus on Iraq is taken from Peter L. Bergen, *The Longest War: The Enduring Conflict between America and al Qaeda* (New York: Free Press, 2011), pp. 52–53.

12. Bruce Riedel, *The Search for al Qaeda: Its Leadership, Ideology, and Future* (Washington, DC: Brookings Institution Press, 2008), p. 10.

13. Alan Cullison, "Inside al Qaeda's Hard Drive," *Atlantic*, Sept. 2004.

14. Gary C. Schroen, *First In: An Insider's Account of How the CIA Spearheaded the War on Terror in Afghanistan* (New York: Ballantine Books, 2005), p. xii.

15. Bergen, *The Longest War*, p. 85.

16. David Rohde and David E. Sanger, "How a 'Good War' in Afghanistan Went Bad," *New York Times*, Aug. 12, 2007.

17. Paul Wolfowitz, testimony to the Defense Subcommittee of the House Appropriations Committee, Mar. 27, 2003.

18. Ricks, *Fiasco*, p. 100.

19. "Interview with Ricardo Sanchez," *CNN Late Edition with Wolf Blitzer*, July 27, 2003.

20. "Bush Takes Heat for WMD Jokes," CNN, May 3, 2004.

21. George W. Bush, State of the Union Address, Jan. 29, 2003.

22. Eric Schmitt, "Rumsfeld Says U.S. Has 'Bulletproof' Evidence of Iraq's Links to al Qaeda," *New York Times*, Sept. 28, 2002.

23. For the remarkable story of how Libyan protesters used dating websites as an organizing tool, see Jeffrey Kofman and Ki Mae Heussner, "Libya's 'Love Revolution': Muslim Dating Site Seeds Protest," *ABC News*, Feb. 24, 2011.

24. Senior American intelligence analyst, e-mail to author, Apr. 13, 2011.

25. "Remarks by the Vice President at the Air National Guard Senior Leadership Conference," Federal Document Clearing House, Dec. 2, 2002.

26. Kenneth M. Pollack, "Next Stop Baghdad?" *Foreign Affairs*, Mar./Apr. 2002.

27. Quoted in Rohde and Sanger, "How a 'Good War' in Afghanistan Went Bad."

28. Ibid.

29. Barton Gellman and Dafna Linzer, "Afghanistan, Iraq: Two Wars Collide," *Washington Post*, Oct. 22, 2004.

30. Vanda Felbab-Brown, "The Drug-Conflict Nexus in South Asia: Beyond Taliban Profits and Afghanistan," in *The Afghanistan-Pakistan Theater: Militant Islam, Security and Stability*, ed. Daveed Gartenstein-Ross and Clifford D. May (Washington DC: Foundation for the Defense of Democracies Press, 2010), p. 90; "Addiction, Crime and Insurgency: The Transnational Threat of Afghan Opium," United Nations Office on Drugs and Crime, Oct. 2009.

31. James Fallows, "Bush's Lost Year," *Atlantic*, Oct. 2004.

32. Andrew Exum, interview with author, Washington, DC, Feb. 9, 2011.

33. "Millions Join Global Anti-War Protests," BBC News, Feb. 17, 2003.

34. "Outrage at 'Old Europe' Remarks," BBC News, Jan. 23, 2003.

35. Frederic Wehrey et al., *The Iraq Effect: The Middle East after the Iraq War* (Washington, DC: RAND, 2010), p. xiii.

36. Noah Schactman, "The Baghdad Bomb Squad," *Wired*, Nov. 2005.

37. Patrick Henson, interview with author, Baghdad, May 2007.

38. Kelly McEvers, "Iran Asserts 'Soft Power' Influence in Iraq," *Morning Edition*, National Public Radio, Aug. 3, 2010.

39. Michael Eisenstadt, "Iran and Iraq," in *The Iran Primer: Power, Politics, and U.S. Policy*, ed. Robin Wright (Washington, DC: U.S. Institute of Peace, 2010).

40. Mohsen M. Milani, "Meet Me in Baghdad," *Foreign Affairs*, Sept. 2010.

41. Quoted in Taysir Allouni, "A Discussion on the New Crusader Wars," trans. Open Source Center, Al Jazeera, Oct. 21, 2001.

42. Neil MacFarquhar, "For Arabs, New Jihad Is in Iraq," *New York Times*, Apr. 2, 2003.

43. "Syria Mufti Calls for Suicide Operations," United Press International, Mar. 27, 2003.

44. Emily Wax and Alia Ibrahim, "TV Images Stir Anger, Shock and Warnings of Backlash," *Washington Post*, Apr. 10, 2003.

45. Quoted in Dana Priest and Josh White, "War Helps Recruit Terrorists, Hill Told," *Washington Post*, Feb. 17, 2005.

46. National Intelligence Council, "Trends in Global Terrorism: Implications for the United States," National Intelligence Estimate, Apr. 2006, p. 2.

47. Peter Bergen and Paul Cruickshank, "The Iraq Effect: War Has Increased Terrorism Sevenfold Worldwide," *Mother Jones*, Mar./Apr. 2007.

48. Ricks, *Fiasco*, p. 3.

49. Amy Belasco, "The Cost of Iraq, Afghanistan, and Other Global War on Terror Operations Since 9/11," Congressional Research Service report, Sept. 2, 2010.

50. Joseph E. Stiglitz and Linda J. Bilmes, *The Three Trillion Dollar War: The True Cost of the Iraq Conflict* (New York: W. W. Norton, 2008).

51. Joseph E. Stiglitz and Linda J. Bilmes, "The True Cost of the Iraq War: $3 Trillion and Beyond," *Washington Post*, Sept. 5, 2010.

52. "Bin Laden Addresses American People on Causes, Outcome of 11 Sep Attacks," trans. Open Source Center, Al Jazeera, Oct. 29, 2004.

7. One Step Forward

The chapter epigraph is from Joseph R. Biden Jr., opening statement in the Senate Foreign Relations Committee, "Hearings on Iraq: The Administration's Plan," Jan. 11, 2007.

1. Ahmed S. Hashim, *Insurgency and Counter-Insurgency in Iraq* (Ithaca, NY: Cornell University Press, 2006), p. xv. A number of books chronicle the beginning of the American invasion, including Bing West and Ray L. Smith, *The March Up: Taking Baghdad with the 1st Marine Division* (New York: Bantam Books, 2003); Evan Wright, *Generation Kill: Devil Dogs, Iceman, Captain America, and the New Face of American War* (New York: Berkley Caliber, 2004); Karl Zinsmeister, *Boots on the Ground: A Month with the 82nd Airborne in the Battle for Iraq* (New York: St. Martin's, 2004).

2. Judy Keen, "Bush to Troops: Mission Accomplished," *USA Today*, June 5, 2003.

3. Quoted in Thomas E. Ricks, *Fiasco: The American Military Adventure in Iraq* (New York: Penguin Books, 2006), p. 136.

4. Ed McCarthy, interview with author, Temple, TX, Mar. 13, 2011.

5. Mark Fineman et al., "Preparing for War, Stumbling to Peace," *Los Angeles Times*, July 18, 2003.

6. Ricks, *Fiasco*, pp. 109–10.

7. Ellen Knickmeyer and K.I. Ibrahim, "Bombing Shatters Mosque in Iraq," *Washington Post*, Feb. 23, 2006.

8. "Holy Shia Shrine Bombed in Samarra," *Iraq the Model*, Feb. 22, 2006.

9. "Sectarian Violence Stalks Iraq on Holy Day," CNN, Feb. 23, 2006.

10. Alex Morales and Caroline Alexander, "Iraq Violence Kills 379 Since Samarra Mosque Bombing," Bloomberg, Feb. 28, 2006.

11. Colonel Peter Devlin, "State of the Insurgency in al Anbar," intelligence assessment, Aug. 17, 2006, p. 2.

12. Peter L. Bergen, *The Longest War: The Enduring Conflict between America and al Qaeda* (New York: Free Press, 2011), p. 271.

13. James A. Baker III and Lee H. Hamilton (cochairmen), *The Iraq Study Group Report* (New York: Vintage Books, 2006).

14. Bergen, *The Longest War*, p. 282.

15. Andrea Seabrook and Madeleine Brand, "House Passes Resolution against Troop Increase," *Day to Day*, National Public Radio, Feb. 16, 2007. Seabrook and Brand note seventeen House Republicans who voted for the resolution condemning President Bush's troop surge.

16. Dana Blanton, "Fox News Poll: Most Think Troop Surge Is Bush's Last Chance in Iraq," Fox News, Jan. 18, 2007.

17. Steven Metz, e-mail to author, June 3, 2011.

18. Jonathan Karl, "Troop Surge Already Under Way," ABC News, Jan. 10, 2007.

19. Vincent Passero, interview with author, Washington, DC, Mar. 19, 2011.

20. Thomas E. Ricks, *The Gamble: General David Petraeus and the American Military Adventure in Iraq, 2006–2008* (New York: Penguin Press, 2009), p. 168.

21. Passero, interview.

22. Niel Smith and Sean MacFarland, "Anbar Awakens: The Tipping Point," *Military Review*, Mar./Apr. 2008.

23. Gary W. Montgomery and Timothy S. McWilliams, *Al Anbar Awakening*, vol. 2, *Iraqi Perspectives* (Quantico, VA: Marine Corps University Press), p. 20.

24. "Forbidden Pleasures Return to Mosul as al Qaeda Melts Away," Agence France-Presse, May 24, 2008.

25. Timothy S. McWilliams and Kurtis P. Wheeler, *Al Anbar Awakening*, vol. 1, *American Perspectives* (Quantico, VA: Marine Corps University Press), p. 10.

26. Ricks, *The Gamble*, p. 62.

27. Montgomery and McWilliams, *Al Anbar Awakening*, vol. 2, p. 12.

28. Sterling Jensen, interview with author, Washington, DC, Mar. 8, 2011.

29. Montgomery and McWilliams, *Al Anbar Awakening*, vol. 2, p. 35.

30. Ricks, *The Gamble*, p. 67.

31. Travis Patriquin, "How to Win the War in Al Anbar," PowerPoint presentation, no date given.

32. Bobby Ghosh, "In Iraq's Old Battlefields: Two Kinds of Americans," *Time*, Oct. 8, 2010.

33. General David H. Petraeus, "Report to Congress on the Situation in Iraq," Sept. 10–11, 2007, p. 5.

34. General David H. Petraeus, "Report to Congress on the Situation in Iraq," Apr. 8–9, 2008, p. 4.

35. Anthony Shadid and John Leland, "Anti-U.S. Cleric Returns to Iraq, and to Power," *New York Times*, Jan. 5, 2011.

36. Splitting the country into three regions was Senator Joe Biden's absurd plan. "Sen. Biden: Divide Iraq into Three Regions," *Day to Day*, National Public Radio, Sept. 29, 2006.

37. Bernard Stancati, "Tribal Dynamics and the Iraq Surge," *Strategic Studies Quarterly*, Summer 2010, p. 108.

8. Two Steps Back

The chapter epigraph is from Ahmed Rashid, *Descent into Chaos: The United States and the Failure of Nation Building in Pakistan, Afghanistan, and Central Asia* (New York: Viking, 2008), p. xxxviii.

1. Peter Bergen, *The Longest War: The Enduring Conflict between America and al Qaeda* (New York: Free Press, 2011), pp. 71–72.

2. See Shuja Nawaz, *Crossed Swords: Pakistan, Its Army, and the Wars Within* (Oxford: Oxford University Press, 2008), p. xxxi.

3. Zahid Hussain, *Frontline Pakistan: The Struggle with Militant Islam* (New York: Columbia University Press, 2007), pp. 19–20.

4. Ibid., p. 20.

5. Abdel Bari Atwan, *The Secret History of al Qaeda* (Berkeley: University of California Press, 2006), p. 180.

6. Zahid Hussain, *The Scorpion's Tail: The Relentless Rise of Islamic Militants in Pakistan—and How It Threatens America* (New York: Free Press, 2010), p. 27.

7. Rashid, *Descent into Chaos*, p. 98.

8. "Osama bin Laden Might Be in Pakistan," *Hardball with Chris Matthews*, MSNBC, Dec. 19, 2001.

9. Johanna McGeary and Paul Quinn-Judge, "Theater of War," *Time*, Oct. 27, 2002; U.S. Department of State, Office of the Coordinator for Counterterrorism, "Country Reports on Terrorism, 2004," Apr. 2005.

10. Bruce Hoffman, interview with author by phone, Mar. 25, 2011.

11. Stationery Office, Intelligence and Security Committee, "Report into the London Terrorist Attacks on 7 July 2005," May 11, 2006; British House of Commons, "Report of the Official Account of the Bombings in London on 7th July 2005," May 11, 2006.

12. One perceptive account written at the time the reports were released is Dan Darling and Steve Schippert, "British 7/7 Bombing Report Ignores al Qaeda," *Threats Watch*, Apr. 10, 2006. Some of the subsequent evidence in this chapter was first compiled in their response to the reports.

13. Zahid Hussain et al., "Top al Qaeda Briton Called Tube Bombers before Attack," *Times* (London), July 21, 2005.

14. Quoted in Sean Alfano, "Video: Two London Bombers Were al Qaeda," Associated Press, July 7, 2006.

15. Hoffman, interview.

16. Ismail Khan, "Al Qaeda No. 3 U.K. Plot Mastermind," *Dawn* (Pakistan), Aug. 16, 2006.

17. "The Pakistan Connection," *Ottawa Citizen*, Aug. 31, 2006.

18. "Agent Infiltrated Terror Cell, U.S. Says," CNN, Aug. 11, 2006.

19. Hassan Abbas, "An Assessment of Pakistan's Peace Agreements with Militants in Waziristan (2004–2008)," in *The Afghanistan-Pakistan Theater: Militant Islam, Security and Stability*, ed. Daveed Gartenstein-Ross and Clifford D. May (Washington, DC: Foundation for the Defense of Democracies Press, 2010), p. 7.

20. Nic Robertson, "In Afghanistan bin Laden Using Culture to Buy Loyalty," *AC360 Blog*, CNN, Sept. 11, 2008.

21. Anne Stenersen, "Al Qaeda's Foot Soldiers: A Study of the Biographies of Foreign Fighters Killed in Afghanistan and Pakistan between 2002 and 2006," *Studies in Conflict and Terrorism*, 2011, p. 186.

22. Hassan Abbas, interview with author by phone, Mar. 26, 2011.

23. Quoted in Rashid, *Descent into Chaos*, p. 45.

24. Abbas, "An Assessment of Pakistan's Peace Agreements," p. 10.

25. Ibid., p. 12.

26. Ibid., pp. 12-14.

27. Sayed G. B. Shah Bokhari, "How Peace Deals Help Only Militants," *News* (Karachi), July 31, 2008.

28. National Intelligence Council, "Trends in Global Terrorism: Implications for the United States," National Intelligence Estimate, Apr. 2006; National Intelligence Council, "The Terrorist Threat to the U.S. Homeland," National Intelligence Estimate, July 2007.

29. Hoffman, interview.

30. Mark Mazzetti and David Rohde, "Amid U.S. Policy Disputes, Qaeda Grows in Pakistan," *New York Times*, June 30, 2008.

31. "Al Qaeda Blamed for Somali Bombing Wave," CNN, Oct. 29, 2008.

32. Spencer S. Hsu and Carrie Johnson, "Somali Americans Recruited by Extremists," *Washington Post*, Mar. 11, 2009.

33. I. M. Lewis, *A Modern History of the Somali*, 4th ed. (Oxford: James Currey, 2002), p. 15.

34. Abdurahman M. Abdullahi, "Perspective on the State Collapse in Somalia," in *Somalia at the Crossroads: Challenges and Perspectives on Reconstituting a*

Failed State, ed. Abdullahi A. Osman and Issaka K. Souaré (London: Adonis and Abbey, 2007), p. 44.

35. Ken Menkhaus, *Somalia: State Collapse and the Threat of Terrorism*, Adelphi Paper 364 (London: Routledge, 2004), p. 56.

36. Ibid.

37. Ibid., p. 60.

38. Quoted in Marc Lacey, "Islamic Militants Declare Victory in Mogadishu," *New York Times*, June 5, 2006.

39. Bruno Schiemsky et al., "Report of the Monitoring Group on Somalia Pursuant to Security Council Resolution 1676," U.N. Security Council Committee, Nov. 2006, p. 42.

40. Andre LeSage, interview with author by phone, Mar. 30, 2011.

41. Michael R. Gordon and Mark Mazzetti, "U.S. Used Base in Ethiopia to Hunt al Qaeda," *New York Times*, Feb. 23, 2007.

42. Marc Lynch, *Rhetoric and Reality: Countering Terrorism in the Age of Obama* (Washington, DC: Center for a New American Security, 2010), p. 30. For other examples of this revisionist view, see Martin Fletcher, "Somalia Is Greatest Victim of President Bush's War on Terror," *Times* (London), Dec. 21, 2009; Nir Rosen, "How Did al Shabaab Emerge from the Chaos of Somalia?," *Time*, Aug. 20, 2010; Matthew Yglesias, "How Bush Failed Somalia," *American Prospect*, Dec. 18, 2008; Editorial, "Haunted by Somalia," *Los Angeles Times*, Mar. 13, 2009.

43. Bill Roggio, "Failing to Understand Somalia," *Weekly Standard*, Dec. 19, 2008.

44. Chris Tomlinson, "Islamic Group Under Scrutiny in Somalia," Associated Press, June 20, 2006.

45. Chris Tomlinson, "Video Shows Foreign Fighters," Associated Press, July 6, 2006.

46. Schiemsky et al., "Report of the Monitoring Group on Somalia," pp. 42–43.

47. Tristan McConnell, "British and American Fighters Respond to Jihad Call in Somalia," *Times* (London), May 23, 2009.

48. For a first-rate profile of Hammami, see Andrea Elliott, "A Call to Jihad from Somalia, Answered in America," *New York Times*, July 12, 2009.

49. J. M. Berger, *Jihad Joe: Americans Who Go to War in the Name of Islam* (Washington, DC: Potomac Books, 2011), p. 172.

50. Bill Roggio, "Al Qaeda Names Fazul Mohammed East African Commander," *Long War Journal*, Nov. 11, 2009.

51. Quoted in David H. Shinn, "United States-Somali Relations: Local, National, and International Dimensions," paper presented at the Center for African Studies, Ohio State University, Apr. 26, 2010, p. 2.

52. For more on these groups in Gaza, see "Radical Islam in Gaza," Middle East Report No. 104, International Crisis Group, Mar. 29, 2011; Yoram Cohen and Matthew Levitt, *Deterred but Determined: Salafi Jihadi Groups in the Palestinian Arena* (Washington, D.C.: Washington Institute for Near East Policy, 2010). For a discussion of how al Qaeda has not formally connected to these groups, see Cohen and Levitt, *Deterred but Determined*, p. 3.

53. Josh Kron, "Uganda Says It Thwarted Possible Fourth Bombing," *New York Times*, July 13, 2010.

54. "Somalia's Islamist Leader Threatens Ugandans, Burundians with Revenge," Xinhua News Agency, July 5, 2010.

55. Josh Kron, "World Cup Bombing Suspects Arrested," *Sydney Morning Herald*, July 14, 2010.

9. The War on Oil

1. Souhail Karam, "Riyadh Says Arrested Militants Planning Oil Attacks," Reuters, Mar. 24, 2010.

2. Osama bin Laden, "Declaration of Jihad against the Americans Occupying the Land of the Two Holy Mosques," trans. Open Source Center, Aug. 23, 1996.

3. "Al Qaeda in Saudi Arabia: Excerpts from 'The Laws of Targeting Petroleum-Related Interests,'" GlobalTerrorAlert, Mar. 2006.

4. Bruce Lawrence, ed., *Messages to the World: The Statements of Osama bin Laden* (London: Verso, 2005), p. 272.

5. "Newly Released Video of al Qaeda's Deputy Leader Ayman al Zawahiri's Interview to al Sahab TV," Middle East Media Research Institute, No. 1044, Dec. 8, 2005.

6. Julie Watson, "Chertoff Urges Safer Mexican Border," Associated Press, Feb. 16, 2007.

7. "An Interview with One of the Most Wanted Men: Abu Hummam al Qahtani (Part 1)," trans. Nine Eleven Finding Answers (NEFA) Foundation, *Sada al Malahim*, Jan. 12, 2008, http://www.nefafoundation .org/newsite/file/nefaqaidayemen1008-4.pdf.

8. "Forum Member Surveys Participants on Best Places to Target U.S.," Open Source Center summary in Arabic, Al Tahaddi Islamic Network, Mar. 22, 2010; "Highlights: Jihadist Web Site Discusses Possible Targets in United States," Open Source Center summary in Arabic, Al Fallujah Islamic Forums, Feb. 2, 2010; Adnan al Ansari, "Jihad—Impact and Fruit," trans. Open Source Center, *Sada al Malahim*, Mar. 22, 2009; International Institute for Counter-Terrorism, Jihadi Websites Monitoring Group, "Oil Installations as

an Attractive Target for Terrorism," *Insights*, Nov. 2009, http://www.ict.org .il/Portals/0/Internet%20Monitoring%20Group/JWMG_Oil_Installations_ as_a_Target.pdf.

9. Gal Luft and Anne Korin, "Terror's Next Target," *Journal of International Security Affairs*, Dec. 2003.

10. Christopher Dickey, "Saudi Storms," *Newsweek*, Oct. 3, 2005.

11. Quoted in B. Raman, "Al Qaeda Attack on Saudi Oil Facility Fails," *International Terrorism Monitor*, Feb. 27, 2006.

12. Khalid R. al Rodhan, *The Impact of the Abqaiq Attack on Saudi Energy Security* (Washington, DC: Center for Strategic and International Studies, 2006), p. 2.

13. "Attack on Abqaiq Oil Facility Foiled," *Arab News* (Jeddah), Feb. 25, 2006.

14. Neil Partrick, testimony to the House of Commons Select Committee on Foreign Affairs, Mar. 2006.

15. Andrew Hammond, "Saudi Arrests Suspects Planning Oil Attacks," Reuters, Apr. 27, 2007.

16. "Saudi Arabia Arrests 701 al Qaeda–Linked Militants Plotting 'Oil Attacks,'" Fox News, June 25, 2008.

17. Luft and Korin, "Terror's Next Target."

18. Robert Baer, *Sleeping with the Devil: How Washington Sold Our Soul for Saudi Crude* (New York: Three Rivers Press, 2003), p. xxv.

19. Quoted in Terry Macalister, "Once Seen as an Alarmist Fear, an Attack on Key Saudi Oil Terminal Could Destabilize West," *Guardian* (Manchester), June 3, 2004.

20. "Iraq Pipeline Watch," Institute for the Analysis of Global Security, last post Mar. 27, 2008.

21. Michael Scheuer, "Al Qaeda and the Oil Target," in *Saudi Arabian Oil Facilities: The Achilles Heel of the Western Economy*, ed. Erich Marquardt (Washington, DC: Jamestown Foundation, 2006), p. 11.

22. Pierre Thomas, "Osama bin Laden Evidence: Al Qaeda 'Interest' in Targeting Oil, Gas Infrastructure," ABC News, May 20, 2011.

23. David Sandalow, *Freedom from Oil: How the Next President Can End the United States' Oil Addiction* (New York: McGraw-Hill, 2008), p. 192.

24. Jay Inslee and Bracken Hendricks, *Apollo's Fire: Igniting America's Clean Energy Economy* (Washington, DC: Island Press, 2008), p. 16.

25. Chris Kahn, "$4 Gasoline in 2011: Oil's Surge Paves Way for Higher Prices at the Pump," *Huffington Post*, Dec. 31, 2010.

26. "Oil Pressure Rising," *Economist*, Feb. 23, 2011.

27. Daniel Indiviglio, "Ten Ways Rising Oil Prices Endanger the U.S. Recovery," *Atlantic*, Feb. 23, 2011.

28. Sandalow, *Freedom from Oil*, p. 23.

10. The Thousand Cuts

The chapter epigraph is quoted in "Jihadist Book Urges 'Indolent' Muslims Follow Jihad, Argues United States 'Weak,'" Open Source Center, Mar. 26, 2010.

1. Michael Lewis, *The Big Short: Inside the Doomsday Machine* (New York: W. W. Norton, 2011), p. 237.
2. "The Crisis: A Timeline," *CNN Money*, last updated Sept. 14, 2009.
3. Ibid.
4. Jeffrey Friedman, "Capitalism and the Crisis: Bankers, Bonuses, Ideology, and Ignorance," in *What Caused the Financial Crisis* (Philadelphia: University of Pennsylvania Press, 2011), p. 2.
5. Ayman al Zawahiri, "The Facts of Jihad and the Lies of the Hypocrites," trans. Nine Eleven Finding Answers (NEFA) Foundation, Al Sahab, Aug. 5, 2009, http://www.nefafoundation.org/newsite/file/Formatted%20 2009-8-zawahiri%20interview%20transcript%20Post%20Version.pdf.
6. "The West and the Dark Tunnel," trans. Open Source Center, Al Sahab, Sept. 22, 2009.
7. Abu Omar al Baghdadi, "To the New Rulers in the White House and Their Allies from among the Leaders of the Other Christian Countries," trans. NEFA Foundation, Nov. 7, 2008, http://www.nefafoundation.org/newsite/file/nefaobama1108-2.pdf.
8. Osama bin Laden, "Address to the American People," trans. Open Source Center, Sept. 14, 2009.
9. Lewis, *The Big Short*, pp. 14–15.
10. Ibid., p. 23.
11. Ibid.
12. "Yemeni-American Jihadi Cleric Anwar al Awlaki in First Interview with al Qaeda Media Calls on Muslim U.S. Servicemen to Kill Fellow Soldiers," Middle East Media Research Institute, release no. 2480, May 23, 2010.
13. Gabriel Weimann, "War by Other Means: Econo-Jihad," *Yale Global*, June 4, 2009.
14. "Highlights: Jihadist Web Site Discusses Possible Targets in United States," Open Source Center summary in Arabic, Al Fallujah Islamic Forums, Feb. 2, 2010.
15. Thomas Hegghammer, "The Case for Chasing al Awlaki," *Foreign Policy*, Nov. 24, 2010. Hegghammer states that the article is "almost certainly written by Awlaki." Head of Foreign Operations [Anwar al Awlaki], "The Objectives of Operation Hemorrhage," *Inspire*, Nov. 2010, p. 7.
16. Matthew 5:39.
17. Ikrimah al Muhajir, "Technical Details," *Inspire*, Nov. 2010, p. 14.

18. Awlaki, "The Objectives of Operation Hemorrhage."
19. Ibid.
20. Editorial, *Inspire*, Nov. 2010, p. 4.
21. Douglas Frantz et al., "The New Face of al Qaeda," *Los Angeles Times*, Sept. 26, 2004.
22. Shaykh Ibrahim al Banna, "Tawaghit Exposed," *Inspire*, Nov. 2010, p. 11.
23. "Highlights: Jihadist Web Site Discusses Possible Targets."
24. Awlaki, "The Objectives of Operation Hemorrhage."
25. Yahya Ibrahim, "$4,200," *Inspire*, Nov. 2010, p. 15.
26. Adam Gadahn, "A Call to Arms," video, Mar. 2010.
27. "Threat Message on Jihadist Forum Names U.S., International Targets," Open Source Center summary in Arabic, Dec. 31, 2009.

11. A Formidable Adversary

1. Bruce Riedel, "Who Was Hiding bin Laden?" *Daily Beast*, May 2, 2011.
2. Leah Farrall, "How al Qaeda Works," *Foreign Affairs*, Mar./Apr. 2011.
3. Lolita C. Baldor et al., "Source: Bin Laden Directing al Qaeda Figures," Associated Press, May 6, 2011.
4. Farrall, "How al Qaeda Works." This is consistent with the analysis offered in Thomas Hegghammer, *Jihad in Saudi Arabia: Violence and Pan-Islamism since 1979* (Cambridge: Cambridge University Press, 2010).
5. For background, see Nic Robertson and Paul Cruickshank, "Sources: Senior al Qaeda Leader Directed Europe Plot," CNN, Oct. 6, 2010.
6. Dina Temple-Raston, "Bin Laden Told Partners to Plan Mumbai-Like Attacks," *Morning Edition*, National Public Radio, Sept. 30, 2010.
7. "Drone Attacks 'Linked' to Suspected Europe Terror Plot," BBC News, Oct. 6, 2010.
8. Scott Helfstein et al., *Deadly Vanguards: A Study of al Qaeda's Violence against Muslims* (West Point, NY: Combating Terrorism Center, 2009), p. 2.
9. Quoted in Lawrence Wright, "The Rebellion Within: An al Qaeda Mastermind Questions Terrorism," *New Yorker*, June 2, 2008.
10. Ibid.
11. Alia Brahimi, "Crushed in the Shadows: Why al Qaeda Will Lose the War of Ideas," *Studies in Conflict and Terrorism*, Feb. 2010, p. 97.
12. H. R. H. Prince Ghazi bin Muhammad bin Talal, "Introduction," in *True Islam and the Islamic Consensus on the Amman Message* (Amman, Jordan: Royal Aal al Bayt Institute for Islamic Thought, 2006), p. xx.
13. Amman Message, *Jihad and the Islamic Law of War* (Amman: Royal Aal al Bayt Institute for Islamic Thought, 2007), p. 63.

14. Jamestown Foundation, "Controversial Gathering of Islamic Scholars Refutes al Qaeda's Ideological Cornerstone," *Terrorism Monitor*, Apr. 9, 2010.

15. Peter Bergen, interview with author, Washington, DC, Mar. 15, 2011.

16. For one representative example of this argument, see Dan Murphy, "Bin Laden's Death Puts Exclamation Mark on al Qaeda's Demise," *Christian Science Monitor*, May 3, 2011.

17. Ayman al Zawahiri, "To Our People in Egypt," trans. Open Source Center, Feb. 24, 2011.

18. Quoted in R. Green, "Jihadists' Reactions to the Libyan Rebellion," Middle East Media Research Institute, Inquiry & Analysis Series Report No.681, Apr. 4, 2011.

19. Yahya Ibrahim, "Protest Focus," *Inspire*, Spring 2011, p. 5.

20. Hani al Siba'i, "Names of the Released Detainees from the Al Aqrab, Al Istiqbal, Al Wadi and Burj al Arab Prisons," trans. Open Source Center, Mar. 17, 2011.

21. Senior U.S. military intelligence analyst, interview with author by phone, Apr. 13, 2011.

22. Mark Landler et al., "Washington in Fierce Debate on Arming Libyan Rebels," *New York Times*, Mar. 29, 2011.

23. "'Al Qaeda Snatched Missiles' in Libya," Agence France-Presse, Mar. 26, 2011; Damien McElroy, "Al Qaeda 'Receive Looted Libyan Weapons,'" *Telegraph* (London), Apr. 4, 2011.

24. "Irtifa Mu'addal al Batalah fi Misr ila 11.9% bil Rub al Awal min al Am al Jari" [High rate of unemployment in Egypt to 11.9% for first quarter of this year], *Al Shorouk* (Egypt), May 25, 2011.

25. Gary Thomas, "'Great Game' Resurfaces in Afghanistan," Voice of America, Nov. 18, 2010; Karen DeYoung, "If U.S. Gets out, Who Gets in, Neighbors Ask," *Washington Post*, Nov. 5, 2010.

26. David W. Barno and Andrew Exum, *Responsible Transition: Securing U.S. Interests in Afghanistan Beyond 2011* (Washington, DC: Center for a New American Security, 2010), p. 9.

27. Syed Saleem Shahzad, "Al Qaeda Sees Opportunity in Peace," *Asia Times*, Apr. 13, 2011.

28. Pervez Musharraf, *In the Line of Fire: A Memoir* (New York: Free Press, 2006), p. 201.

29. Jane Perlez, "Many in Pakistan Fear Unrest at Home," *New York Times*, Feb. 3, 2011.

30. Ibid.

31. Hassan Abbas, *Pakistan's Drift into Extremism: Allah, the Army, and America's War on Terror* (Armonk, NY: M. E. Sharpe, 2005), p. 104.

32. David Steven, "Running Out of Everything: How Scarcity Drives Crisis in Pakistan," *World Politics Review*, May 3, 2011.

33. Nic Robertson and Paul Cruickshank, "Al Qaeda's Training Adapts to Drone Attacks," CNN, July 30, 2009.

34. Peter Taylor, "Drones 'Winning' War against al Qaeda, Says Ex-CIA Head," BBC News, Mar. 20, 2011.

35. Quoted in Mohsen M. Milani, "Meet Me in Baghdad," *Foreign Affairs*, Sept. 20, 2010.

36. Quoted in International Crisis Group, "Loose Ends: Iraq's Security Forces between U.S. Drawdown and Withdrawal," Middle East Report No. 99, Oct. 26, 2010.

37. Timothy Williams and Duraid Adnan, "Sunnis in Iraq Allied with U.S. Rejoin Rebels," *New York Times*, Oct. 17, 2010.

38. Quoted in ibid.

39. Martin Chuov, "Fears of al Qaeda Return in Iraq as U.S.-Backed Fighters Defect," *Guardian* (Manchester), Aug. 1, 2010.

40. Quoted in Lourdes Garcia-Navarro, "Bitterness Grows Amid U.S.-Backed Sons of Iraq," *All Things Considered*, National Public Radio, June 24, 2010.

41. Alexander Smoltczyk, "Uncertainty Reigns as Baghdad Enters New Era," *Der Spiegel*, Jan. 7, 2011.

42. Yasir Ghazi, "Punk'd, Iraqi-Style, at a Checkpoint," *New York Times*, Sept. 3, 2010.

43. Gregory Johnsen, "Welcome to Qaedastan," *Foreign Policy*, Jan./Feb. 2010.

44. Christopher Boucek, testimony to the House Committee on Homeland Security, Subcommittee on Counterterrorism and Intelligence, Mar. 2, 2011.

45. "Al Qaeda in Yemen Adapts to Evade U.S.," Associated Press, Apr. 16, 2011.

46. "Yemen-Based al Qaeda Seizes Swaths from Lodar to Balhaf Gas Port," Xinhua News Agency, Apr. 6, 2011.

47. "Tribal Sheikhs Expel al Qaeda from Their Land," *Al Masry Al Youm* (Cairo), Apr. 15, 2011.

48. Quoted in "Brand al Qaeda," *Sydney Morning Herald*, Jan. 28, 2007.

49. Jean-Pierre Filiu, "Al Qaeda in the Islamic Maghreb: Algerian Challenge or Global Threat?" Carnegie Endowment for International Peace, Oct. 2009.

50. Dario Cristiani and Riccardo Fabiani, "AQIM Funds Terrorist Operations with Thriving Sahel-Based Kidnapping Industry," *Terrorism Monitor*, Jan. 28, 2010.

51. Quoted in Sonia Rolley, "The AQLIM Business," trans. Open Source Center, *Paris Slate*, Dec. 10, 2010.

52. Russell J. Isaacs, "The North African Franchise: AQIM's Threat to U.S. Security," *Strategic Insights*, Dec. 2009.

53. Remy Ourdan, "A Declaration of War on France by bin Laden," trans. Open Source Center, *Le Monde*, Oct. 29, 2010.

54. Bertin Bakouo, "Saharan Space: Is AQIM Challenging Security Forces?" trans. Open Source Center, *Info-Matin*, July 1, 2010.

55. "Clinton: Pay Debt by 2015," *CNN Money*, June 28, 1999.

56. Clark Kent Ervin, interview with author, Washington, DC, Mar. 16, 2011.

57. Robert Heilbroner and Lester Thurow, *Economics Explained: Everything You Need to Know about How the Economy Works and Where It's Going* (New York: Touchstone Books, 1998), p. 108.

58. Malik Ahmad Jalal, "The Number One National Security Threat?" *Harvard National Security Journal*, Mar. 28, 2011.

59. Niall Ferguson, "An Empire at Risk," *Newsweek*, Nov. 28, 2009.

60. Bronwen Maddox, "America Counts Cost of Going to War," *Times* (London), Mar. 29, 2010.

61. Andrew F. Krepinevich Jr., *National Security Strategy in an Era of Growing Challenges and Resource Constraints* (Washington, DC: Center for Strategic and Budgetary Assessments, June 2010), p. 6.

62. Tom Gjelten, "Defense Officials Anticipate Drop in Military Spending," *Morning Edition*, National Public Radio, July 6, 2010.

63. Edmund L. Andrews, "Wave of Debt Payments Facing U.S. Government," *New York Times*, Nov. 22, 2009.

64. Ibid.

65. David J. Lynch, "Balancing Our Priorities; Reducing the Deficit vs. Shoring Up the Economy," *USA Today*, Aug. 2, 2010.

66. Erik Wasson, "Stocks Plunge after S&P Shifts Rating on U.S. Debt to Negative," *Hill*, Apr. 18, 2011.

12. How to Survive al Qaeda

The chapter epigraph is from Stephen Flynn, *America the Vulnerable: How Our Government Is Failing to Protect Us from Terrorism* (New York: Harper Perennial, 2005), p. x.

1. For a skillful explanation of the role played by Karzai's cynical manipulations, see C. Christine Fair, "Explaining the Inexplicable: Murder at Mazar," *Foreign Policy*, Apr. 4, 2011.

2. Una Moore, "This Attack Is Different," *UN Dispatch*, Apr. 1, 2011.

3. Editorial, "Fearmongering on Dubai," *Nation*, Mar. 2, 2006.

4. Matthew Duss, interview with author by phone, Apr. 20, 2011.

5. Editorial, "Obama Selects a Voice of Radical Islam," *Washington Examiner*, Feb. 22, 2010.

6. For a short but good summary of the controversy surrounding Rashad Hussain, see Andrea Elliott, "White House Quietly Courts Muslims in U.S.," *New York Times*, Apr. 18, 2010.

7. Ben Sheppard, interview with author by phone, Apr. 20, 2011.

8. Charlie Allen, interview with author, Washington, DC, Apr. 12, 2011.

9. William McCants, "No New bin Ladens," *Jihadica*, May 8, 2011.

10. Stephen M. Lord, testimony to the House Committee on Science, Space, and Technology, Subcommittee on Investigations and Oversight, Apr. 6, 2011.

11. Erroll Southers, "America Is Not Israel, But . . . ," *Jerusalem Post*, Jan. 13, 2009.

12. "Security Specialist: Canada's New Airport Security Scanners a Waste of Money," *Homeland Security Newswire*, Apr. 23, 2010.

13. Quoted in Dan Milmo, "How to Spot the Terrorists: BAA Wants Review of Airport Security," *Guardian* (Manchester), Nov. 29, 2010.

14. Sheldon H. Jacobson, "The Right Kind of Profiling," *New York Times*, Jan. 4, 2010.

15. Senior U.S. intelligence analyst, interview with author, Alexandria, VA, Apr. 14, 2011.

16. Douglas A. Brook and Cynthia L. King, "Federal Personnel Management Reform: From Civil Service Reform Act to National Security Reforms," *Review of Public Personnel Administration*, Sept. 2008.

17. U.S. Department of Labor, Bureau of Labor Statistics, "Career Guide to Industries, 2010–2011 Edition," http://www.bls.gov/oco/cg/cgs041.htm.

18. Daniel Byman, interview with author by phone, Mar. 29, 2011.

19. Clark Kent Ervin, interview with author, Washington, DC, Mar. 16, 2011.

20. Quoted in Jerome H. Kahan et al., "An Operational Framework for Resilience," *Journal of Homeland Security and Emergency Management*, Jan. 2009.

21. Ben Sheppard, interview with author by phone, Mar. 8, 2011.

22. Lawrence Freedman, foreword to *The Psychology of Strategic Terrorism: Public and Government Responses to Attack*, by Ben Sheppard (London: Routledge, 2009), pp. ix–x.

23. Ben Sheppard, *The Psychology of Strategic Terrorism: Public and Government Responses to Attack* (London: Routledge, 2009), p. 2.

24. Bert Tussing, interview with author by phone, Apr. 21, 2011.

25. John Maldonado, interview with Kyle Dabruzzi by phone, Oct. 11, 2006.

26. City of Phoenix, "What Is CERT?" http://phoenix.gov/cert/whatis.html.

27. Newsletter of the Phoenix Citizen Corps Committee, Sept.–Oct. 2005.

28. Nicholas D. Kristof, "The Case for a No-Fly Zone," *New York Times*, Mar. 9, 2011.

29. Joshua Foust, "And Now, a War against Libya?" *Need to Know*, PBS, Mar. 18, 2011.

30. John F. Kerry, "A No-Fly Zone for Libya," *Washington Post*, Mar. 10, 2011.

31. Lloyd Grove, "Bill Clinton Endorses No-Fly Zone," *Daily Beast*, Mar. 11, 2011.

32. Bruce Drake, "Obama Should Impose No-Fly Zone on Libya and Aid Insurgents, Senators Say," *Huffington Post*, Feb. 27, 2011.

33. Slobodan Lekic, "U.S. to Withdraw Strike Jets from Libya Mission," Associated Press, Apr. 4, 2011.

34. Daniel Byman and Matthew Waxman, "Kosovo and the Great Air Power Debate," *International Security*, Spring 2000, pp. 5–38.

35. Thomas E. Ricks, *Fiasco: The American Military Adventure in Iraq* (New York: Penguin Books, 2006), p. 15.

36. Todd Harrison and Zack Cooper, "Selected Options and Costs for a No-Fly Zone over Libya," *CSBA Backgrounder*, Mar. 2011, p. 7.

37. Jeremiah Gertler, "Operation Odyssey Dawn (Libya): Background and Issues for Congress," Congressional Research Service, Mar. 30, 2011; "U.S. Intervention in Libya Cost $608 Million," *Defence Web* (London), Apr. 13, 2011.

38. Marine Corps officer, interview with author by phone, Apr. 19, 2011.

39. P. J. Crowley, Twitter post, Mar. 27, 2011, https://twitter.com/PJCrowley/status/52038549448564738.

40. Jeffrey Goldberg, "Libya, a Seventh-Tier Problem for America," *Atlantic*, Mar. 21, 2011.

41. Ken Silverstein, "Greening the Transport Sector," *EnergyBiz Insider*, May 7, 2008.

42. Bruce Dale, interview with author by phone, Jan. 4, 2011.

43. Eric Evarts, "Higher Fuel Economy Standards Take Effect for 2012 Models," *Consumer Reports*, Jan. 5, 2011.

44. White House, Office of the Press Secretary, "President Obama Announces $2.4 Billion in Grants to Accelerate the Manufacturing and Deployment of the Next Generation of U.S. Batteries and Electric Vehicles," Aug. 5, 2009.

45. David Victor, interview with author by phone, Jan. 5, 2011.

46. Kateri Callahan, interview with author by phone, Jan. 5, 2011.

47. Robert Zubrin, *Energy Victory: Winning the War on Terror by Breaking Free of Oil* (Amherst, NY: Prometheus Books, 2007), pp. 94–95.

48. Bruce Dale et al., "Biofuels Done Right: Land Efficient Animal Feeds Enable Large Environmental and Energy Benefits," *Environmental Science & Technology*, 2010, pp. 8385–8389.

49. Jay Inslee and Bracken Hendricks, *Apollo's Fire: Igniting America's Clean Energy Economy* (Washington, DC: Island Press, 2008), p. 161.

50. See S3303, 110th Cong. (2008); HR6559, 110th Cong. (2008).

51. Gal Luft, interview with author by phone, Jan. 4, 2011.

Index